To Those Who Served Before The Mast

Low pressures with their howling gales
Was what real sailors sought
When battling on with wind filled sails
Through mighty seas they fought

Those ships of wood and men of steel
Through the forties they did sail
They knew the hardships and the strife
They knew when not to fail

Around the Horn from Liverpool
Or the Cape for eastern teas
Its welcome to the toughest school
The hard and cruel seas

From captain down to first trip boy
Each had his part to play
To bring his ship home safely through
The hazards of each day

For Angela and Charlotte

Cutty Sark arrives at Shanghai on her maiden voyage in 1870

Cutty Sark - Ferreira

John Richardson

The Front Cover picture of this book, which has been supplied by Mrs Nancy Barnes of Southport Lancashire, portrays the tea clipper *Cutty Sark* as she appeared on her maiden voyage in 1870.

First published in 2007 by Richardson Publishing PO Box 2148 Amesbury Wiltshire UK.

Copyright 2007 John Richardson who is to be identified as the author of this publication; it has been asserted to him in accordance with the copyright design and patents act of 1988.

British Library Cataloguing in publication data. A catalogue record for this book is available from the British Library.

ISBN-10: 0 9537242 2 0
ISBN-13: 978-0-9537242-2-2

All rights to this book are reserved. No part of this book publication may be produced in any manner without prior permission from the author or publisher.

Printed and bound in England.

BUCKINGHAM PALACE

    I have been associated with 'Cutty Sark' ever since the Cutty Sark Society was founded in 1951, with the purpose of buying, restoring and exhibiting this famous sailing ship to the public. Built as a tea clipper, she only found her best form as a wool clipper on the run from Australia to London. Even in her dry dock at Greenwich, she still has the looks of an ocean thoroughbred.

    I warmly welcome this excellent book. It is expertly written and very well illustrated. The author combines his artistic skill with a wide knowledge of the sea, and an exceptional ability to tell a dramatic story in clear and concise language. The brilliant account of her tragic dismasting off the South African coast during the First World War adds a new and previously little-known incident in her long career. She made a remarkable recovery, but it marked the beginning of the old ship's gradual decline. This was only ended when she entered her special dock at Greenwich in 1954. It is good to know that, after 50 years on public display, Cutty Sark is to be given a thorough overhaul, which, we all hope, will give her a new lease of life as one of the finest examples of the last generation of sailing ship design and construction.

His Royal Highness The Duke of Edinburgh Patron of 'The Cutty Sark Preservation Society.' Seen here being welcomed aboard his ship on 28 May 1953. His visit marked the beginning of a long programme of refurbishment and overhauls for the ship's future preservation.

Photo - Cutty Sark Trust

Contents

Foreword	4
Illustrations	7
Author	8
Introduction	9
Basil Lubbock	16
Hercules Linton	17
Letter From Lisbon Maritime Museum	21
Ferdinand de Lesseps	22
Alfred Holt	23
Cutty Sark	24
Cutty Sark's Crew List	28
Cutty Sark's List of Voyages	29
Cutty Sark's Maiden Voyage Crew	30
Loading Tea Cargoes	35
Captain George Moodie	36
Captain FW Moore	44
Captain WE Tiptaft	46
Captain JS Wallace	50
Captain W Bruce	54
Captain F Moore	61
Captain R Woodget	65
Crew Deserters	86
The End for the Tea Clippers	88
Cutty Sark's Different Appearances	105
Ferreira's Dismasting	107
Masting	126
Captain Wilfred Dowman	146
Heavy Lifts	156
Badly Loaded Cargoes	157
A Sailor From The Past	159
Picture Glossary	165 - 199
Torrington	200
Ann McKim	201
Rainbow	203
Stornoway	205
Scawfell	206
Thomas Stephens	207
Blackadder	210
Thermopylae	213
Torrens	219
Norman Court	225
The Tweed	227
Lightning	228
Westward Ho	229
Index	230
Glossary	235

Illustrations

5	HRH The Duke of Edinburgh	130	Fore T'gallant Cut Away
8	Author	131	Main T'gallant Cut Away
12	Capt Emilio da Sousa	132	The Bent Lowe Mainmast
14	John Willis	133	Mainmast going Over
17	Hercules Linton	134	After the Part Dismasting
22	Ferdinand de Lesseps	135	SS Kia Ora
23	SS Agamemnon - Alfred Holt	136	SS Indraghiri Towing
25	Tam O' Shanter	137	Arrival at Table Bay
34	Cutty Sark	138	Ferreira Re-Rigged
39	Cutty Sark racing Thermopylae	139	Ferreira
39	Captain George Moodie	140	SS Indraghiri
42	Cutty Sarks Jury Rudder	141	SS Kia Ora
43	Cutty Sarks Jury Rudder	142	Ferreira
45	Captain FW Moore	143	Maria di Amparo
52	Captain JS Wallace	144	Maria di Amparo
58	South China Sea Map	145	Maria di Amparo
64	Captain F Moore	149	Captain Wilfred Dowman
70	Cutty Sark's Sydney Visitors	150	Cutty Sark - Capt Woodget
71	Cutty Sark's Crew Members	152	Cutty Sark
74	RMS Britannia	153	Cutty Sark deck Scenes
74	Overhauling RMS Britannia	155	Titania - Herzogin Cecilie
78	Icebergs	156	A Frame
79	Captain Woodget's Dogs	158	Loading Diagram
84	Captain R Woodget	163	MV Willesden
95	Ferreira at Pensacola	165-198	Picture Glossary
97	Shipping Water	199	Lahloo
98	Ariel and Taeping	202	Ann McKim
99	Cutty Sark	204	Rainbow
100	Cutty Sark	209	Haloween - Thomas Stephens
101	Cutty sark	216	Thermopylae
102	Cutty Sark Hove To	218	Thermopylae
103	Cutty Sark Under Stun'sls	221	Torrens
104	Cutty Sarks Different Appearances	224	Torrens After Collision
106	Cutty Sark at Sydney	227	The Tweed
108	Ferreira	228	Lightning
109	Ferreira		
123	Ferreira Under Tow		
124	Ferreira and Maria di Amparo		
125	Harbour Master's Log		
127	Schomberg - Mast Partners		
128	Ferreira		
129	Ferreira Rolling		

About the Author

Born at Liverpool in 1937, John Richardson spent two years at the Wellesley Nautical School before joining the Merchant Navy in 1953. Self taught through a lot of trial and error, he spent much of his spare time drawing and painting ships. He left the merchant service to join the South African Navy in 1975, and in his subsequent sea going duties served aboard various supply and auxiliary vessels as a rigger. On invitation he later became the marine artist for the navy, and was thereafter commissioned to paint various warships. But in being a rigger he always held a special interest for the square rigged sailing ships of bygone times Before leaving his last ship and retiring from the service in 1990, not only did he paint many of the South African Navy warships but numerous sailing vessels as well. He then took up his new pastime of writing. which included a book describing his first trip to sea, and also about his paintings and the ships they portrayed. The author now lives in Wiltshire with his wife Barbara and their two sons. The eldest of whom chose a military life in the army, whilst the youngest who opted for a life at sea is presently serving as a master mariner.

The author putting the finishing touches to one of his oil paintings. The ship is a British seventy four gun Man O' War anchored in Simon's Bay off Simonstown.

Introduction

Ever since man first took to the water on a log before discovering the use of oar and sail, continuous efforts were made to improve his waterborne craft. Maritime transport over the centuries has since become more efficient, and during the slow and tedious development from the aforesaid log to the fully rigged ship, those waterborne craft became bigger, faster and safer. In the nineteenth century however, after thousands of years of development, sail finally reached its epitome, and in doing so surrendered its domination of the seas to the 'tin kettle' smoke belching steam ships.
Nevertheless, on reaching the pinnacle of their design and development, and after having ruled the oceans of the world for so long, those ships of sail were to have one last defiant fling at their coal burning challengers. Indeed, those ship of sail after countless years of progression, became the thoroughbreds of and the aristocrats of sail. They were 'The Clipper Ships.'
The Americans were the innovators of those ocean greyhounds known as clippers, and indeed, it was from their sleek Baltimore schooners that the concept of clipper ships began. The new breed of sail was so named ... or termed, 'clippers' because of their ability to sail faster than the clumsy bluff bowed ships of the day. They clipped valuable time from their passages, therefore, the new name of clippers and clipper ships originated. Furthermore, despite the fact there was no such rig as a 'clipper rig' the name somehow stuck.
Some people will say the fine lined *Ann McKim* of 1832 was the first ever fully rigged clipper ship, but in view of the curious difference in her draught between fore and aft, others claim that *Rainbow* built eleven years later laid claim to the honour. Nevertheless, nobody will ever be able to say for certain just which was the first ever clipper ship, and neither will anybody be able to say which was the first to be built in Britain. In those days there were no standards, rules or guidelines as to the design of a clipper on either side of

the Atlantic. There was no such rig known as a clipper, it was a slang word, so how could any shipyard claim to be the first to build one?

After that successful American development however, Britain quickly followed suit and began its own programme of clipper ship building; the result was the *Scottish Maid* coming from the yard of Alexander Hall in 1839. She was a two masted topsail schooner or brigantine of 142 tons. Because of her fine lines and good dead-rise, she arguably had some claim to being Britain's first clipper. Then came the 145 ton schooner-rigged *Torrington,* a vessel which in 1845 also came from the yard of Alexander Hall. Had this vessel been of normal design, she may well have been referred to as an 'opium carrier.' But because of *Torrington's* large dead rise which enabled her to travel at as much as fourteen knots, she too was graced with the newly fangled pseudonym of being a clipper ship, but referred to as an 'opium clipper.'

After the schooner rigged *Torrington* came the ship rigged *Reindeer*, the first British built fully rigged ship to be called a clipper. Later on the full riggers *Stornoway* and *Chrysolite* came off the stocks. The *Stornoway* has been accredited as to being the first ever, ship-rigged vessel to have been specifically built for the tea trade - the first ever British tea clipper as it were. From then on the newly termed clipper ships took to the water in greater numbers. In some un-written law however, concocted from some equally un-known source, it then transpired that any vessel which was to be known as a clipper should be ship rigged. It would be fine lined with a larger dead-rise than normal and also have a Baltimore or Aberdeen bow. However, it goes without saying that because of the greater speed attained by those so called clippers, the sacrifice they paid with their larger dead-rises, was quite a large reduction in cargo space.

After the clipper ship building started, it took over twenty years and towards the end of the 1860s before the zenith of clipper ship design was finally reached. One of the ships built at the end of that period was the fabulous and much celebrated *Cutty Sark.* A ship which incorporated the very latest designs in ship-building; she was composite built, had iron wire rope for her standing rigging and split topsails. She also adopted the new idea of having her shrouds secured inside the bulwarks, thereby doing away with the age old system of outside channels. To give the vessel her proper credentials, *Cutty Sark* was, and is, a full rigged ship, then to add to its pseudonym, she is an 'extreme clipper.' The term 'extreme' has been bestowed on only a small number of ships, the absolute aristocrats of design and sailing ability.

Compared with *Stornoway's* 527 tons, *Cutty Sark* was built at 921 tons. Indeed, it was this latter tonnage which appeared to be the benchmark for the tea clippers of the era. In their carrying of tea cargoes, the 900 - 1,000 ton ships had the best combination of size, loading and discharging, sailing ability, carrying capacity, and the requirement of crew numbers. Although those tea clippers were noted for their speed, they were not however, as fast as the so called 'Liverpool Yankee Clippers' of the 1850's. Those American ships which were built for Liverpool's Black Ball and White Star Lines were much larger in size, and when comparing the tonnage of the *Cutty Sark* of 1869, to *Lightning* of 1852, the latter was over twice her size. Despite the fact that many British tea clippers were extremely fine lined, the extra size of the American built *Lightning* enabled her to power her way through heavy seas much better than the dainty little *Cutty Sark.* On the other hand however, *Cutty Sark* was able to ghost along through the lightest of winds or cat's paws much better than the big Yankee Clippers.

When *Cutty Sark* was sold to the Portuguese in 1895 and renamed *Ferreira,* and despite many enquiries and searches by the author, it would appear that from those times until 1922, little in the way of the ship's logs or records had been preserved. Consequently, this manuscript has been composed from what scant information has become available. At the time of *Ferreira's* part dismasting in May 1916, the First World War was at its height. Communications at sea were extremely poor and primitive, and only a small number of ships carried radio. These were warships, passenger vessels and large cargo liners from well found merchant company's, and certainly not sailing vessels. Furthermore, because she was only able to carry 1,100 tons of cargo, an obsolete old sailing ship like *Ferreira* was of little value at that particular time. Therefore, scant attention was paid to the her when she arrived at Table Bay under tow in May 1916.

However, what prompted the writing of this particular book, and what may possibly contribute a little towards history, was an incident which took place at Cape Town in 1990. I was there to watch the start of the Cape to Lisbon yacht race, an event in which my son was taking part by crewing for *Dunkelly*. Knowing I had a passion for ships of sail or anybody who'd sailed them, my son introduced me to the skipper of an opposing yacht named *I G Insurance*. Her skipper was Emilio da Sousa, a well and truly weather beaten old Portuguese sailor. My son knew I'd be interested in meeting this Old Salt, because he was a relation of Captain Frederik Vincenzo da Sousa, a man who in 1916 had been the master of *Ferreira,* the ex *Cutty Sark!* During our lengthy all day conversation, I learned that Captain Emilio da Sousa had served at sea since leaving school and possessed a foreign going master's certificate. Of his numerous maritime adventures, his latest had been to sail a replica of the fifteenth century caravelle *Bartolomeu Dias* from Lisbon to South Africa. That historic voyage which followed the ageless wind patterns of the Atlantic Ocean, began on 8 November 1987 and ended in Mossel Bay ten weeks later. His feat of sailing was to correspond with the South African landing of Bartholomew Diaz in February of 1488.

Emilio and I had a good talk on the subject of *Ferreira's* dismasting, and as can be

Top: The author on the left with Emilio da Sousa.
Bottom Left: Preparing for the 1990 Cape to Lisbon yacht race, Captain Emilio da Sousa and two of his crew load victuals aboard their yacht *IG Insurance*.
Bottom Right: The caravelle replica which Emilio da Sousa sailed from Lisbon to Port Elizabeth. The sea passage which lasted two months marked 500 years of the Bartolomew Diaz voyage of discovery to South Africa.   Photos Johan Swarts - West Parow SA

imagined he was extremely well informed on the matter. His forebear had told him of the *Ferreira* episode some years previously, and Emilio was pleased that someone showed an interest. For quite some time as I helped him load his stores for the race, I made notes and sketches on every scrap of information he was able to give me. The facts I was given on *Ferreira's* dismasting were so interesting and informative, they added greatly to the small amount of information I already had upon the subject. Consequently, I told Emilio that one day in the future, I'd do my best to make an illustrated manuscript of *Ferreira's* dismasting and have it published. However, a book on *Cutty Sark - Ferreira,* could hardly be completed without making some reference to the history of *Cutty Sark* and her competitors of the day. Therefore, despite the fact the main emphasis of this book is on the part dismasting of *Ferreira* ... and in order to make the manuscript more complete, a number of *Cutty Sark's* rivals in the tea and wool trade have also been included.

But more was to come! In 1995 after completing the Whitbread round the world yacht race, my son then introduced me to Robert Linton at his Highlander Restaurant in Southport. He is the great grandson of Hercules Linton designer of *Cutty Sark*, and once again I was given valuable information on the ship.

With regard to the pencil drawings on the following pages, it must be explained that a number of these relate to *Ferreira* in heavy weather. In reality, when a ship is labouring under such conditions of gales, hurricanes, and mountainous seas, a large amount of spray tends to fill the atmosphere; this in turn reduces visibility to a minimum. With this in mind I have omitted much of the spray which should have been evident in some of the drawings the sake of clarity.

In this book imperial measurements are used throughout. Also, and unless otherwise stated, ship's lengths are at all times given as being between perpendiculars, ie; from the rabbet at the inside of the stem to the inside of the stern frame.

Therefore a given ship's length does not include the bowsprit, jib-boom or the overhang of the stern.

Vessels of whatever rig they may be, may at times be referred to as being a ship, even if they are barques, schooners steamers or other.

John Willis
Owner of *Cutty Sark*

Cutty Sark Society

Cutty Sark laying at Falmouth after being restored to her original state.

Basil Lubbock

Probably the greatest of all British maritime writers on ship's of sail was Alfred Basil Lubbock. He spent many years at great expense to himself, in chronicling the clipper ships and windjammers of yesteryear, and without his efforts in life, the world of maritime writers and researchers would be much the poorer. Basil Lubbock as he is better known was born in Sussex, England on 9 September 1876. He was the son of Alfred Lubbock the seventh son of Sir John Lubbock, second baronet and brother to the first Lord Avebury. Coming from an established family Basil was educated at Eton. Adventurous and daring from the start he went to Canada in 1897 to join in on the Klondike Gold Rush, a feat accomplished by his going over the Chilcoot Trail. At a later date joined the British four masted barque *Ross Shire* on 12 July 1899. On that ship where he signed on as an ordinary seaman at San Francisco, he made a passage around Cape Horn to the UK. That tough rounding of The Horn must have sewn into him the seeds for his great love for sail, as indeed, it resulted in him writing his first book 'Round the Horn Before the Mast.' He took part in the Boer War where he held a commission, and in 1912 married Dorothy Mary, the widow of Commander TU Thynne RN. At the start of the First World War, he was once again a commissioned officer of the Wessex Brigade Royal Field Artillery. In that regiment he served in both India and France. During the Great War when Basil Lubbock had fought in the trenches, he was awarded the Military Cross. At the end of the First World War in 1919, he devoted his life to the priceless research and documentation for which we remember him so well today. It was James Brown, later known as of Brown Son & Ferguson of Glasgow, who published his many books. Basil Lubbock died aged almost 68 on 4 September 1944 at Monk's Orchard, Blatchington, Seaford, Sussex.

Hercules Linton

Hercules Linton the designer of *Cutty Sark* was born at Inverbervie, Kincardineshire on 1 January 1836. Coming from a family of means where his father was one of Lloyd's surveyors, Hercules was educated until the age of 19. He was then apprenticed to Alexander Hall & Son, a firm which in 1855 were the leading shipbuilders of Aberdeen. After serving his apprenticeship he continued with the company until his rose to a reasonably high position. In 1862 however, he changed employers to become the register surveyor of Lloyd's in their Liverpool office, there he served for six years as assistant to John Jordan the Chief Surveyor.

In May 1868 he went into a partnership with William Dundas Scott to form the ship building firm of Scott & Linton. However, the £1,200 they needed to set the business up had to be borrowed. Scott's £600 was provided by his father, whilst that of Linton came from the re-mortgaging of his house as well as the pledging of his life policies. In ship building and surveying circles, both Scott and Linton were highly regarded in the field of ship design and construction, but most unfortunately, neither of them were proficient in the art of business or money matters.

From the outset Hercules Linton managed the design and ship building side of the firm, William Scott attended to the finances and engineering, whilst John Rennie became their chief draughtsman. In May 1868 the new firm rented part of 'The Woodyard' a site in

Dumbarton which was formerly used by the ship builders Denny Brothers & Co. The first order Scott & Linton received was for a small iron steamer named *Camel*, but when signing the contract for its building with J Bibby & Co, no provision was made for either a deposit or any interim payments. The result of that lapse of business expertise soon developed into cash flow problems for the firm. The end result being they had to borrow from the banks, whereas, the usual deposit and interim payments would have been more than sufficient to take care of their financial problems.

In January 1869 they were approached to construct a composite built fine lined clipper ship for Captain John Willis. The reason Scott & Linton were chosen for such a state of the art vessel, was probably because of Linton's noted qualifications as a designer. Captain Willis was an extremely shrewd business man, and armed with the knowledge that Scott & Linton dearly wanted the contract …. in order for them to enhance their reputations as ship builders …. he included a number of clauses into the contract. At that particular time the going rate for the building of a composite ship was £21 a ton. But Willis who had an option of builders cleverly squeezed the price down to £17, on the grounds that he was taking a risk due to Scott & Linton being a fledgling firm.

The contract implied that after Willis had paid the required deposit there would be seven interim payments, each of which were to be paid on the completion of each state of construction. Other clauses written into the contract were that a superintendent would oversee the ship's construction, and a £5 a day penalty would be incurred for each day of late being on every stage of construction. The contract agreement was reached and signed on 1 February 1869, and the composite ship was to be to the standard of A1 at Lloyds for 19 years with a completion date set for 30 July 1869.

It has always been a well known fact that Captain George Moodie superintended the building of the composite ship, and also, that he and his *aide de campe* Henry Henderson his master shipwright, rejected every piece of material which showed the slightest fault or blemish. Such a procedure of having a superintendent put the completion date back by a considerable time, moreover, as well as a having a pile of rejected material in their yard, the £5 a day penalty hit the builders hard.

The merciless treatment meted out to Scott & Linton by Captain Willis, is assumed to have been caused by the involvement of Hercules Linton's father Alexander Linton. At that particular time Linton senior was one of the Lloyd's surveyors at Glasgow. Furthermore, he became heavily involved in the ship's construction. Indeed, it was on his direction that the bilge areas of the ship had to be strengthened, which resulted in a long, costly and unforeseen delay.

Another clause in the building contract was that Denny Brothers & Co would complete the building of the ship should Scott & Linton fail. This was brought about when Scott &

Linton ran out of both money and credit. At the same time Captain Willis would not budge an inch on the contract by releasing any cash to the struggling firm. It was widely believed that Willis's reluctance to forward any money to Scott & Linton, was due to the obstinacy of the father of Hercules Linton. Due to their complete lack of finances, Scott & Linton were compelled to suspend all work on the ship in September 1869. At that particular time the construction of the ship was almost complete, but Willis remained adamant not to forward any money to finish the project. Scott & Linton had no redress, and Willis was not a man to mix business with sympathy. Indeed, it may well appear that from the very outset of the ship being built, John Willis and the firm of Scott & Linton had crossed swords.

It may also appear that Willis had since set out to destroy Scott & Linton, and maybe that led to so many rejections in the building of the ship. It so happened that *Blackadder* and *Halowe'en* were being built at the same time by Maudsley Sons & Field in Deptford for Willis. No merciless examinations of materials took place on those two ships even if they were built of iron. Indeed, it later turned out that *Blackadder* was dismasted on her maiden voyage, and all due to shoddy workmanship. Nevertheless, despite the many recriminations from the people of Dumbarton which followed him for many years, Willis who cared nought for the ship builders or the gossip which surrounded him, took the contract away from the little firm. It was an action which resulted in Scott& Linton going bankrupt and out of business

At the time of the firm's collapse, Hercules Linton's wife gave birth to a son in October 1868 … at the same time his house was taken from him. The unemployed Linton then joined Gourlay Brothers & Co in Camperdown, Dundee, as an assistant manager. That job lasted two months before one at Leckie, Wood and Munro was undertaken. But he resigned and went to Morton Wilde & Co who had taken over The Woodyard which he himself had previously operated. But that firm also collapsed in November 1870 after just twelve months. Hercules Linton was appointed as a Fellow of the Antiquaries of Scotland in 1876. Further employed at London he returned north to Montrose where his tenth and last child was born in December 1884. His wife Marjorie died in the following month of January 1885. Moving back to his birthplace of Inverbervie Linton was elected to the Town Council in 1895, but *Cutty Sark's* designer died in Leith at the age of 64 on 15 May 1900.

;;

Since his excommunication from *Cutty Sark* before her completion, Hercules Linton the designer probably watched the ship's progress through the years with mixed feelings. He must have thought her performances were reasonable enough, but except for the odd flash of brilliance, there was nothing to suggest that his *Cutty Sark* was in any way outstanding. It would have appeared to many that *Cutty Sark* was just another fine lined clipper, and one which would become outmoded by both the steamers and the modern windjammers. But if they were Linton's thoughts, one which may have eluded him at the time, was she'd never had a captain with the ability to maximise her design and building capabilities.

Enter Captain Richard Woodget in 1885! Master mariner of the highest order, and one who showed the sailing world just what Linton's creation was really capable of. Indeed, it was whilst under his command, that both his talents and those of Hercules Linton's were tested to the absolute limit. One of these was in the incident which took place on 28 June 1891. Little has been written about that winters day in southern hemispheres of 1891, the day when *Cutty Sark* rode out and beat, what is in modern days referred to as being a 'Rogue Wave.' Although it was never measured, that huge wave which tracked *Cutty Sark* was probably 80 - 100 feet in height. In his explanation of the gigantic wave which hit the ship, Captain Woodget said Linton's counter stern lifted the ship to such a height, that she was lying bows down at a precarious angle of 45 degrees. Nevertheless she rode the monster wave perfectly.

Those natural phenomemena known as rogue waves have roamed the oceans since time began, some ships which have encountered them have survived to tell the tale, but the number is extremely small. Even in the 21st century, behemoth sized ships of 200,000 tons and more, still arrive in port smashed and battered, and all after encountering one of those monsters which rear up and travel across the ocean at speed.

After Captain Woodget had proved his talents for the world of sail to see, possibly another of Linton's thoughts which may have crossed his mind, was that Woodget should have been her captain from the start. If he had, then those tea clipper records of the 1870's would have shown the name of *Cutty Sark* with much more regularity.

But even after all the records *Cutty Sark* did create, there is one thing Hercules Linton would never have even dreamed of, which was that not only would his *Cutty Sark* outlive every other clipper ship in existence, but she'd even last right up until the twenty first century. Indeed, the masterpiece of Hercules Linton presently lays at rest in Greenwich for all the world to see and admire.

Information for the above article has been supplied by Robert Linton from his Southport restaurant 'The Highlander. Scotsman Robert Linton is the great grandson of Hercules Linton.

S. R.

MINISTÉRIO DA DEFESA NACIONAL

MARINHA

MUSEU DE MARINHA

N.º 2897 Processo: 449.05

Assunto: CO-OPERATION

Referência: Your letter dated 19/7/95

Mr. J. Richardson

Ainsdale, Southport, Merseyside

PR8 3LQ

United Kingdom

Dear Sir,

We are afraid that's impossible to get the *Ferreira* ship's log as well as her crew lists. In fact these documental elements were lost forever. We could find a few data about that ship, but we are sure that you already have those simple informations. About the harbour movements of *Ferreira* perhaps you could try to pick up some informations near the portuguese customs services. Anyway, a complete list of *Ferreira's* movements it's out of question, even if supplied by the customs services. You can contact the customs archive writing for the following adress:

Direcção das Alfândegas de Lisboa - Biblioteca
Largo Terreiro do Trigo
1100 Lisboa

About the pictures of the *Ferreira*, we have a few, as you can see by the photocopies enclosed. The costs of these photographs depends on the printing of your book, but they are between 14.000$00 and 16.400$00 for each one. So, if you really want some of these pictures, let us know about the printing numbers of your book, to makes us possible to send you a final budget for this set of photographs.

With the best regards,

Lisbon, 13-09-95

THE DEPUTY DIRECTOR,

Pedro Luís da Costa Gomes Lopes
Captain, PO Navy

(a) Unidade, serviço, estabelecimento ou organismo.

Above: 16 November 1869 was the opening day of the Suez Canal.
Left: Ferdinand De Lesseps, the French engineer responsible for the creation of the Suez Canal.
Right: Ferdinand De Lesseps in his old age after his unsuccessful attempt to build the Panama Canal.

Photo - Frank Richardson

The Suez Canal had been planned and begun long before *Cutty Sark* had ever came into existence … or was even on the drawing board. In reality and as far as world trade was concerned, the Suez Canal was a major industrial advancement. But for sailing ships it was the final nail in their coffins. The canal had been designed and planned by the Frenchman Ferdinand de Lesseps, and a statue of him was erected at the canal's northern entrance at Port Said. Unfortunately, it was pulled down during the re-claiming of the canal by the Egyptians in 1956.
The opening of the Suez Canal marked a dramatic development in favour of the steamships, they could reduce the time taken by steaming out to the far east by a number of weeks. As an example; on her maiden voyage in 1862, the Alfred Holt steam ship *Agamemnon* took 82 days to reach Shanghai from Liverpool via the Cape of Good Hope. No sailing ship had ever come close to those figures. But on the opening of the canal in 1870 … when *Agamemnon* was the seventh ship to pass through, she made the same passage in 42 days!
That was just a few weeks before *Cutty Sark* began her maiden voyage. She couldn't go through the canal! The towing, passage and pilot fees were too high, as well as the fact that the Red Sea is often a windless zone. Sailor men cursed the Suez Canal calling it 'the ditch' … .and well they should, because soon afterwards commercial sail had gone forever.

Oil Painting by the author

Above:

The 2,600 ton SS *Agememnon* built in 1862 was the first of Alfred Holt's Blue Funnel Line. She was indeed the one ship above all others which spelt the death knell for sail. Soon afterwards her two sister ships SS *Ajax* and SS *Achilles* joined the company.

On the right is Mr Alfred Holt in his old age. A brilliant engineer in steam, and the man who pioneered the double compound steam engine.

John Willis the diehard owner of *Cutty Sark* believed whole heartedly in sail, whilst Alfred Holt believed the future lay in steam. Alfred Holt was the undoubted winner.

Cutty Sark

On succeeding his father in the shipping business, Captain John Willis already owned a few ships in the tea trade. But despite the fact his company was successful and showing a profit, Old White Hat Willis, or Willis of the White Hat, as he was generally referred to, wanted something really extra and special. For quite some time he'd been watching in envy at the other the tea clippers as they won great acclaim with their staggering runs in bringing the teas back to London. It was the mode or craze of the day, and just like so many other ship owners he dearly wanted to emulate them all. It was in those times the greatest desire of any ship owner to possess the fastest clipper ship, and although his flagship *The Tweed* was his favourite, Willis knew her chances of being first home with the first tea were remote.

The Willis dream was to have a clipper ship which was absolutely second to none. His vision was to own a perfectly designed and built ship, a ship which combined beauty with power and strength. In being reasonably wealthy Willis was in a position to have such a ship built. He also knew enough about ships and their designs to open negotiations. But he wasn't one of those ship owners who had inherited wealth by engaging managers to run his business then live off the fat of the company profits. He was indeed an extremely active person, and one who in the days of coach and horses and the early steam trains, travelled regularly between London and the Clyde to operate his business. He had himself been to sea in his father's ships, and at the age of 12 had started from the bottom as a ship's boy. Indeed, he had learned the hard way before attaining his master's certificate. He also knew what a day's work was - and the value of every penny he earned and possessed!

Willis had a ship which had recently been built at Dumbarton, Her construction had been started by Scott & Linton but finished off by Peter and William Denny. In those days a ship's name was often a well kept secret until its actual christening, and such was the case of the ship to be launched. The naming of any ship whether it be a mighty battleship, a huge passenger liner, or just a little sailing ship always holds the same significance. It is indeed a solemn occasion and often one of great celebration. Consequently, on a cold grey day of 23 November 1869, with just a few people in attendance - due to the unpopularity of Willis, the finished ship was launched at Dumbarton by Mrs Janet Moodie. She was the wife of her first captain to be, and the man who had supervised her construction. As the champagne bottle showered against the ship's bows, she named the ship with the time honoured words of "I name you *Cutty Sark*, may God bless you and all who sail in you." Neither William Scott, Hercules Linton nor John Rennie were invited to attend the launching ceremony. The people gathered at the launch were rather bemused at the strange name of *Cutty Sark,* but in being a Scotsman thorough and through, John Willis was a man with a great love for Scottish poetry.

Amidst the roars of thunder and lightning, the terrified Tam O' Shanter was chased through the graveyard, by Nannie the witch.

He had chosen the name of his new ship from 'Tam O' Shanter' a poem written by his much beloved Scots poet Robert Burns. One of the passages in the poem relates to a group of witches performing unholy rites in a graveyard, when quite suddenly! Tam O' Shanter on horseback comes upon them. Amongst the gathering of ugly old witches there was one exception - Nannie! A beautiful young witch wearing a cutty sark o' paisley harn. She is described by Robert Burns as chasing Tam O' Shanter as he gallops away in terror on his mare named Meg. In the thunder and lightning the chase goes on through the graveyard, until with her left arm outstretched to catch Tam O'Shanter, the beautiful young witch was only able to only pull a handful of hairs from the horse's tail.

On 21 December 1869, the new ship was towed across the River Clyde to Greenock, there she was rigged and fitted out with the very latest style of rig and sail plan. *Cutty Sark* set sail towards London to load her first cargo for Shanghai in January 1870. It would appear that due to the economics of the day, a run crowd from the builders had sailed the ship down to London then paid off at the arrival port. Run crowds are a group of sailors who sign on to the ship's articles, but are simply hired to take a ship on short port to port passages.

Ship owners or their captains never signed crews on until the last day or so before the ship sailed, and in many cases crews were signed on sailing day! Money had always been tight for ship owners, and the wastage of pay by keeping a full crew on board was out of the question. Indeed, her first crew were signed on 11 February 1870 after the ship had been at London for a month. Alternatively, had *Cutty Sark* signed a Glasgow crew which would have seemed more appropriate, they would have been idle on pay for a month. But it was Captain George Moodie who sailed *Cutty Sark* from the Clyde to London. It has been said in much later times that if he hadn't been so contrary in his examination of all the materials which went into *Cutty Sark's* building, then that ship would not be where she is today ... in Greenwich!

Indeed, of all the known surveys the ship underwent during her working career, it is true testimony to her builders ... and Captain Moodie, that her hull never showed any sign of deterioration. At sea and except for routine turnings over, her bilge pumps were hardly ever used. Consequently, *Cutty Sark*'s figure head was made by the noted wood carver Francis Hellyer of Blackwall. It is that of Nannie the witch wearing her 'cutty sark' o' Paisley harn. She is portrayed with her left arm outstretched and her long black hair flowing into the wind. In later times when the sailors of *Cutty Sark* had been painting over the ship's stem - and knowing both the origin of the ship's name and its figure head, it is said they often put a handful of rope yarns in Nannie's left hand, a replacement for the hairs she grasped from the horses tail.

Translated from Scottish Gaelic, a cutty sark is a short chemise, a scanty little nightgown, or a short shift, an item of clothing which was worn by Nannie the witch. After the figurehead had been carved by Hellyer, Willis then instructed him to position a number of beautiful naked witches around the ship's counter stern. Also on the squared stern was a carving of Tam O' Shanter on his mare. The figures depicted the witches chasing the horseman through the graveyard. Many of the London populace roundly applauded the entertaining design of *Cutty Sark's* stern, but in those years there were also a large number of narrow minded people who held a strict Victorian stance. No doubt many of them were clerics, and to escape the wrath of those people in high places and especially the church, the end result was the female figures had to be removed, or else any his hopes of getting cargoes from London might be jeopardised!

Cutty Sark, was built at 921 nett, 963 gross, and 1,200 deadweight tons. She has a length between perpendiculars of 212 feet, whilst the overall length of the vessel, from the outer end of her jib boom to the after end of the spanker is some 280 feet. With a beam of 36 feet, the moulded depth of the vessel is 22 feet 5 inches Her main truck at the time of building was 151 feet above the loaded waterline line and 145 feet above the deck. In those days there were no Plimsoll Load Lines. On the mainmast she crossed a skysail and had the usual arrangement of stunsails; in all, the Cutty *Sark* spread over 32,000 square feet of canvas Being composite built, *Cutty Sark* had a comparatively much stronger and lighter hull than her fore runners, added to which, she had wire rope for her standing rigging and did not have to use outside channels, an item which although allowing for a greater spread of the shrouds, served to somewhat hinder a ships speed.

Cutty Sark was fitted lavishly with teak wood, and as well as being able to load a cargo of 1,200 tons was extremely fine lined and built specifically for the tea trade. The ship was, or is, as the term goes … a thoroughbred, an out and out clipper of the highest order.

15 February 1870 was the time when *Cutty Sark* began her maiden voyage. But more importantly and as far as commercial sail was concerned, it was also the month in which the first steam ships passed through the Suez Canal!

Much of the information on the following pages has been condensed from SF Bailey's 1989 book 'The Crews of The Cutty Sark.' These descriptions which were taken from the original logs of *Cutty Sark*, are presently in The National Maritime Museum at Greenwich. They cannot in a minority of cases be ascertained as being 100%. This is due to some of the storage systems of the times, as well as poor handwriting and the illiteracy of some of the sailors of the day.

Maiden Voyage Crew List of *Cutty Sark* 11 February 1870

Name	Rank	Origin		Monthly Wage	Age
Moodie G	Master	Fife		…..	39
Low J	1st Mate	Aberdeen		£8	30
Guthrie J	2nd Mate	Banff		£5;5;0	34
Henderson H	Carpenter	Perthshire		£6;6;0	29
Dryburgh A	Carp - Mate	Fife		£3;10;0	20
Johnson C	Bosun	London		£3;10;0	38
Frank W	Sailmaker	Memel, Russia		£4;10;0	38
Ambrose W	AB	Antigua	WI	£2;10;0	29
Bain J	AB	Glasgow		£2;10;0	28
Brown W	AB	St Vincent	WI	£2;10 0	25
Cook G	AB	Bedford		£2;10;0	29
Cooper	AB	Scotland		£2;10;0	22
Costello J	AB	Valparaiso Chile		£2;10;0	21
Davis H	AB	Antigua	WI	£2;10;0	25
Ennew	AB	London		£2;10;0	20
Fisher R	AB	British Guiana		£2;10 0	24
Fletcher W	AB	Southampton		£2;10;0	46
Hanlon J	AB	Guernsey		£2;10;0	20
Jackson S	AB	Dumfries		£2;10;0	31
Johnson H	AB	Riga, Russia		£2;10;0	22
Johnston A	AB	Finland		£2;10;0	26
Parker W	AB	London		£2;10;0	18
Richards W	AB	Liverpool		£2;10;0	25
Spears J	AB	Bristol		£2;10;0	21
Swinson P	AB	Sweden		£2;10;0	24
Vaughan E	AB	Bangor		£2;10;0	22
Wellesley J	AB	London		£2;10;0	46
Hegarty W	Ord Seaman	London		£2; 0; 0	19
Korpi J	Ord Seaman	Finland		£2; 0; 0	19
Rae J	Cook	West Indies	WI	£3;10;0	52
Ferguson J	Steward	Jamaica	WI	£4; 0;0	26

. Ship's Company Thirty One

The Voyages of *Cutty Sark* Under the Red Ensign

	Signed on at	Dates From and To	Days	Captain
01	London	11-2-70—14-10-70	245	George Moodie
02	London	5-11-70—21-12-71	403	George Moodie
03	London	3-2-72—19-10-72	259	George Moodie
04	London	20-11-72—3-11-73	348	Francis W Moore
05	London	4-12-73—21-10-74	321	William E Tiptaft
06	London	10-11-74- 25-10-75	349	William E Tiptaft
07	London	19-11-75—27-9-76	313	William E Tiptaft
08	London	16-10-76- 11-10-77	360	William E Tiptaft
09	London	1-11-77—16-11-77	15	William E Tiptaft
10	London	29-11-77—13-1-80	776	Tiptaft - JS Wallace
11	New York	13-2-80—9-3-80	25	James Smith Wallace
12	London	13-5-80—10-4-82	706	JS Wallace - Wm. Bruce
13	New York	1-5-82—2-6-83	397	F Moore
14	London	13-7-83—21-3-84	220	F Moore
15	London	11-6-84—27-2-85	226	F Moore
16	London	30-3-85—21-12-85	273	Richard Woodget
17	London	15-2-86—7-6-87	477	Richard Woodget
18	London	15-8-87—10-3-88	208	Richard Woodget
19	London	14-5-88 —21-1-89	251	Richard Woodget
20	London	2-5-89 —17-1-90	260	Richard Woodget
21	London	12-5-90—17-3-91	309	Richard Woodget
22	London	21-4-91— 29-1-92	283	Richard Woodget
23	London	9-8-92—17-4-93	251	Richard Woodget
24	Antwerp	28-7-93—28-3-94	243	Richard Woodget
25	London	22-6-94—26-3-95	277	Richard Woodget

Cutty Sark's Maiden Voyage Crew

At times when just one or possibly two ships were looking for a crew, whilst at the same time a large number of ship-less sailors were looking for employment, a ship's captain was able to take his choice from those unemployed sailors. Therefore, he would advertise for a crew by having a notice placed at the bottom of his gangway. Sailors who combed the docks seeking employment would take heed, and on a given date would congregate on the quay side beneath the poop deck in the hope of being selected. The ship's captain and his first mate would then arrive on deck to choose the men they required. No doubt some of the faces in the crowd would be known to both master and mate, and by this method of crew selection, any known trouble makers or incompetent seamen could be excluded from their choice.

However, having a 'stand' on the quayside which all captains liked to have was not always the case, and more often than not it wasn't. On many occasions when there were a large number of ship's captains looking for a crew, whilst at the same time there were not enough sailors to fill the posts, then the positions previously described were completely reversed, it was then the seaman who could pick and choose. It would indeed appear from crew list on the preceding page, that except for the master, his first and second mates as well as the two carpenters who were all hand picked Scotsmen, the other twenty six of the ship's company were somewhat of 'a mixed bag' of stragglers.

The fact that *Cutty Sark had* arrived in London from the Clyde as a gleaming and sparkling new ship about to make her maiden voyage, seemed to have held little esteem or respect for those who were looking for employment. Possibly because many seamen of the day opted for the more comfortable steamers, Or it may have been that any new ship of sail held hidden terrors in being untried, or if she had been poorly rigged she may well be a workhouse on her sailing with unwanted repairs aloft. Or quite possibly and more than likely, it could have been the names of Willis and Moodie who put them off. Indeed, it was no secret in the local taverns that those two men had brought Scott & Linton down through their ruthless business activities, and many sailors might have expected similar harsh treatment on the ship when it sailed. There were a number of sought after shipping companies who sailors of the day looked out for, but according to the maiden voyage crew list, it would appear that John Willis & Co was not one of them.

When *Cutty Sark* did sign her first crew on 11 February 1870, sailors must have been in short supply, because at that particular time Captain Moodie did indeed sign on a rag tag mixed bag crew - and they were probably all he could get! In those days there were no Merchant Navy Pools where seamen could register. It was either being a 'Company's Man' - a sailor who stayed in the same ship trip after trip, the company's office, or else combing the docks looking for a ship.

It was always the policy for a seamen to draw a month's advance of wages when signing on a ship, this was for him to either pay off his lodging debts etc, or to buy clothing for the voyage. In many cases however, the money was used for a drinking spree, and some of the men never recovered enough from their jollifications to join the ship when it sailed. The advance of wages was no loss to the ship owner. If a seaman failed to join and sail with the ship after accepting an advance of wages, that loss fell upon the money lending ship chandler or pawnbroker who cashed the advance note for the seaman. If and when a ship's chandler cashed an advance note, he would invariably do so on the proviso that on top of the 10% - 15% deduction for his fee, the seaman also bought clothing from him.

All seamen of the day had to provide their own bedding. This which consisted of a straw mattress was a main seller at ship's chandlers, and because of their straw content those items were referred to by their users as 'donkey's breakfasts.' After having drawn an advance note when signing on *Cutty Sark,* H Fletcher of Southampton and A Shinper of Dover failed to join the ship. Only one replacement AB named W Ennew could be found, he joined as a Pier Head Jump when the ship anchored off Gravesend on 15 February. The ship weighed and sailed at 4 am on the following day of 16 February 1870.

On the ship's arrival at Shanghaai, 104 days after leaving London, two AB's named Bain and Hanlon were dismissed on 13 June for allegedly broaching cargo. Two more AB's were also paid off on the same day for other offences. Those four men were replaced on 15 June 1870 by J Durr of London, E Evans of Aberayon in Wales, J Jones also of Aberayon, and J Kinseller of Dublin. A week later W Emmen of London was signed on as AB, whilst in order to work his passage back to the London, W Christo an AB from Aberdeen signed on as a supernumerary at £1 a month. During the homeward passage which began on 25 June 1870, one of the AB's named Richard Fisher who was 24 years old and came from British Guiana, died of dysentery and was buried at sea on 21 July.

Beating down the China Seas against headwinds, currents and calms for the first 37 days after leaving Shanghaai, the ship made just 728 miles. That is just about the same distance as between John O' Groats and Land's End. An average which was less than one knot or 20 miles a day. However, on picking up the winds and after a 110 day passage, *Cutty Sark* arrived in London on 13 October 1970 to complete her maiden voyage.

The crew of *Cutty Sark* for her maiden voyage which included her Shanghaai replacements, consisted of at least ten different nationalities which were as follows.

8 Scotsmen, 9 English, 3 Welsh, 4 West Indians, 2 Russians, 2 Finns, 1 Guernsey, I Swede, 1 Irish 1 from British Guiana 1 Chilean, the cook J Rae was from a WI unknown origin .

The position of cook on any ship in those days was one of great esteem, he was normally the most respected man on the ship and the one most unlikely to leave …. unless of course he was a bad 'un! Likewise the mate or bosun would hardly leave of their own accord after one voyage. On the day after the ship's arrival at London however, the following crew members were paid off. No doubt many if not all of those 22 listed below were dismissed by the no nonsense captain.

1st Mate J Low - Bosun C Johnson - Ship's Cook W Rae - as well as 19 AB's -W Ambrose - W Brown - W Christo - J Cooper - J Costello - A Dryburgh - J Durr - E Ennew - E Evans - W Hegarty - S Jackson - H Johnson - A Johnston - J Jones - J Kinsellar - W Parker - J Spears - P Swinson and E Vaughan.

Due to the ship not having a half-deck, apprentices were not carried on *Cutty Sark's* first two voyages. On the third voyage, Alexander Moodie the captain's son became the first of the ship's apprentices. When the half-deck was constructed in 1872, three apprentices were carried on voyage number 4. The half-deck had berths for eight apprentices

GREAT RACE
OF THE
TEA SHIPS,
WITH THE FIRST
NEW SEASON'S TEAS.

PRICE OF TEAS REDUCED.

THE "Taeping," "Ariel," "Fiery Cross," and "Serica" have arrived, with others in close pursuit, with something like FORTY-FIVE MILLION POUNDS OF NEW TEA on board—half a year's consumption for the **United Kingdom**. This enormous weight coming suddenly into the London Docks, Shippers are compelled to submit to **MUCH LOWER PRICES**, in order to make sales.

We are thus enabled to make a Reduction of FOURPENCE in the pound.

4/0	down to	3/8
3/8	"	3/4
3/4	"	3/0

And so on downwards.

We may add the above Ships have brought a few lots of most unusual fine quality.

Reduction takes place on Friday the 21st inst.

135, OXFORD STREET;
57, STRETFORD ROAD; and
171, STRETFORD ROAD—
"Great Northern."

BURGON & CO.,
TEA MERCHANTS.

Courtesy National Maritime Museum, London

Poster advertising the Great Tea Race of 1866. Like most advertising, somewhat misleading; the tea cargo of the four leaders was approximately four and one half million pounds, not forty-five million as the poster states.

Cutty Sark
From a Line Drawing by Max Millar

Cutty Sark Society

Loading Tea Cargoes

The preceding page drawing of *Cutty Sark's* sail plan, shows her as she appeared in 1870, it also provides an inside view of the hold after the ship had been loaded with tea chests. Tea could be a very complex cargo to load onto clipper, and especially when the ship would be taking part in a race from the Far East to London. To participate in such a race, the ship had to be perfectly balanced to get every last yard of speed out of her, and the manner in which a ship was loaded played a crucial part.

When a ship is laying light at anchor before the loading of the tea begins, her sailors would scrape barnacles and seaweed from the ship's side as far down as possible. A cleaner under body would give the ship a swifter and smoother passage through the water. Alternatively, with a barnacle encrusted bottom, even a reduction of half a knot of speed would mean a loss of 12 miles a day - or 1,200 miles over a 100 day passage, which in turn might well mean 4 -10 days of extra sailing.

When a tea clipper is fully loaded and ready to sail, those tea chests by themselves would be insufficient in weight to send the ship down to the required level. Therefore, extra stiffening weight which may be bags of sand or the like, would be floored out on the bottom of the hold to send the ship a little further down in the water. Needless to say, a good or experienced captain would know exactly how much stiffening he needs to attain the required deadweight. On the other hand, too little stiffening would result in the ship having a bigger freeboard, whilst too much stiffening would mean a reduction in the tea which could be loaded. In the years of the tea clippers there were no compulsory load lines, and on a racing clipper ship, their captains didn't want or even need them.

It is a well known fact that when the ship is at sea, a clipper captain would spend most of his life on the weather rail, but when loading tea, he would be down in the hold supervising the placement of the chests. Tea chests were not all the same shape or size, and because of a clipper's extremely fine lines, some of them were half chests or even wedge shaped to fit into the every nook and cranny in the odd corners, thereby maximising every square foot of cargo space. Once the cargo has been loaded and the ship is ready to sail, the captain would at all times want his ship a little down by the stern.

Captain George Moodie

Born at the fishing village of East Wemyss in the County of Fife in 1831, George Moodie quickly became acquainted with the sea. Seamanship, carpentry, fishing nets, fishing boats and their construction were all part of his future education, and indeed the young George Moodie learned well. At the age of 16 he signed his indentures with Johnstone Brothers of Grangemouth, a textile company who sent him to join the brig *Lively Maria*. At the age of 23 he married Janet Cassels also of East Wemyss, and after serving as an AB, then from second to first mate, George Moodie gained his master's certificate at the age of 30. He then joined the fleet of John Willis to serve on *The Tweed* as first mate under Captain Stuart, in what was to be the ship's first voyage after her conversion from a paddle wheeler. After just one trip in that ship he was given command of the tea clipper *Laurel* on which he made a voyage to the east. In the following year his employer John Willis went along as passenger. Some passenger! Old White Hat soon learned that not only was his new captain a sound and forceful master, but was also quite an authority on ship design and construction.

In 1868 after George Moodie had became master of the tea clipper *Lauderdale,* John Willis who was by that time well aware of Moodie's ship building skills, took him off the ship to discuss plans for the building of a new clipper ship, and then for him to superintend the construction of it. Willis's favourite and pride of the fleet was *The Tweed*, a strong and powerfully built vessel which had once been a paddle wheeler built of Malabar teak at Bombay in the early 1860's. Much has been written about *The Tweed*, a ship from which the new ship's lines and other of her attributes were taken for *Cutty Sark's* building. Indeed, a lot of credit should be given to the Bombay ship builders for the subsequent lines of *Cutty Sark* as well other ships in the Willis fleet. A short article on *The Tweed,* has been included near the end of this book.

When Willis's new ship was being built at The Woodyard in Dumbarton, George Moodie who superintended her building went to great lengths in selecting only the very best of materials for her construction. Needless to say, the ship builders Scott & Linton later went bankrupt and out of business, and all because of the hard headedness of both Moodie and Willis. However, it was not Captain Moodie himself who examined all the timbers which went into the construction of the ship, it was in fact Henry Henderson the shipwright. Indeed, it was he who reported his interpretation of faulty materials to his captain. The unfinished ship building contract then went to the guarantor Peter Denny & Brothers for its completion. The ship which was named *Cutty Sark* on her launching on 23 November 1869, was christened by George Moodie's wife Janet.

Cutty Sark's maiden passage under Captain Moodie was acceptable but nothing out of the ordinary. The trip from London (Gravesend) to Shanghaai which began on 16 February 1870 took 104 days; however, on one occasion on 14 April 1870 she did record 360 miles in a 23½ hours, an average of fifteen knots. During the passage *Cutty Sark* had encountered teething problems with some of her iron work which was normal for new ships of the day; then like many of the other outward bound tea clippers, *Cutty Sark* was continually held up by calms and light winds in the China seas.

Captain Moodie's first two voyages on *Cutty Sark* will be remembered as being normal enough, but it was his third trip on the ship which will place him in the annals of maritime history. Indeed, his performance on that voyage became one of the greatest seamanship feats of all time. At the time both *Cutty Sark* and her great rival *Thermopylae* were engaged in a race to land the first teas in London. Both ships had loaded at Shanghai and at near identical times they sailed from Woosung on 17 June 1872.

After the usual struggle down the China Seas both ships set their courses for London. The biggest problem for Captain Moodie at the time was, that the ship's owner John Willis had his brother Robert on board. Robert the youngest of the family had little knowledge of either ships or the sea, but in thinking that blood is thicker than water tried to lay the law down to the captain. Apparently Robert Willis had been abroad for health reasons and was taking passage back to London in his brother's ship. In the Willis family the father John and two brothers James and John had all become master mariners, James had been lost at sea and that possibly influenced Robert not to pursue the life.

Racing neck and neck with her arch enemy, *Cutty Sark* was within sight of, and just a few miles ahead of *Thermopylae* on 1 July 1872, but that was when the two ships lost sight of each other. Nevertheless the race continued across the Indian Ocean. But on 15 August after all kinds of gales and high seas had pounded the ship, a time when *Cutty Sark* was unknowingly almost 400 miles ahead of her rival, disaster struck! A big sea tore *Cutty Sark's* rudder off and she could not be steered The ship's position at the time was 34.26S and 28.1 E. The nearest places of refuge for repairs were the South African ports of either

East London or Port Elizabeth, both of which were about 170 miles away. But Captain Moodie knew that even if he were able to get a tow or use his sails and drogues to get to either port, there would be little or no repair facilities available in those fledgling seaports. Alternatively Cape Town where repairs would be available was 650 miles away, but even if a steam tow did become available it would be out of the question, because such a tow would take much more than a week, and by that time Captain Moodie was confident he could have made the repairs himself.

Nevertheless, the unknowing and the inexperienced Robert Willis demanded that the captain should put into port to make the necessary repairs. The captain refused and plans were made to repair the damage by making a jury rudder and fitting it at sea. The arguments became furious between both master and the ship owner's brother, so fierce, that at one point Captain Moodie threatened to clap the insubordinate passenger in irons. Needless to say, the ship's master asserted his authority on Robert Willis as to who was in charge of the ship. On that particular voyage and because the half deck had not yet been built, there was just one apprentice the 15 year old Alexander Moodie, who as the captain's son made just the one voyage in the ship. At that time Apprentice Moodie was the assistant to Henderson the shipwright, who after having assisted in the ship's building had signed on as its carpenter. The young Apprentice Moodie was given charge of the brazier and bellows as a forge was set up on the deck.

On the day after the rudder catastrophe the weather had moderated to just a big swell, but the hapless ship could only wallow and roll in it. Henderson was a John Willis favourite and a person who was amply paid at £6 guineas a month, a wage which was higher than any of *Cutty Sark's* carpenters during the whole time the ship was under the Red Ensign. As well as taking part in the ship's construction, Mr Henderson stayed in the ship for her first five voyages and served under three different captains.

Captain Moodie's description of the rudder replacement.

The making of the rudder was the simple part of it. The connecting of it to its post, and securing it to the ship in order for it to work …. and then for it to be of sufficient strength when positioned, was the most difficult part of the job. The connection was made by putting eye bolts in both the rudder post and the rudder, then placing them so that each would just clear the other. A large bolt made from an awning stanchion was then passed through them and clenched both ends. In this way we had five eye bolts in both the rudder and the post, both locked with strong bolts which would bear considerable weight.

The securing the whole of it to the ship was of the next importance, but it soon became apparent that this could not be carried out in the recommended manner, which was by

On 1 July 1872 *Cutty Sark* and *Thermopylae* were racing neck and neck, but on 15 August when *Cutty Sark* was 400 miles ahead of her rival, she lost her rudder in heavy weather.
                                                                Painting by the author

Captain George Moodie

placing chains along the ship's bottom and leading them to the hawse pipes. This is because *Cutty Sark* is too sharp for any chain to lay along the keel, as well as the fact that her length is too great. It would be too difficult to bind the post tightly owing to the great length of chain. I therefore concluded to take two guys through the after mooring pipes, fitting the lower one with a bridle under the keel, 16 feet from the heel of the ship, so that from post to bridle there would be little down pull to prevent post and rudder from rising.

The next thing was to get the steering gear connected to the rudder, the trunk was too small to admit anything but the false sternpost which emerged 30 inches above the deck but when wedged around formed good support. The steering gear then had to be secured to the back of the rudder and led to a spar placed across the ship about 15 feet before the taff rail, which led the steering chains clear of the counter then inboard to the wheel. Of course all the gear was attached to both rudder and post before it was put over the stern. Having a small model of the ship, I took all the measurements from the chains which enabled me to place it near the truth. By the time *Cutty Sark* had set sail again on 20 August 1872, she had drifted a nominal few miles to a position of 34.38S and 27.36E.

Against the prevailing winds and having to shorten down for fear of the jury rudder carrying away, *Cutty Sark* rounded the Cape and picked up the South Easterly Trade Winds. At all times a close eye was kept on the jury rudder, but more importantly the eyebolts which began showing signs of failure. On 12 September Ascension Island was passed, but on the 20 August when the trade wind gave out, so too did the last of the rudder eyelets. The whole contrivance then had to be hauled aboard in what at the time was calm weather, but within a day the repairs had been completed. To get the rudder stock up through the trunk way, the whole of the rudder and its associated parts were dropped over the stern and the ship's sails filled in the gentle breeze to move her ahead.

Once the semi submerged rudder was a little astern of the ship, the sails were backed to send the ship itself slowly astern, in that manner the stock could be hauled up the trunk way much more easily and the rudder was soon connected and working again. Nevertheless slow progress still had to be made as there was no spare gear left to fashion out any more rudder parts. Quite disappointingly for Captain Moodie, his race with *Thermopylae* had to take second place.

;;;

Thermopylae arrived at London on 11 September 1872 after a 115 day passage and was declared the winner. But after clawing her way home under reduced sail and speed for over 7,000 sea miles, *Cutty Sark* docked just over seven days behind her rival. After his continuous altercations with Robert Willis and despite the pleas of Old White Hat Willis

Cutty Sark's Oerts type rudder under normal circumstances.
She lost her rudder on three known occasions during her life span

Captain Moodie's jury rigged rudder - made from hatch boards, chains spars and outriggers.

for him to stay on as captain, both George Moodie and his son paid off *Cutty Sark* on 19 October 1872. Apparently Captain Moodie joined a Glasgow steamer of the State Line.

In those years ships had supporters just like sporting teams have today. *Cutty Sark* and *Thermopylae* both had their admirers, and much had been said as to which ship won the race. It was argued that *Cutty Sark* was almost 400 miles ahead of her rival when the rudder carried away, and although Captain Kembal of *Thermopylae* denied such a claim in being so far behind, he refused to produce his log book to his doubters for examination.

As for the tea race itself, *Titania* arrived at London on 19 September after 116 days and was first home with the teas for that year. She was followed by *Duke of Abercorn* which left Foochow on 18 June and took 114 days. Although *Thermopylae* and *Undine* were joint third in coming home after 115 days, the shortest passage of 1872 was apparently accomplished by *Normancourt*, a ship owned by the London bankers Baring Brothers. She took 96 days from Macao to The Lizard.

Captain Francis William Moore

There were two captains of *Cutty Sark* with the surname of Moore. The first of these was Francis William Moore of Flamborough, a captain who on 20 November 1872 took over *Cutty Sark* from George Moodie. The 50 year old Captain Moore had been in the employ of John Willis for a number of years and subsequently had 36 years of sea time behind him. A that particular time on November 1872 he was the 'ship's husband' (Shore Superintendent} for the Willis fleet. But because Old White Hat had previously been short of a captain for *Blackadder,* Captain Moore had been asked to come out of his seagoing retirement to take command of that ship. However, after a single voyage in *Blackadder* when he'd retired for the second time he was once again called out. This time and due to Captain Moodie's hastily made resignation it was to take command of *Cutty Sark.* During the ship's stay at London in 1872 the apprentice's half deck had been constructed, and three apprentices William Gibson, Frederick Hill and Henry Simmons were signed on for Voyage number four.

Due to the steamers taking the lion's share of the tea trade in the early 1870's, cargoes were getting thinner by the year. Therefore, *Cutty Sark* like a number of other tea clippers changed tack, and went out light ship to Sydney to load coal for Shanghai, then hang around in the hope of getting a cargo of tea for London. After a promising run in ballast, *Cutty Sark* under Captain Moore anchored in Sydney Harbour on 11 February 1873 after being 69 days out. On loading 1,200 tons of coal she then sailed on 1 April towards Shanghai, arriving there on 12 May after 41 days. But it was only after a close shave with a typhoon. Indeed, her near sister ship *Blackadder* who was sailing quite close whilst on the same charter was not so lucky and had to cut her masts away.

On arrival at Shanghaai a consignment of tea was loaded for London and *Cutty Sark* departed on 9 July 1873, two days ahead of her rival *Thermopylae*. Extremely bad weather was experienced in the China Sea, and because Captain Moore was one of those 'rather safe than sorry' captains he took no undue risks. Consequently, by the time he passed Anjer on 28 July, he discovered that *Thermopylae* had also passed Anjer, but 12 days earlier on 16 July. After having started out two days behind *Cutty Sark,* her rival *Thermopylae* docked in London after a 101 day passage, whilst *Cutty Sark* which arrived on 3 November took 117 days.

After just one voyage on *Cutty Sark,* Captain Moore hung up his sea boots for the third time and paid off on 3 November 1873, then returned to his position as ship's husband.

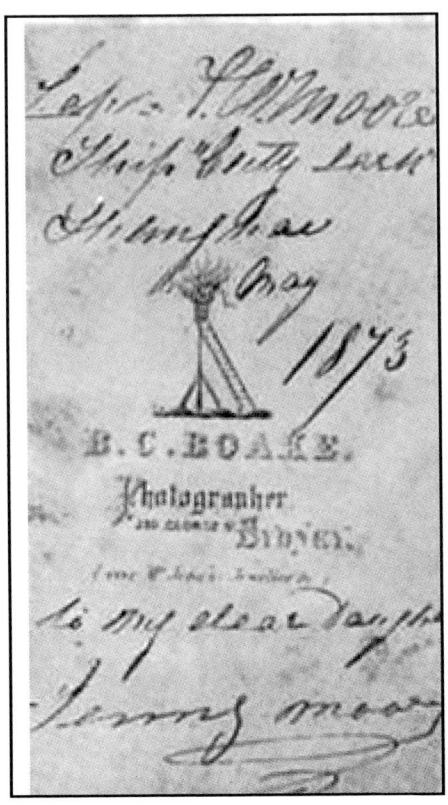

The photograph of 51 year old Captain FW Moore was taken at Sydney in May 1873 and is inscribed to his daughter.
The photographer was BC Boake of 330 Georges Street Sydney.

Captain William Edward Tiptaft

Born in 1843 at Coldstream on the River Tweed, a border town between England and Scotland, that little town is just a few miles from where the Willis family originated at Berwick on Tweed. When aged fifteen and just like John Willis his future employer, William Tiptaft moved to London to begin his sea career. After serving as ordinary seaman and then on becoming an AB, he entered the John Willis fleet three years later in 1861. On joining *Whiteadder* as AB and staying in the ship for four years, he rose to second mate in 1865. Later on he was promoted to first mate, then at the age of 27 became master of the ship after relieving Captain Frederick Moore in 1870. He stayed in command for two years before being transferred to another Willis ship *Merse*. But two years later when the other Captain Moore, namely Francis William Moore, wanted to leave *Cutty Sark* to continue with his ship's husbandry duties, Captain Tiptaft was sent to *Cutty Sark* as his relief.

(The two captains with the surname of Moore should not be confused. Frederick Moore was the captain William Tiptaft relieved on *Whiteadder*, whilst Francis William Moore was the captain he relieved on *Cutty Sark*.)

William Tiptaft was not noted for driving any of his ships, and just like Captain FW Moore before him, he held the 'rather safe than sorry' attitude. These points were made abundantly clear over the following years, when Captain Tiptaft made six so called 'rather mediocre' voyages on *Cutty Sark*.

The fifth of *Cutty Sark's* voyages began on 4 December 1873 when Captain Tiptaft first signed on. It was the ship's second voyage out to Sydney, but this time she loaded a general cargo for the Australian port. After discharging at Sydney Tiptaft took his ship to Shanghaai with coal, then found that after being the first to arrive for the new crop, was sent by the agents Jardine & Matheson up the Yangzte River to load tea at Hankow. The passage back to London with 1,270,651 pounds of tea, began at Woosung on 24 June, and ended 118 days later at London's East India Dock on 20 October 1874.

Voyage time - 321 days.

The sixth voyage of *Cutty Sark* and the second under Captain Tiptaft, began with her signing on at London on 10 November 1874, then leaving for Sydney four days later. That passage ended after 73 days on 2 February 1875. *Cutty Sark* repeated her previous voyage by loading coal for Hankow and sailing towards the Chinese port on 19 February 1875, arriving at Shanghaai 48 days later on 14 April. The passage back to London with tea began from Woosung on 21 June, and ended on 21 October 1875 after a 122 day passage.

Voyage time - 349 days.

After signing on again at London on 19 November 1875, William Tiptaft's third voyage on *Cutty Sark* began two days later on 21 November. However, after a collision with *Somersetshire* off Gravesend, *Cutty Sark* was compelled to return for a new main t'gallant mast and some of her ground gear. That delay cost the un-insured *Cutty Sark* four days as well as the repair bill. A spar of the required length could not be found as a replacement when the new main t'gallant mast was fitted in November 1877. Therefore, when the shortened version was shipped the skysail had to be dispensed with..

Since the *Blackadder* episode of 1870, when poor workmanship had resulted in that ship being dismasted on her maiden voyage, the insurance company had refused to pay out. This was on the grounds that the faulty workmanship was completed with the full knowledge of John Willis. From then on John Willis carried his own insurance.

Despite the fact that Captain Tiptaft was not a noted driver, *Cutty Sark* sailed 2,163 miles in the Southern Ocean on her passage towards Sydney, thereby creating a six day sailing record. *Cutty Sark* arrived at Sydney on 12 February 1876 and left three weeks later on 5 March with coal for Shanghai. She arrived at her destination on 23 April after 49 days. Loading tea for London she docked there in the nominal time of 111 days on 27 September 1876.

Voyage time - 313 days.

Captain Tiptaft's fifth voyage on the tea clipper began when he signed articles on 16 October 1876, then sailed for Sydney five days later on the 21st. Another cargo of coal for Shanghai, and another of tea for London saw *Cutty Sark* leaving Woosung on 6 June 1877. The tea clipper arrived with her cargo of 1,334,000 pounds of tea at the East India Dock on 11 October 1877.

Voyage Time 360 Days.

Captain Tiptaft signed on for his fifth voyage in *Cutty Sark* on 1 November 1877 and left Gravesend three days later. But the next two weeks were to test his resolve to the utmost.

After leaving Gravesend on 4 November for Sydney, the ship hit a ferocious storm in the English Channel. With the pilot still on board *Cutty Sark* put back into the shelter of The Downs. But so vicious did the weather become, that even in the lee of the land there was great danger of colliding with the dozens of ships which had already anchored. Those ships which included a number of large steamers had also sought refuge from the dreadful English Channel weather.

Captain Tiptaft waited in the anchorage for the gale to blow itself out, but instead of that it intensified into hurricane force. Lifeboats from one end of the English Channel to the other were putting out to assist ships in distress, but in the prevailing heavy weather many ships the length of the Channel were lost. Both of *Cutty Sark's* anchors were out to the bitter end, but so too was the ground gear of all the other ships in the bay. Many cables parted sending their ships ashore in the screaming hurricane, blue lights were to be seen everywhere as all the ships in the vicinity violently pitched, rolled and collided with each other. After that great storm of November 1877, there was hardly a ship in The Downs, that came through unscathed. Five were sent ashore, and dozens of sailing vessels had lost their masts and spars.

Both *Cutty Sark's* anchor cables had parted which sent her adrift. That resulted in her colliding with two different vessels which were also adrift. *Cutty Sark's* headboards and port bulwark was stove in, yards were swinging wildly with every roll and the deck was awash with sheets, braces and many other ropes which swirling around in the water had come off their belaying pins. Captain Tiptaft who made an attempt to get some sail on the ship, eventually got a lower topsail up to carry him somewhat clear of the carnage of smashed up ships. At that time the newly signed first mate JS Wallace played a heroic part in helping the ship to hold her own. That Scotsman's seamanship, courage and leadership were indeed one of the major factors in *Cutty Sark's* survival. Nevertheless the hurricane continued and all Captain Tiptaft could do was to keep his ship hove to.

Blue lights and rockets were set off for assistance and these were seen by the tug *MacGregor*. The tug arrived just in time to get a towline on board as *Cutty Sark* had been blown dangerously close to the Goodwin Sands. However, the little tug wasn't powerful enough to make much headway and Captain Tiptaft signalled for further assistance. This came by the way of the tug *Benachie,* and between those two, they towed *Cutty Sark* to the anchorage off Greenhithe.

In the subsequent claim for salvage, the tug owners who claimed £8,000 were awarded £3,000. *Cutty Sark* was uninsured, and John Willis had to pay for his for his own repairs for the damage sustained by the hurricane. That bill could have been a lot more had not Henry Henderson the eagle eyed carpenter dispensed with wreckage of another ship from off *Cutty Sark's* decks. Indeed, in one of the collisions in that chaotic storm, *Cutty Sark* had collided through her own fault with another ship. But despite the battering she'd received *Cutty Sark* was much luckier than a large number of other ships during that ferocious hurricane of November 1877.

No damage was sustained in the cargo, and after repairs to the ship and then on signing new articles 29 November 1877, *Cutty Sark* on her tenth voyage and Tiptaft's sixth, once again sailed for Sydney on 2 December. Her passage which took 72 days was the best of all the sailing ships out to Australia that year. Once again coal was taken to Shanghaai, this time in a 40 day passage which on 22 April 1878 saw *Cutty Sark's* arrival. But by that time and due to the ever increasing number of steamers, the tariffs for tea were rock bottom. Furthermore, all the agent could get for *Cutty Sark* was a half cargo, and to take half a cargo all the way to London would have meant the ship not paying her way

Undeterred, Captain Tiptaft took a cargo of coal from Shanghaai to Nagasaki, leaving the Chinese port on 18 September he arrived a week later then returned for another Shanghaai coal cargo. The bad news was that none could be had, but the worst news of all came at Shanghaai on 12 October 1878 when Captain Tiptaft took ill and died. His death was given as probable heart disease and stress brought on by overwork. His age was 35.

First Mate James Smith Wallace then took command of *Cutty Sark*.

Captain James Smith Wallace

James Smith Wallace who was born at Aberdeen in 1853, was yet another of those Scots who at the age of twelve began his seafaring life on fishing boats. Then after serving his apprenticeship in sail, and at the age of 25, he signed on *Cutty Sark* as her first mate on 1 November 1877. However, just a few days later when *Cutty Sark* had sailed for Sydney, and after going through that tempestuous November 1877 storm off The Downs, it was in that hurricane where First Mate James Wallace exemplified himself in his seamanship qualities. After that most inclement weather, the ship put back to London for repairs where Wallace paid off until the ship was made good. Then on 29 November he once again signed on as first mate at a monthly wage of £8. Under the command of Captain Tiptaft the ship sailed to Sydney, Shanghaai, Nagasaki and back to Shanghaai. It was in that latter port however, where the unfortunate Captain Tiptaft died. As a consequence, on 12 October 1878, 25 year old James Wallace assumed command of *Cutty Sark*.

Captain Wallace was most popular with the crew, he was also the fearless driver that *Cutty Sark* required to get the best out of her. Indeed, it was widely viewed at the time, that the ship had never been given the chance to prove her undoubted qualities. But Captain Wallace had a most unfortunate start to his captaincy. In the first instance, *Cutty Sark* like a few more of the tea clippers of 1878 was unable to secure a tea cargo from Shanghai for London. Indeed, the steamers had taken the lot, which simply meant that the days of the tea clippers were well and truly over. To add to his bad luck, the new captain was compelled to return to Sydney in a 51 day passage where all he could get was another cargo of coal for Shanghai. On leaving Sydney with 1,150 tons of coal on 11 March 1879, *Cutty Sark* arrived back at Shanghaai on 2 May after 45 days.

With the tea cargoes forever gone to the steamers, Captain Wallace left in ballast for Manila where he arrived in September 1879. Then with a cargo of sugar for New York he left the Philippine capital on the 23 September. *Cutty Sark* arrived at the America port on

12 January 1880 after 111 days at sea. Signing new articles at New York for voyage 11, and leaving New York behind on the homeward run towards London, *Cutty Sark* hit some heavy weather in the North Atlantic. Coming through those elements, Captain Wallace came upon a derelict timber carrier named *Ulster*. Registered in St Johns she had not been so lucky with the weather and was found abandoned and swept clean. With no sign of life on board the derelict, *Cutty Sark's* passage continued and after 19 days she docked in London.

During those years the crew numbers of all sailing ships were being reduced owing to lack of work, as a consequence *Cutty Sark's* crew numbers had been lowered from the original 31 of her maiden voyage down to the mid or lower twenties. John Willis then decided to have *Cutty Sark's* rig cut down, which in turn would give him the option of reducing the ship's crew even further. Therefore, after her London arrival the lower masts were reduced in height by between seven feet at the mizzen and nine feet six inches at the main, whilst the topmasts and t'gallants were cut down accordingly. The reduction of the overall height of the mainmast from deck to truck was fourteen feet. The yards were also shortened to give a more balanced appearance, whilst the skysail, stunsails and their booms were all discarded.

Voyage number 12 for *Cutty Sark* was to the Far East with best quality steam coal for the American Navy. But trying to get a crew for the voyage had been almost as hard as getting the charter. On leaving London for the South Wales loading port of Penarth, a crew of just 21 were signed on to take the ship around the land. It is not known whether or not a tow was taken. The crew for that passage was apparently.

Captain Wallace, First Mate SW Smith, Second Mate GH Rogers, Apprentices CA Sankey, HL Stoughton, WR Beaumont, FFC Kirby, HWS Parton, and WI McCausland, Carpenter E Holford, Sailmaker A Jansen, Cook TW Wells, and AB's J Camando, F Clark, W Edwards, C Louis, W Lynch, N Nicholasen, TCE Nothroth, J Rowlands, J Stern, and G Taylor.

But after leaving London and then on her arrival at Penarth on 22 May 1880, two of the AB's named Clark and Lynch were discharged, whilst Rowlands, Stern and Taylor packed their bags and deserted. The exodus of those five sailors was probably due to the bullying First Mate 'Bucko Smith.' Moreover, and because of the mate's bad reputation which quickly spread through the taverns of the South Wales seaports, namely Swansea, Cardiff and Newport, Captain Wallace had to drag the dregs of the coal ports to get a crew together. However, although he was probably looking for ten, he eventually managed to round up just six AB's.

The first three of those six who all signed on at £2-10-0 a month were American. Sam Carson of Savannah, John Dorsey of North Carolina and William H Francis of Chicago.

There was also Joseph Reynolds of Jamaica, George Alexander from Trieste, and J Downie from Bangor, the latter of whom who failed to join. But GE Williams from Cheltenham and John Somers of London signed as an ordinary seaman at £2 per month. *Cutty Sark* sailed from Penarth with a complement of 23. There is no mention in the records of a steward being carried.

William H Francis from Chicago was a 35 year old Negro, who signed on at Cardiff whilst the ship lay at Penarth. He and the first mate quickly came to despise each other, and because of their aggressive attitudes and conflicting personalities, they were both unpopular with the crowd. *Cutty Sark* sailed from Penarth towards Anjer for orders in June 1980, and from that date, First Mate Smith and AB Francis had a number of verbal altercations. They even had a fight on the deck which was witnessed by all hands. But it all came to a head in the middle watch of 11 July when the ship was about a week short of Anjer. Smith and Francis were in the same watch, and on being given an order Francis refused to obey then attacked the mate with a capstan bar. The mate wrested the weapon from him and smashed it over his head killing him.

Captain Wallace had a certain amount of sympathy for his chief officer. But he was compelled to have him locked up in his cabin until the ship's arrival at Anjer for the trial of his first mate for murder. Somehow or other Smith managed to break out of his cabin on the ship's arrival at Anjer, the general talk in the foc'sle however, was that Captain Wallace had assisted him in his escape. The sailors who wanted to see justice done to the hated Smith refused to turn to. Indeed, and despite their high regards they had for their captain, their refusal to work ship lasted a whole week whilst still at Anjer. However, after the mate was nowhere to be found they reluctantly turned to, and after receiving orders for Yokahama *Cutty Sark* sailed.

On 4 September 1880, the distraught and traumatised Captain Wallace was up on the poop deck at 4 am when he suddenly jumped over the taff rail and into the sea. Despite the helmsman's best efforts of throwing two lifebuoys into the water after him, the 27 year old Captain Wallace was never seen again. More than likely in his suicide, Captain Wallace was suffering from the pressures of the recent past and had weighted himself down before taking his plunge. So ended the life of a fine captain who was most popular with the whole of his crew and especially the apprentice boys to whom he gave regular instruction in navigation as well as seamanship. It has been said that the sailors blamed themselves for putting their immensely popular captain under so much pressure.

Whilst *Cutty Sark* was sailing towards Yokahama, the incompetent second mate then became master, but he declined taking the ship any further due to both his apparent bad eyesight and poor navigational skills. Consequently, the senior apprentice who was the most reliable navigator sailed *Cutty Sark* into Singapore. At that port a telegraph relating recent events was sent to John Willis in London.

Some three years later, the despised First Mate Smith was recognised in New York, reported to the police, later tried in the UK, and sentenced to seven years hard labour. for the manslaughter of WH Francis. On his release from prison he resumed his sea life under the auspices of John Willis who assisted him in passing the necessary examinations to eventually be given command of a steamer.

Captain William Bruce

William Bruce was not selected on merit to be the captain of *Cutty Sark*. Indeed, the 42 year old Aberdonian's appointment to the post was due a number of adversities; a series of events which began with the death of WH Francis followed by the escape of First Mate Smith which led to the suicide of Captain Wallace. At the time of those unfortunate episodes William Bruce was serving as first mate on *Hallowe'en,* another of the Willis ships which at that particular time was lying at Hong Kong. But because of his poor qualities as a seaman, Bruce was neither popular nor wanted by Captain Fowler of *Hallowe'en.*

So when John Willis received a telegraph informing him of the recent calamity on *Cutty Sark,* and then on asking *Hallowe'en's* master by telegraph if he could recommend and supply a replacement captain for *Cutty Sark*, Captain Fowler had no hesitation in volunteering the name of William Bruce to get rid of him. The result being, that on 24 September 1880, William Bruce signed on *Cutty Sark* as her master at Singapore. It was his first command, but by the time of his arrival most of *Cutty Sark's* crew had paid off by mutual consent. The new crew members signed on at Singapore were;-

Captain W Bruce; First Mate C Smith; Second Mate ST Reynolds; AB's - Canty; Collins; Foley; Hansen; Kellam; Lampig; Larson; Sharff; Shore, and Wilson. In the meantime the coal cargo for the US Navy destined for Yokahama had been diverted and discharged at Singapore. Nevertheless, with a new crowd of sailors, *Cutty Sark* sailed towards Calcutta on speculation looking for anything on offer.

By holding prayer meetings each day, Bruce soon made himself most unpopular with the new crowd. He was a heavy drinking hypocrite and soon proved to be a poor sailor as well. Indeed, in his first passage on his new ship towards Calcutta, this became most apparent to his sailors who regarded him as a coward, and all due to his inability to carry sail when the chance arose. However, *Cutty Sark* arrived at Calcutta in November 1880.

Because there were no cargoes available at the port, Bruce who expected a long wait to get one was obliged to pay the new sailors off. As a consequence the ship lay at Calcutta for nearly four months until her agent finally secured a cargo of tea and jute for Melbourne. Indeed, that cargo resulted in the first tea ever to be imported into Australia! Another new crew of sailors were signed on at £2-10-0 per month; as well as a first mate on £7 a month and a second mate on £3-10-0. But because Captain Bruce was unable to sign a full crew, there were seven who signed on at 1/- a month at Calcutta just for the run and free ride to Melbourne. There were also a few who had lived ashore and signed back on the ship again, they included the two ordinary seamen signed on at Penarth and the sailmaker. That sailmaker named Alexander Jansen was a 56 year old Russian who was unfavourably referred to as 'Vanderdecken,' a most unpopular Jonah who constantly prophesised doom and gloom for the ship. *Cutty Sark* sailed for Melbourne on 5 March 1881.

The new first mate was 25 year old William H Rutland of London, a bucko slave driver who quickly became the sanctimonious and hypocritical captain's drinking partner. After a tumultuous passage of booze daily prayers and self righteousness to Melbourne, Bruce got *Cutty Sark* to her destination on 14 May 1881. On arrival at the port an AB named William McGregor from Glasgow went overboard and was drowned. At Melbourne the seven men on the run job paid off; they were Second Mate A Selbie and four AB's J Caffey, J Carlson, G Fairhurst, and J Leary, as well as Ordinary Seaman A Delaney. Apprentice Stoughton also signed off the ship, but that was due to the hard time the mate had been giving him. Captain Bruce was then compelled to sign on replacements for those who had left. But there was a difference! - the new sailors would demand to be paid the Australian rate of £4 a month, 60% higher than that of the London wage! In Melbourne whilst alongside, the heavy drinking Captain Bruce held prayers on the deck of the ship each day, an act which was supposed to proclaim his piety to those who were watching from the quayside.

In the place of those run sailors came Second Mate H Carne, AB's O Allen, T Thompson, and J Leary; the latter who signed on again for another run, and two ordinary seamen H Peart and W Gerrard. Also signed on was the steward JA Cave of Sunderland. It was no secret in those days that captains despised anybody on Australian wages, whilst their foc'sle mates were either filled with jealousy or envy. With her three highly paid replacement AB's, who at £4 a month were on more wages than any second mate in sail, *Cutty Sark* discharged her tea and jute then sailed for Sydney via Port Phillip. But Captain Bruce's big worry was, how many of his sailors would skin out when he arrived at Sydney, thus giving him more problems of sailors on Australian pay.

On arrival at Sydney three AB's Edwards, Leary and Thompson who were on that run job for 1/- a month were paid off, but Oscar Allen who was on £4 stayed on. The cook JM Bosher of Kent as well as two ordinary seamen Meinke and Peart disappeared over the wall with their bags, whilst JH Hackley an AB who drew a £4 advance vanished with immediate effect. Therefore, Bruce was compelled to sign on a cook, J Barker at £4-10-0, five AB's, T Dunton, G Billings, W Blood, W Hall, and B Sullivan at £4 a month, H Horning an OS at £2 and deckhand Sydney Ormiston at £1. There were at the time nine AB's on £4 a month! Captain Bruce was not a happy man, but over a bottle of hooch, both he and the first mate hatched a plot to put those Aussie wage sailors in their place.

Cutty Sark left Sydney on 2 July 1881, and after a reasonably good 46 day passage arrived at Shanghai on 17 August. But after the hold had been emptied of its coal, the slave driving bucko mate done his best to work the overpaid Sydney AB's out. He did that by keeping them working non stop down the hold day and night until they cracked. Four of them who could take no more of the mate's hazing paid off by mutual consent. But that's when a cholera epidemic hit the ship. After a month two of the £4 a month Sydney AB's and another AB named McCarthy died with cholera at the Shanghai Isolation Hospital. The six Sydney sailors and McCarthy were happily replaced by Captain Bruce, who by that time had just three of his expensive hands to get rid of. He then signed four AB's on, A Foley, G Nichol, J Shubert, and C Wilson at the Shanghai rate of £2-15-0, and apprentice HWS Parton. The senior apprentice was promoted to third mate.

Due to the cholera and after missing out on a passage across the Pacific to Portland for timber, *Cutty Sark* eventually sailed towards the Philippine Island port of Cebu where a London cargo of jute awaited her. Once there however, and after having joined the queue, a wait of six weeks was experienced before the baled jute was loaded. But by the time loading had been completed, the cargo had been re-sold and the ship's orders had been changed for New York. Captain Bruce was noted for his two faced activities. One minute he'd be most cordial, friendly and god loving towards his crew. But in the next he could become the complete opposite. Due to his unfavourable attributes he supplied those before the mast with a few bottles of Philippine firewater. Then when they started fighting amongst themselves, he had William Blood locked up ashore for insubordination, drunkenness and riotous behaviour.

Blood who came from Hamburg was the seventh of the Sydney sailors to go, but it was quite evident to those around that he'd been framed by the captain. Blood was given a 60 day jail sentence and his place was taken by one of the Cebu natives Feliciano Guilleras for a £1 a month wage. That stroke of genius by the captain meant a further £3 a month saved on just one of the Sydney sailors. By ridding himself of seven of the nine Sydney sailors and replacing them with others on a lower rate of pay, Captain Bruce had therefore saved a massive £11-15-0 on the monthly wage bill. That episode of getting rid of four of the highly paid Sydney hands, notwithstanding the three who had died, had been very cleverly orchestrated by Captain Bruce and his first mate. But there were two more to go!

On her passage towards New York *Cutty Sark* left Cebu on 6 December 1881, with the crew in turmoil at what lay ahead. That mayhem started immediately the ship set sail when the captain and his first mate hit the bottle. In company with them was the steward who by acting as waiter joined in on the drinking session. The high powered rotgut booze soon had the revellers legless, senseless and acting in a most dangerous manner. However, the 21 year old Liverpool Second Mate Henry Carne who could see the dangers which lay ahead had other ideas. He therefore and most purposefully plied the captain with so much drink that he became completely incapable. Then whilst the captain was in such a state, the second mate threw his booze out through the porthole.

In their connivance with the sailors, the second and third mates sailed the ship 20 miles to the east and anchored off Cape Saint Nicholas Island. There she stayed for two days until the captain staggered up on deck! Despite his still drunken state he was flabbergasted in finding the ship at anchor, and on questioning the mates and apprentices as to how the anchoring came about, those men didn't offer any explanation. Captain Bruce said nothing about his cache of booze, he was in such a state his probable thoughts were that he, the mate and steward had drunk it all. Meanwhile, and due to the power of the alcohol, the first mate was still flaked out in his cabin. Once again the ship set sail towards New York via Anjer Point. Without any booze on board!

After baffling winds and light airs Anjer was reached by the 'dry ship' four weeks later on 3 January 1882. It was there that Captain Bruce surprisingly dropped his anchor, but that was only to load up with more booze. Enough to last him and his drinking partners, the mate and the steward, until the ship arrived at New York. No attempt was made to re-provision or water the ship, and as soon as *Cutty Sark* weighed anchor the boozing in the saloon began without delay.

When good captains have well drilled and contented sailors, such things as tacking ship is commonplace and an almost an everyday occurrence. Nevertheless, tacking has to be carried out with perfect timing, discipline and precision. But when sailors are poorly fed and badly treated, they most naturally go about their work in a sullen and dispirited manner. Therefore, when Bruce attempted to tack away from the Anjer anchorage, the discipline of his sailors as well as the timing to his own orders, was not what it might have been. The result was the ship being caught in stays with *Cutty Sark* being sent rushing astern almost hitting the rocks before the sails could be straightened out.

The captain and his first mate became engaged in a violent argument during their next drinking session. Eventually they both became so inebriated that the mate staggered to his cabin and locked himself in. The sailors were well aware of both their captain and the

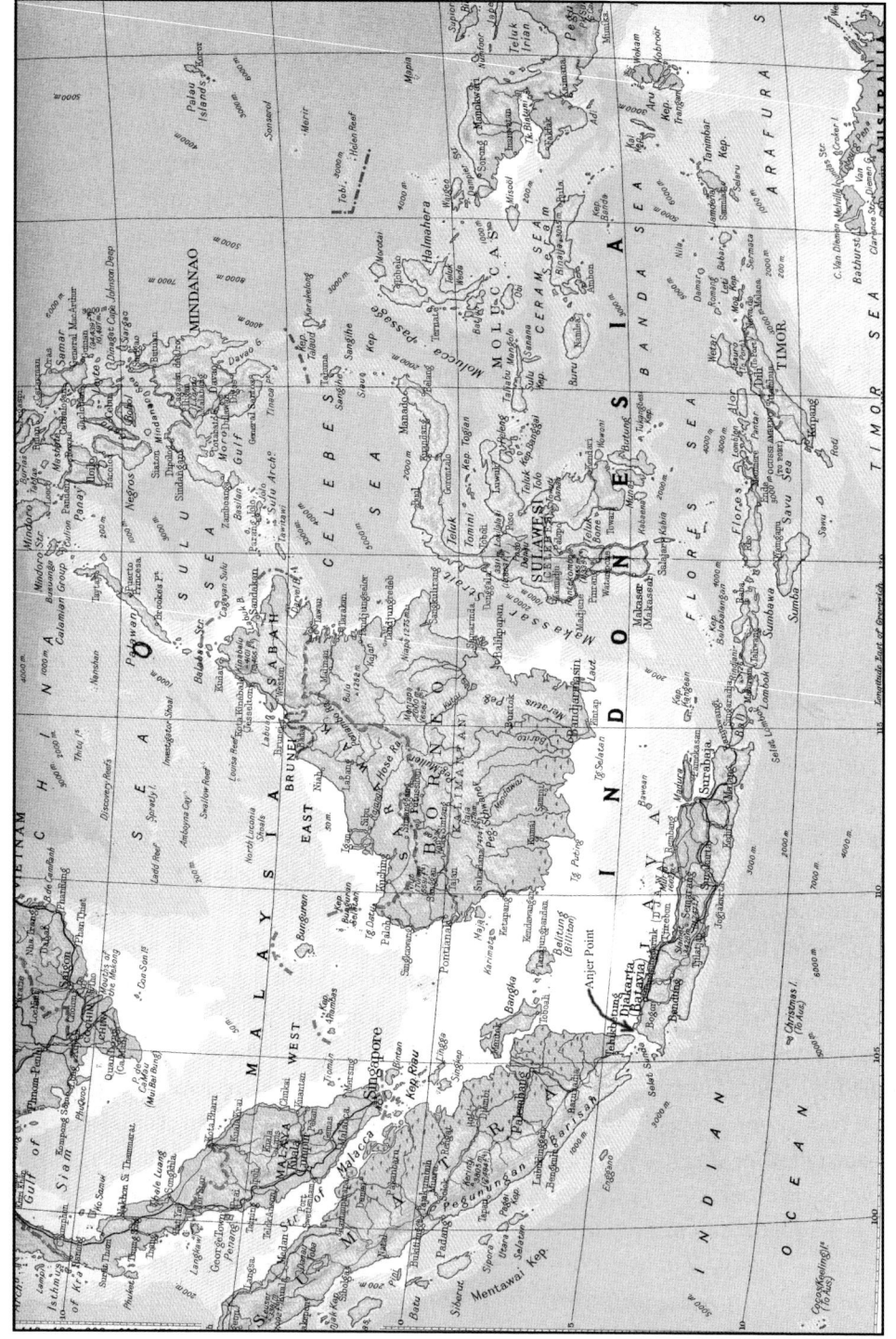

Anjer was a major staging point in the days of the tea clippers, but because it was wiped off the map by the Krakatau Earthquake, and is no longer shown on a modern atlas, this map has been inserted to show where its position was at the north end of the Sunda Strait.

mate's drinking, and for fear of their own safety, pleaded with the second mate to assume command. But the 21 year old knew that if he did so, and even with all hands backing his actions, The Board of Trade and the law of the land in Britain would have a different opinion on the matter. In a word it would be called mutiny!

On 4 February 1882, a month after leaving Anjer, the third Mate believed to be Charles Sankey and AB Thomas Dunton were climbing the starboard ratlines on the weather side to work aloft. At that particular time the starboard clew of the mainsail had been hauled up to allow the foresail to draw better. But when those two men were half way up the ratlines, the mate who was hanging around on deck suddenly let go the spectacle clew iron, tack and sheet blocks without any warning.

All that heavy gear then came down with a rush, knocking able seaman Dunton backwards out off the ratlines and over the side, whilst the third mate could only hang on to the main shrouds. "Man Overboard" came the cry. But despite lifebuoys being thrown into the water by the helmsman, and then on a boat being launched, the Hampshire sailor Thomas Dunton was never seen again. He was the eighth of the expensive Sydney hands to go! Those in the foc'sle and half-deck were outraged at the mate's actions, whilst the old sail maker Vanderdecken claimed his prophesies of doom and gloom had been all been justified.

Soon afterwards the provisions started giving out. The first shortages which came to light were the sugar and lime juice, items which at the loading port of Cebu were plentiful and cheap to buy. Then when *Cutty Sark* was off Table Mountain and half way to her New York destination the ship could quite easily have put into Cape Town to re-provision, but Captain Bruce had other ideas. Then the flour became short as the ship passed St Helena, but again the captain had no thoughts of replenishing the stores. He had enough for himself and that's all that mattered. Burgoo, a thin watery oatmeal substance soon became the only thing left to eat, and shortly afterwards when there was nothing left at all, some of the sailors began to feel the effects of scurvy.

Most fortunately for Captain Bruce his ship was in the busy shipping lanes. Passing ships were alerted as to the plight of *Cutty Sark,* and the flag signals being flown from her gaff proclaimed the fact that she had run out of provisions. Some ships stopped to give what little they could, but many of them who came from ill found companies were themselves hard pressed to give much away. Eventually the wooden built screw corvette HMS *Thalia* stopped to help out. After being rowed across to the warship by his apprentices, Captain Bruce went aboard the Man O' War.

What little tale Bruce told Commander AK Bickford, with regards to his being short on provisions can only be guessed at or imagined. (In later years Commander Bickford became a full admiral.) Nevertheless it must have been a good story, because a whole boat load of provisions including fresh bread - still hot from the galley oven, was thrown into Bruce's apprentice propelled boat and taken back to the clipper ship. If however, the real story about the provisions had come out, the warship's captain would probably have had Bruce clapped in irons and thrown into the corvette's brig to await trial.

But the trials and tribulations of *Cutty Sark's* crew were far from over; and because of their stance against the un-necessary ill treatment and starvation, both the second and third mates had been given a torrid time from their superiors since they had left Cebu. However, Captain Bruce who was indeed a fine navigator if nothing else, began softening up as the American coast came closer. For the first time he gave terrestrial and navigation lessons to the apprentices, and even tried to adopt a stance of friendliness with the scurvy ridden helmsmen. *Cutty Sark* arrived at New York on 10 April 1882, 125 days after leaving Cebu.

No sooner had the ship berthed alongside when the second and third mates requested to be paid off. But Bruce refused on the grounds that the voyage was not yet over. However, Second Mate Carne who had in fact been keeping diaries of the ship's daily events paid a visit to The British Consul. The second mate then showed him what the crew had been subjected to ever since Bruce had been appointed as the ship's master. Needless to say, the horrified consul sent a telegraph to John Willis in London to inform him of the atrocities which had taken place on one of his ships. Furthermore, the cable stated that food had to be begged from one of Her Majesty's Ships, and all after the opportunities of re-provisioning at Anjer, Cape Town and St Helena had all been bypassed.

Like all ship owners John Willis had always been a man to keep his eye on the pennies, but by being a former sailor himself, he had always ensured that his ships were well maintained and his crews given more than enough food to sustain their health and well being. He was most embarrassed by the fact that one of his ships had to beg food at sea, and horrified at what the sailors had to endure. At a subsequent Marine Enquiry held at New York, the certificates of both Captain Bruce and First Mate Rutland were suspended. On that infamous twelfth voyage of *Cutty Sark,* which lasted 12 days short of two years, a total of 79 men had signed on the ship whereas only 23 had started the voyage. During that voyage of 709 days there were seven deaths, and seven desertions.

Captain F Moore

When Captain William Bruce was sacked from the ship and out of the company, Captain F Moore joined *Cutty Sark* at New York in 1882. But on the ship's articles there appears to be no records as to that captain's birthplace - or even his first name. However, at New York on 1 May 1882, he did sign on as F Moore, born in England in 1839. Captain Moore like so many other sailors before him began his sea career at the age of twelve, and more than likely came from the Tyneside area. After serving his apprenticeship on the North East collier brigs, he worked his way up the promotional ladder in both steam and sail, to become first mate of the SS *Leda* before eventually becoming her master. On that ship he sailed between South Shields, the Baltic and the Mediterranean.

In 1873 he became master of the 433 ton barque *Teviot*, a vessel which was once owned by the Royal Mail Steam Packet Co, but whilst Captain Moore was in command, *Teviot* was in the Mauritius instead of the South American trade. After that ship he took command of the 1,293 composite built *Dilharee,* formerly a trooper on the Indian run and owned by John Lidget of London. That ship had been built as a full rigger, but after being cut down to a barque like so many of her rig, she became a New Zealand emigrant ship before being converted to a general cargo carrier.

But when Captain Moore was master of that ship, and whilst transporting a 2,000 ton grain cargo from Portland to Queenstown, the steering gear jammed in the Columbia River whilst the ship was under tow to get her across the Bar. At the time there were two tugs in attendance, but due to the inclement weather his ship stranded on Peacock Spit where she later broke up. At the marine enquiry held at Portland, no blame was apportioned to Captain Moore, and neither were the tug skippers held responsible due the mechanical fault as well as the wild weather conditions.

Captain Moore then joined the Willis fleet to captain the old 1845 built *Coldstream* for a short while. He was relieved on that ship by Captain Richard Woodget, then appointed to *Blackadder* as her master in 1881. However, when he was on his third voyage of

Blackadder, and whilst his ship was berthed alongside *Cutty Sark* at New York, that ship was in complete turmoil due to the improprieties of Captain William Bruce. Indeed, as a consequence of a marine enquiry, both Bruce and Rutland the mate were sacked from the ship and out of the company At that enquiry a number of *Cutty Sark's* crew had testified against their captain and the mate, the latter being with regard to the death of Thomas Dunton, the hazing of the crew, and the way in which eight of the nine sailors on Australian wages had been worked out of the ship. Oscar Owen from North Wales was the only AB on Australian wages to come through the ordeal.

The enquiry also decreed that because the ship had been out of the UK for almost two years, the other 21 of the crew were to be paid off. However, the deckhand Feliciano Guilleras who had signed on at Cebu, and a man who had proved to be an excellent worker as well as being most popular with all on board, was nowhere to be found when it came to him collecting his pittance of a wage. Indeed, as soon as *Cutty Sark's* first berthing rope was as the quayside bollards at New York, the Philippino disappeared at speed never to be seen or heard of again. Nevertheless and thanks to the British Consul, the whole of *Cutty Sark's* crew were paid off, furthermore, and as well as their wages, the convening enquiry awarded them a cash payment of one extra quarter of their ration allowance since the ship had left Cebu 125 days previously.

But by the time of - and during the marine enquiry, *Cutty Sark's* cargo of jute had been discharged and one of case oil for the Far East already loaded. That cargo consisted of 26,816 cases of oil, each case containing ten gallons of paraffin in two cans. However, with *Cutty Sark* having no captain or crew, and as she was shortly due to sail, John Willis had *Blackadder's* complete outfit of 23 men transferred to *Cutty Sark.*

Quite often there is some confusion with various writers on the spelling of ship's crew's names. This is because many people of the day were either unable to read or write - had poor handwriting which resulted in an undistinguishable scrawl - were unable to spell their names correctly - or else got somebody else to write their name down for them when they were signing on. Therefore, the spelling of a man's name may differ from one writer to another. Of all the men who signed on *Cutty Sark* **between 1870 - 1895, 14% of them were unable to read or write However, the names listed below were taken from the New York ship's articles of agreement of 1 May 1882 and are as follows.**

Captain F Moore - First Mate JP Lyviel - Second Mate JG Smith - Third Mate H Upjohn - Apprentices, JW Jaques - GD Jackson - FR Paramore, - JH Sykes - FA Ryoff - RW Gordon. Carpenter, - T Mattince - Cook, L Morris - Steward, E West AB's, Barvig, - Hartman, - Dreney, - Leerberg, - Le Norman, - McLane, - Nilson, -Norman, - W Abram, - plus one un-named**.   Ship's Company 23.**

For some unknown reason, those 10 AB's transferred from *Blackadder* to *Cutty Sark* were all signed on at a wage of £1-10-0 a month instead of the usual £2-10-0. Moreover, with *Cutty Sark's* crew having been reduced from the original 31 down to 23, the original posts of bosun and sailmaker had been dispensed with.

On 4 May 1882 *Cutty Sark* left New York making the line on 1 June with Anjer being reached on 2 August 1882. After watering the ship sailed for Samarang where she arrived on 20 August to discharge her cargo of case oil. Then in ballast to Madras with half the crew full of fever. All of them recovered except for 31 year old William Abram from Lancashire. He died at sea on 5 November just two days before Madras was reached on the 7 November 1882.

Anjer was no more than a village on the Java mainland in the Sunda Straight, 27 miles ENE of Krakatau Island which itself is 6S and 105E. It was however, a major staging post for ships sailing to and from China and the Far East. When ships arrived there from the UK, it was usually a welcome break for their crews as they could replenish with water and acquire much needed fresh fruit and vegetables. But Anjer was wiped off the map after the Krakatau Earthquake of 1883, and for that reason, Anjer is never shown on a modern day atlas.

Three days after Christmas day sail was made for Bimlipitam for a part cargo of horns, hides and jute, the ship then went to Cocanda for topping up with much of the same cargo, then sailing for home on 31 January 1883. London was reached after a 122 day passage, and *Cutty Sark* paid off on 2 June 1883 after a 397 days voyage.

Captain Moore began his second voyage on *Cutty Sark* by signing on at London on 13 July 1883. The ship left two days later with a general cargo for Newcastle NSW, a port which she reached on 10 October after a 79 day run from Gravesend. But instead of the usual Newcastle coal being loaded, one of baled wool was stowed into *Cutty Sark's* hold instead; it was the ship's first cargo of wool. The homeward passage was *Cutty Sark's* first around Cape Horn, and to the Deal anchorage the passage took a creditable 82 days. Indeed, it was the fastest wool passage of the season with *Cutty Sark* beating all the other wool ships by a month or more.

It must be stated that in most cases sailing ships going out to the Antipodes from the UK usually ran their easting down. Those outward bound passages were assisted by the prevailing westerly winds of the Southern Ocean. Then by using the westerly winds whilst homeward bound, those same ships of sail normally went back to the UK via Cape Horn, thus resulting in a round the world voyage. However, by using the Cape Horn route with a westerly wind, passages back to the UK invariably took longer as the distance was greater. It must also be added, that the only reason ships of sail were able to get any work in the carrying of wool from Australia, was because the steamships of the day had not quite established enough coaling stations for the route. Captain Moore's third and final voyage on *Cutty Sark* began with the ship signing on at London on 13 July 1884, then leaving Gravesend two days later on 15 July. Destination Newcastle NSW with a general cargo which included 80 tons of gunpowder. On that voyage when there were eight AB's and eight apprentices, Jacques the senior apprentice was made third mate. Newcastle was reached on 5 September 1884 after an 82 day passage from Gravesend, but it was to be a three months wait before 4,300 bales of wool were loaded for London. The homeward passage to London via the Horn took 80 days, and once again Cutty Sark overhauled all who sailed before her winning the wool race once more.

After paying off Captain Moore was transferred to the company flagship *The Tweed*.

Captain F Moore

Captain Richard Woodget

Over the centuries Great Britain has produced countless numbers of sailors who have served in both sail and steam. Amongst that endless list of seafarers however, there lies an inner or elitist group, a group made up by those who because of their seamanship and other shipboard skills, clearly stand out in the world of maritime deeds and heroics. Those men of the sea who because of their exploits and feats of bravery, have since been inscribed into the annals of maritime history, and indeed, the name of Richard Woodget is most deservedly within their midst.

Richard Woodget who took his farming father's name, began life in 1845 at Burnham Norton in the county of Norfolk. His education at the village school of Burnham Market, resulted in him signing his indentures with Bullard, King & Co in 1861, and then joining the small ship *Johns*. It was indeed the start of a career which made Richard Woodget one of Britain's greatest sailor captains.

His first ship was employed in the Home Trade between the Tyne and Thames, but a year later, Apprentice Woodget was sent to the schooner *Peace*. Then in 1863 he went to the 196 ton brig *British Ensign*, a vessel on which he signed foreign articles and sampled his first taste of life abroad. On that ship he visited the Eastern Mediterranean, South Africa and the West Indies. On the expiry of his indentures in 1865 he was transferred to the 50 ton *Faith*, another coaster on which he was the only mate, and a vessel on which he kept watch and watch with his captain. On vessels of that size there was usually a crew of no more than five.

From then on with his second mate's certificate, he moved around the east coast on Geordie Collier Brigs until gaining his first mate's, then master's certificate. The sailing vessels on which he served during that period were the barques *Dolphin* then *Charles Lambert* both of which were about 350 tons, the brig *Tweedsdale,* the ship rigged

Alexandra, the barque *Princess Dagmar* followed by *Abbotsford, Isabel* and *Nina,* then first mate of the 98 ton schooner *Freak,* mate of the barque *Priscilla,* then in 1874 firstly as second, and then as first mate he signed on his largest ship to date, the 876 ton ship rigged *Copenhagen,* a vessel on which he served for six years. In 1881 he was given his first command of the John Willis owned *Coldstream,* a 756 ton fully rigged ship on which he stayed until 1885, indeed, a ship on which he proved to his employer that he was both a sailor and a captain of the highest quality.

Whilst on board *Coldstream*, Captain Woodget must have been green with envy as he watched folornly as just about every ship of sail left him in its wake, and especially those of the clipper breed which only too often left him hull down in the same watch. Indeed, the old teak built and heavily soaked *Coldstream* was as old in years as Woodget was himself. She was a rather clumsy old slow coach which needed a stiff wind on either quarter to get anything like ten or even nine knots out of her, moreover, her captains had found it hard to make her pay. However, Captain Richard Woodget was one person who did get the best out of the old ship, and quite unlike the captains before him he even made small but steady profits for his employer. John Willis was greatly impressed with both the seamanship and business skills of his captain. So when *Coldstream* arrived back in London from Australia in March 1985, John Willis took him down to the East India Dock to where *Cutty Sark* was loading. The date was March 1885.

As the beautiful and elegant clipper ship stood before them, Willis told Woodget that Captain Moore who had been her master for the past three voyages was about to be transferred to his flagship *The Tweed,* and as a reward for his endeavours, Captain Woodget was to be given command of *Cutty Sark.* To Richard Woodget it must have been like a dream come true, and especially after some of the ships he'd sailed in. But Captain Woodget had not been given command of *Cutty Sark* just for his own benefit, he'd also been sent to that ship to do what she'd been designed and built for, and what no captain to date had been capable of - to drive her, get the very best out of her, and to put *Thermopylae* firmly in its place by creating some sailing records! Indeed, in an era when many captains had opted for the more comfortable steamships, master mariners in sail were increasingly hard to find, but as it turned out at a later date, Richard Woodget had been an absolute jewel in the crown.

One thing *Cutty Sark's* owner and her new captain did have in common, was they were both committed men of sail and both opposed to steam, a fact borne out by Willis having no steamers in his fleet, and Woodget who could easily have had command of a steamer, chose instead the ships of sail. Therefore, on 30 March 1885 Richard Woodget signed on *Cutty Sark* as her master. The irony of it all however, was he was to be the ship's last seagoing captain under the Red Ensign. Moreover, if he had been given command of

Cutty Sark many years earlier, when tea clippers raced home from China with the first crop, then maritime history may well have been very different. Captain Moore who had in fact inherited a run down and bedraggled *Cutty Sark* from Captain Bruce, had done everything a good captain should in bringing her back up to a proper state of respectability and seaworthiness; even if it had taken him three trips. But when Moore transferred to *The Tweed,* not only had he left *Cutty Sark* in pristine condition, but took with him his trusted apprentices. At the same time those half deck boys from the flagship went to *Cutty Sark*. Also transferred from *The Tweed* with the apprentices was the cook Tony Robson, a man of oriental descent who along with Captain Woodget, was to spend the following ten years on *Cutty Sark.*

The crew of *Cutty Sark* for her sixteenth voyage were as follows:
Captain R Woodget - First Mate J Dimmint - Second Mate JW Jaques - Third Mate RL Andrewes.
 Six Apprentices, OJ Bowers - TF Dixon - LK Durant - CE Irving - WE Smith - J Weston.
Bosun, J Murphy - Sailmaker, A Burden - Steward G Thompson - Cook, T Robson - ABs - J Barrett, W Drummond, CF Ersson, J Johansen, C Landin, W MacEvoy, H Ohlensen, O Owens, E Whicker. P Conway, and ordinary Seaman AO Perry.
Total ship's complement 25

Leaving London on 1 April 1885, to Captain Woodget it must have felt that he'd been riding cart horses for the past twenty five years, and then with the wave of a wand, there he was sitting astride a high class racing horse, indeed, a thorough bred of the highest quality. The ship must have felt like a living thing as he put *Cutty Sark* through her paces on the run out to Sydney, and despite poor winds for much of the way, he arrived at his destination on 20 June (mid winter) after 77 days, thereby beating all his competitors on the outward run.
On arrival at Sydney, P Conway an AB and Ordinary Seamen A Perry who had been working their passage at 1/- a month were paid off. E Whicker an AB was discharged (probably through illness) and two other AB's CF Ersson and O Owens as well as the sail maker deserted ship. That left the captain with nineteen hands all told, but he knew and trusted them all as they trusted him. Therefore, no new expensive Sydney hands were signed, so Captain Woodget as well as saving on the wages of four AB's and a sail maker, was quite confident he could get his ship safely home, even with such a reduced crew.
After a wait of three months for the wool clip, *Cutty Sark* left Sydney for London on 16 October 1885 with 4,465 bales of wool and other commodities used as stiffening. Captain

Woodget was to take his ship around Cape Horn, a further route than the one he had taken on the outward passage, but one where strong winds were generally more available. Although he had been around the Horn before, it was the first time he had done so in command. To get the desired strong winds, he took his ship a nominal 58 South where the sight of icebergs was commonplace. In his run to the Horn the usual damage aloft was sustained in the screaming gales, but the gallant little ship took it all in her stride rounding the Horn on 8 November after 23 days. Then by taking 20 days to reach the line, *Cutty Sark* took the 21 day 'Horn to Line' record of from *Heather Bell*.

The run home from the line was fine until Ushant was reached. But from there and by sailing on a wind, the ship made just two or three knots headway for five consecutive days, and indeed, spoiled what would otherwise have been an excellent passage for Captain Woodget. However, on her arrival at London on 29 December 1885, after a 74 day passage, *Cutty Sark* beat all the other wool clippers by over a week, and that included her great rival *Thermopylae*. John Willis was so pleased with both Captain Woodget and *Cutty Sark,* that he had a replica 'cutty sark' night gown cut from a sheet of brass to be secured to the main-mast head as an in port weather vane. However, and despite her great performance, the ship was unable to get a general cargo and had to be satisfied with one of scrap iron for Shanghaai.

On her seventeenth voyage *Cutty Sark* signed articles at London on 15 February 1886. Her complement numbered 25. Included in the crew were 21 year old Robert Andrewes the third mate, and his eighteen year old apprentice brother Walter. Poor winds were experienced for most of the passage, and on calling in at Anjer after ninety six days, where the captain bought two monkeys, *Cutty Sark* arrived at her destination after a long and tedious 124 days on 24 June 1886. The scrap iron was discharged but there was no cargo to be loaded. Joseph Murphy the 54 year old bosun quite sadly died at Shanghaai on 25 September 1886. He was replaced by John Usher an AB from Surrey. After a wait of three months when no cargoes offered, the ship sailed in ballast for Sydney in October, but on her arrival on 5 December she was too late for the wool crop, and three months too early for the next.

On 23 March 1887 Carl Lundberg a Swedish AB signed on at 1/- a month to work his passage back to London. Then three days later the ship sailed with 4,296 bales of wool on 26 March 1887. *Cutty Sark* was caught in calms for the first four days after leaving Sydney, but after having run south, she sailed through the icebergs in westerly gales to round Cape Horn on 19 April. Those hard gales continued right up as far as the River Plate, a region where Apprentice Walter Andrewes was washed overboard in heavy seas. At the same time his elder brother the third mate who was working alongside him could only watch on in horror. But not for the first or last time in maritime history, the young apprentice like so many men before and after him, was washed back inboard on the ship's next roll to leeward. But more drama was to follow on the run home, when off the Western Isles the ship was caught aback in a sudden shift of wind. Most fortunately the light weather sails were on the yards, and although they quickly blew to ribbons, the consequences of having the heavy weather canvas up would surely have brought the masts down. The run to London ended on 6 June 1887 after a 72 day passage, and needless to say, *Cutty Sark* had once again beat all before her and recorded the fastest passage of the year from the colonies. The irony of it all for Captain Woodget was her having been held up for four days on leaving Sydney.

One of the apprentices on the voyage was the 14 year old Toby Mayall making his first trip to sea. He was the son of a leading London photographer, and when during the voyage Captain Woodget learned of his father's profession, he later contacted the photographer through his son. After which, he purchased all the necessary photo equipment to began a new pastime in photography. During the rest of his tenure on *Cutty Sark,* Captain Woodget took and developed many historic photographs, some of which are printed within this book.

Signing on at London on 15 August 1887 for voyage 18, *Cutty Sark* left two days later on passage towards Newcastle NSW. Crossing the line 32 days later on October 19, she passed Tristan and Gough to set an easterly course. However, three days later the ship was partly dismasted. The incident occurred just after midnight in 39 South 45 East on 22 October 1887 when the middle watch turned to. Romping along with a new man at the wheel and a new officer of the watch on deck, the wheel was hard up with the yards on the backstays. But the wind suddenly changed direction to come from the starboard to port bow; both First Mate Jerry Dimint and the man on the wheel were too slow to react. The end result was the fore t'gallant mast went over the side taking with it as well as some of its associated gear, the main t'gallant and its topmast head. Captain Woodget heaved to in order to effect repairs.

By daylight the strong wind had most fortunately dropped to a gentle breeze, a passage of time which allowed Captain Woodget to salve all the spars and rigging which had come down in the darkness, much of this was hanging over the side dragging along. Jury rigging took two days, but whilst repairs were taking place the ship was still making good way. Furthermore, even when sailing under her jury rig the ship still managed to average over 200 miles a day, and on 11 November she made as much as 330 miles in 23½ hours. Arriving at Newcastle on 17 November 1887 and despite her misfortunes, *Cutty Sark* had taken 89 days to make her passage.

After her general cargo had been discharged and 4,515 bales of wool loaded for London , *Cutty Sark* spent the Christmas at Newcastle before sailing on 28 December 1887. Once

Above: *Cutty Sark* drying her sails in Sydney Harbour.
Below: A group of *Cutty Sark's* Sunday afternoon visitors in Sydney. Captain Woodget who is wearing his Tam O'Shanter is leaning on the rail and is third from the right.

It is thought that Captain Woodget took and developed a large number of photos on board.

Above: Cutty Sark's sailmaker working a piece of canvas. On the left stands an apprentice.
Below: Left to right. Second mate, first mate and Tony Robson the cook.

Photos by Captain Woodget.

again she headed south to where the strong winds of the roaring forties emanate. So far south did Woodget take his ship, that for two weeks he stayed below the 60º mark, and then to get his required wind he actually touched 64º 50' South on 16 January 1888. Needless to say, and even if it was summertime in the southern hemisphere, there were plenty of bergs about with plenty of ice in the rigging as well. Cape Horn was passed on 22 January, 25 days after leaving Newcastle, with the equator being crossed on 15 February. *Cutty Sark* had a good run home, and after a passage of 71 days arrived in London on 10 March 1888. Once again *Cutty Sark* had come home first, and in doing so beat the whole wool fleet by between 12 and 59 days.

Voyage 19 began with the ship signing on at London on 14 May 1888. Probably because of the dismasting episode on the previous voyage, 48 year old First Mate James Dimint left the ship and was replaced by Second Mate Thomas W Selby. Also included in the ship's complement was 15 year old Apprentice Richard Woodget, the captain's eldest son making his first trip to sea. But captain's son or not, young Richard was granted no favouritism whatsoever from a father who treated every man on board with equality. Leaving the East India Dock for Sydney on 17 May 1888, *Cutty Sark* loaded a supplement of gunpowder at Gravesend, and on sailing the following day, she cast off her tug at Dungeness.

Cutty Sark's passage to Sydney was nothing out of the ordinary, her best day's run being 320 miles on 27 July. Arriving at her loading port on 5 August 1888, she had to wait for over a month before stiffening and 4,496 bales of wool was screwed into her hold. Leaving Sydney on 26 October for London, Captain Woodget had apparently loaded too little stiffening which resulted in him having a larger freeboard. Three days after sailing on 29 October, the ship went on her beam ends in heavy weather due to her crank load. With that the captain sent down the royal yards and upper staysails.

On 31 October disaster struck when the ship was 46 South and 162 East. During the middle watch at 3 am, the watch on deck were on the starboard side working on the braces in heavy weather. It was then that a huge wall of water came thundering over the deck from the weather side. Those who saw or sensed it coming jumped for it, in such cases there is hardly time to warn others, as indeed, each must have a sixth sense which is only to be gained with experience. Most unfortunately 17 year old Apprentice Sidney Cooke who was making his first trip to sea never had that experience. He tried to hang on to a brace rope as the deck quickly filled to the bulwark top, but in the blackness of the night the young lad was washed over the safety nets into the raging sea. Most unfortunately, nothing more was seen of the young apprentice.

In such cases there is nothing at all which can be done by the captain to attempt a rescue. First and foremost, the boy was heaviliy dressed in oilskins and seaboots, and due to that he would have sunk like a stone. Secondly, even if the captain could have turned the ship around it would have been dangerous both for the ship and all on board. Due to the inclement weather he would have had to gibe the ship and then try to ascertain the position where the man went overboard; and even if he could have done those things, the weather was too heavy to lower a boat - and it was dark.

Cutty Sark went past 64 South to find the winds, but all that came were easterlies which resulted in Cape Horn being passed on 3 December after 38 days, 13 days longer than usual. The ship's best day's run on the homeward passage was 306 miles. *Loch Vennacher* won the wool race to London that year with an 84 day passage, *Salamis* was second with 85, whilst *Cutty Sark* came in third with 86. *Cutty Sark* paid off on 21 January 1889. After the steamers had taken the tea trade from the sailing ships, coaling stations had been better established on the route to Australia, furthermore, the modern triple expansion steam engines gave the smole belchers a greater steaming range. The results were that cargoes for the sailing ships even as far out as the Antipodies were becoming harder to secure. Due to those facts and after paying off in January of 1889, *Cutty Sark* had to wait three months before she could load a cargo.

Signing her articles on 2 May 1889, and then on leaving the East India Dock two days later, the clipper ship took on her usual load of gunpowder at Gravesend to begin voyage number twenty. On that voyage 8 AB's and nine apprentices had been signed on. Yorkie Atkinson was made third mate and the ship's complement was 23. Nothing out of the ordinary was experienced on the passage out, but that was until the ship neared the South East coast of Australia. Between the dates of 23 and 24 July, *Cutty Sark* had experienced a good run and recorded 332 miles, but on the following day when Wilson's Promontory, the most southern tip of Australia - was sighted, the ship's course was altered to ENE.

Shortly after noon when the wind had slowed, *Cutty Sark* was making between 10 and 11 knots when the crack P&O liner RMS *Brittania* passed to her westward. Steaming at a speed of 15 knots, the pride of the mighty P&O line left *Cutty Sark* hull down by dark. But after Cape Howe was passed when *Cutty Sark* altered course to North by East, the wind came around to a strong steady south westerly. That freshening wind sent the clipper ship surging ahead at her greatest speed.

The clipper ship bounded forward like a greyhound. As usual her Old Man was on the poop deck's weather rail; a position where he spent most of his life whilst at sea. Then in the first hour of the middle watch as the clipper tore forward, a myriad of passenger ship's lights appeared fine on *Cutty Sark's* port bow. Indeed, It was the same ship which had passed *Cutty Sark* earlier in the afternoon. Moreover, it was the brand new mighty RMS *Brittania!* The time and date was recorded as being 1 am on 26 July 1889. With her t'gallants bowed dangerously forward and stretched to breaking point, the clipper ship

Top: *RMS Britannia* had three sister ships *Victoria, Oceana* and *Arcadia*. They were built between 1887 and 1888 to commemorate the Golden Jubilee of Queen Victoria.

Bottom: *Cutty Sark* overtaking *RMS Britannia*. - From a Painting by the author

powered on through a wind and sea that was perfect both for her and for the occasion.

No doubt every single person on board *Cutty Sark* whether on watch or not, was aware of the situation - as well as the name of the ship ahead they were overhauling! Furthermore, in order to take part in the historic feat of their captain's sailing abilities, those off watch sailors must have tumbled out their bunks at speed to turn to on deck in order to assist in any way they could. Sailor men just loved to go past a steamer.

Lookouts on steamships are never obliged to report lights abaft the beam, so the man in *Britannia's* crows nest probably never even bothered to look aft. But up on the bridge of the passenger ship, which at the time was reputed to be the fastest merchant steamer in existence, Second Mate Robert Olivey saw a red light fine on his starboard quarter. Seeing there were no mast head lights to accompany the single red light, he must have thought it rather strange as only a ship of sail would show such a light. Surely it couldn't be a sailing ship trying to overtake *Britannia!* Even the latest warships of the Royal Navy would have a struggle to even keep up with - let alone go past her. But when that red light began gaining on him, the stunning truth finally hit home. Indeed, a lowly ship of sail was overtaking the mighty *Britannia.*

The officer of the watch sent below for Captain Hector to come up and witness the unbelievable spectacle for himself. However, with *Cutty Sark* tearing along at over seventeen knots - or twenty miles an hour, she soon came abeam of the mail boat at a mile distant. Quite unlike the big steamer which left a boiling wake astern of her, the clipper ship left just a thin slip stream. Then as the fastest sailing ship in the world came abeam of the fastest steamer, her red port light slowly faded away as she drew away. It was replaced by one of white. *Cutty Sark's* a stern light! From then on a clean pair of heels were shown to the liner before the end of the middle watch. The finality of it all was, that the fastest steamer in the world had been overhauled and passed by a ship of sail.

All sailors of the day liked nothing more than to give a steamer the go by, and especially a passenger liner. To have passed her was the greatest overtaking achievement of all time, as well as being the talking point in the taverns for many years to come. What a pity it was dark at the time of that historic passing, an event which denied *Cutty Sark's* sailors the privilege of trailing a rope over their stern. Sarcastically inviting their 'tin kettle smoke belching' victim to take a tow!

In the continuance of her epic sprint however, and after anchoring in Sydney harbour, *Cutty Sark* was just finishing stowing her sails by the time the mail boat arrived an hour later at 10 am. In the previous twenty years *Cutty Sark* had gone past many steamers, but to go past *Britannia* the world's fastest merchantman, to those men of *Cutty Sark* it was their greatest ever achievement. The golden cutty sark at the ship's mainmast head must have glinted brightly that day in the Sydney sunlight. Jock Willis back in London must have been delighted on hearing the news of *Cutty Sark's* most famous scalp, and no doubt telegraphs of his congratulations were quickly wired through to the Sydney agents for Captain Woodget's attention.

The 6,525 ton RMS *Britannia* was built by Caird & Co of Greenock and launched on 18 August 1887. On her sea trials of 15 October 1887, her triple expansion engines gave a speed of 16.5 knots Accepted on the following day she served the P & O line until broken up at Genoa in 1909.

Waiting in the bay until 23 October, *Cutty Sark* was obliged to be last in the queue of the ships loading wool. This was because the shippers wanted all the wool carriers to arrive in London at roughly the same time for the wool sales. Therefore, the slowest ships were first in the queue whilst the fastest brought up the rear. The result of that ruling meant that *Cutty Sark* who was last in the queue, had to wait in the bay for twelve weeks before going alongside. Ten days after going alongside she had 4,577 bales screwed in on top of 200 tons of chrome ore stiffening, then after leaving her berth took her departure for London on 3 November 1889.

Whilst *Cutty Sark* was at Sydney, a new Zealand born AB named William Paris deserted on 22 October. He was replaced by Oscar Hausen who after drawing an advance of wages failed to join, he was further replaced by SA Frazer from New York who did join. The second Mate William Naylor was discharged on 19 August and replaced by one of the AB's Robert Walker on 1 November. This man promoted to second mate is further described in the chapter 'A Sailor From Another Age.' In order of merit with regard to their speeds, the other wool clippers which left Sydney before *Cutty Sark* were - *Derwent, Cairnbulg, Orontes, Woolahra, Cimba, Sophocles, Serica,* and *Rodney*. There were also the wool ships *Loch Vennacher* and *Salamis* from Melbourne and *Blackadder* from Brisbane. With *Derwent* having a 20 day head start on *Cutty Sark* the race to London was on. A poor run of 30 days by *Cutty Sark* to Cape Horn was followed by a good one of 23 days to the line, and a further 22 to London. In all *Cutty Sark* took 75 days from Sydney to London, the feat was equalled by *Cimba*. The first away *Derwent* was actually first to reach London after 80 days, but the race was won by *Cutty Sark* and *Cimba* who finished joint first. On *Cutty Sark's* arrival in London on 17 January 1890 she paid off.

Another long wait for a cargo was experienced at London, until the 22 man crew for voyage 21 was signed on 12 May 1990, in the meantime she dry-docked for a bottom clean. On this voyage Captain Woodget had two sons aboard as apprentices. They were 17 year old Richard John and 15 year old Harold. There were only eight AB's for the trip, but there were eight apprentices to make the numbers up. The steward took a trip off and Tony Robson acted as cook - steward for the voyage. On that passage out to Australia *Cutty Sark* had mixed fortunes with the winds, her best run being 340 miles in the

Southern Ocean, whilst the worst was just two miles. Despite the fact she overhauled many of her wool trade rivals on the way, the passage to Sydney was a relatively normal one for *Cutty Sark* in being 75 days. However, she did overhaul RMS *Britannia's* sister ship RMS *Victoria* off Otway on 31 July 1890. On arrival at Sydney the great Maritime Strike was in progress. The result of that was a long wait for all ships of sail, and all because when the wool did come down to the dock warehouses, the steamships which were faster and more reliable took just about all the wool available.

It wasn't until 7 November that *Cutty Sark* began loading, but due to the strike the bales of wool were arriving in dribs and drabs, but by 14 December she had loaded 4,617 bales on top of her stiffening. There were no desertions at Sydney that trip, but Apprentice Charles Tite paid off sick at Sydney in the first week of December. The ship sailed on 14 December 1890 hoping to catch the March wool sales. But with it being slow going from the off, if it wasn't head winds then it was the calms that compelled the ship to take 33 days to Cape Horn. The line was crossed on 13 February 1891, and after a passage of 93 days London was made on 17 March 1891. Her longest run from Australia to date, but nevertheless she once again won the wool race as the nearest ship to her, *Salamis* of the Aberdeen White Star Line was eight days behind her.

Voyage 22 from London began with the signing of the 22 crew on 21 April 1891. William Turner the Peterhead carpenter who had been in the ship since 13 July 1883 had made eight voyages. He left the ship and was replaced by J Hornberg of Finland. At the same time, Esplin the steward returned after missing voyage 21 to resume his duties as steward. Once again there were eight AB'S and eight apprentices as well as two mates to make up Captain Woodget's crew. The senior apprentice would take up the third mate's post, whilst another would be the lamp-trimmer. Bosuns and sailmakers had not been carried for a number of voyages and the trend continued. Captain Woodget believed that all sailors should be sailmakers, whilst the mate on watch acted bosun.

Leaving London for Sydney on 23 April 1891, *Cutty Sark* made the run from Dover to Portland in 24 hours. With that excellent start she crossed the line on 20 May, but inconsistent winds for the rest of the passage resulted in her taking 79 days to reach her destination. But even if it was a slow time by *Cutty Sark's* standards, she still managed to beat the rest of the outward bound wool fleet. The most outstanding point of interest during the passage occurred on 28 June when the ship was in the Roaring Forties. Captain Woodget's log records that during the forenoon watch whilst in a rough sea, he saw the biggest following sea he'd ever seen in all his life roll up from astern.

So big was the huge crested growler, he thought the ship was going to be swamped and buried forever. But it was then that the brilliance of Hercules Linton her designer shone through. The squared counter stern which had come from the design of *The Tweed,* as

Captain Woodget was a keen and dedicated photographer. He learned the art and took a large number of photos while on *Cutty Sark*. **Ice bergs were one of his fascinations.**

Captain Woodget had a boat lowered to take this picture of *Cutty Sark* in mid-ocean. He also bred and trained prize pedigree dogs on the ship. - Photos Capt. Woodget

well as the ship's quarter section designed by Hercules Linton, really played their part to the full. That counter stern did indeed lift the after end of the ship as it was designed to. But as it buoyantly rose, the crest of the wave enveloped the steering position. The solid wall of water then raced forward before it came crashing down on the main deck engulfing the apprentice's half deck. The half-deck house was filled almost to the level of the deck-head. The sailor's foc'sle was also filled, but only to the level of the bottom bunks as the giant following sea roared over the ship.

Indeed, if the stern had not lifted when it did, that monster wave would have pooped the ship and swept away everything including the boats and deckhouses. The 21 year old Second Mate Norman Canning of St Mary's, Jersey, recalls that as he was standing outside the carpenter's shop looking aft, he saw a huge crested wave rearing up. Canning said it reached well over the level of the crojack yard, and for fear of his being swept away he made a dive into the chippy's shop and slammed the door behind him. The invading water then rushed along the deck from aft with such terrific force, that both the second mate and the chippy who was also inside the shop thought they were done for, but after roaring forward over the level of the portholes, the rogue wave carried on past the ship. Captain Woodget remarked that when the stern lifted it went so high in the air, the ship was momentarily at an angle of 45 degrees from aft to forrard. Then when the ship raced down the face of the mountain of water, she must have been travelling twice as quick as the fastest she'd ever sailed before, and that meant 35 knots plus!

Modern day yachtsmen say that when their vessel runs down the face of a huge sea, as *Cutty Sark* did on 28 June 1891, the speed recorder usually shows at least a doubling of their normal speed reading.

At the time of the deluge there were two men at the wheel, an AB and the captain's son Richard. Captain Woodget concluded that if those two men had not been lashed down, both would have been washed away with no chance of rescue. The watch on deck were fortunately working close to their accommodation, because they also saw the massive wall of water coming aboard, and dropping everything made a dive for their foc'sle door. But before they could slam it shut, enough seawater had entered to flood the compartment as high as the bottom bunks. Making Wilson's Promontory on 11 July, *Cutty Sark* arrived at Sydney two days later on 13 July 1891. That was after averaging 14.5 knots for the previous 48 hours.

Another long wait of twelve weeks occurred before the agents finally secured a wool cargo. With the usual 200 tons of stiffening on the ceiling, the loading of 4,638 bales began on 27 October and ended eight days later on 4 November. Sailing for London on the following day, 5 November 1891, Captain Woodget changed his normal route and went to the North of New Zealand instead of sailing through the ice. Although Captain

Woodget did get a few good runs in, his change of plan resulted in him taking a day longer to reach Cape Horn than did the Aberdeen White Star Line ship *Salamis*. That ship had sailed from Geelong eight days earlier than *Cutty Sark*. Then *Salamis* beat him by a day to the equator, and from there by another day to London. Indeed, *Salamis* was the winner of the wool race that year by taking 82 days to London, whilst *Cutty Sark* came second with a run of 85 days. Variable light winds, calms and head reaching had resulted in *Cutty Sark* taking 85 days from Sydney to London. There she paid off on 29 January 1892, and then began a long wait for her next cargo, and indeed, it was over six months before she secured a general cargo for Newcastle NSW. Signing a new crew on at London on 9 August 1892, voyage 23 began with a crew of 22. On this voyage Richard Woodget junior, who at the time was the senior apprentice, was promoted to second mate at a wage of £4.10.0 a month. Leaving the West India Dock on 12 August 1892, the passage out to Newcastle was without any notable incident, except that it took *Cutty Sark* until 7 November, and 87 days, to reach her destination.

After discharging at Newcastle where no cargoes offered, Captain Woodget took his ship 60 miles south to Sydney. But the steamers had once more taken the lion's share and all Woodget could get was a consignment of wool for Antwerp. But on a more promising note, a record stow of 4,723 bales were screwed into the ship, 87 more than her last cargo, and 434 more than her first wool cargo taken by Captain Moore on his 1882-83 voyage. But whilst loading at Sydney one of the apprentices 16 year old Percy French Mortlock a first tripper deserted ship. Another deserter was 19 year old HN Maitland who had signed on as a boy for 1/- a month. To make up the shortfall, An Australian AB from Sydney named Thomas Lewis was signed. Also signed on was 53 year old Edwin Laister who at 1/- a month was working his passage to Antwerp. Loading was completed on 7 January 1893 and *Cutty Sark* sailed on the same day.

She had baffling winds for the first few days, but Captain Woodget went south towards the ice where the winds were generally stronger and more consistent. But a few weeks later when Captain Woodget was in 50 South and 46 West he was surprised to find himself surrounded by icebergs for a number of days. It was most unusual to find such a large number of bergs so far to the north, but at a later date it was discovered that a huge portion of ice which had broken away from the Antarctic plateau, was breaking up as it moved north. Moreover, every ship traversing Cape Horn that year encountered unusually large numbers of icebergs. Fortunately it was summer in the southern hemisphere and those icebergs could be seen more easily, *Cutty Sark* passed Cape Horn on 5 February 1893. For Captain Woodget the voyage had gone reasonably well. But that was until disaster struck with fateful consequences at 2.15 pm on 2 April 1893. On that date *Cutty Sark* was in position 47 North and 52 West. There was an unpleasant cross sea running and with the wheel hard up and two men at it, the yards hard up against the backstays Captain Woodget was indeed a sail carrier, but with the glass dropping and the wind intensifying, he ordered both the main royal and the outer jib to be taken in. After the main royal had been made fast, two sailors went out on the jib-boom to lash down the outer jib sail. At that particular time the helmsman was the new AB Thomas Lewis who had recently signed on at Sydney. The ship was yawing from side to side in the big swell, and due to that Lewis allowed the ship to occasionally run off course. The captain who at the time was on the poop deck advised him of the two men out on the jip-boom.

But while they were lashing down that headsail in the strong wind, Lewis once again let the ship go off course and that allowed the ship to run head on into the deep swell. As a consequence, the jib boom dipped and went right under washing the two men from off the footropes. On realising what had happened Captain Woodget immediately threw two life-buoys into the water. But the two overboard men struggled to keep afloat as they were heavily dressed in oilskins and seaboots. Furthermore, as the ship continued yawing they were too far out on the starboard beam and could only struggle helplessly. The sea was too big for a boat to be lowered, but even if one had, after the two sailors had struggled for a few moments nothing more was seen of the them. Those two men were highly regarded by their captain and referred to as being excellent sailors, they were 30 year old John Doyle from Dublin, and 22 year old John Clifton of Brighton. Captain Woodget grieved deeply at the loss of the two young men, and also remarked that in the seven years of his captaincy of *Cutty Sark,* it was the first time he had ever seen her put the jib-boom under. It must have been quite a sad ordeal for the master to compose letters of regret to the mothers of the two North Atlantic victims.

In poor winds which constantly came from ahead, progress from the Western Isles was slow all the way to Antwerp, a point from where it took *Cutty Sark* 23 days, and until 15 April 1893 to reach port. Whilst at Antwerp the ship was literally laid up. No badly needed bottom scrape or repairs to the copper bottom, which Captain Woodget knew needed attention. Indeed it must have appeared to him, that Willis the owner was pulling the purse strings ever tighter. However, a cargo was eventually obtained for Sydney and whilst loading at the Belgian port, *Cutty Sark* signed on a new crew on 28 July 1893 for voyage 24. On that trip the captain's son Richard who had been second mate took the trip off, he was replaced by a 21 year old German named R Littmann. At the same time, Henry Norman who had been first mate on voyage 22, and who had taken voyage 23 off, had returned for voyage 24. The captain's youngest son 15 year old Albert also joined the ship, but because he had not signed any indentures, he joined as a boy at a wage of 1/- a month. *Cutty Sark's* voyage number 24 began with the signing of her articles on 28 July 1893 at Antwerp. On that occasion 10 AB's one O/S and a boy were signed, the reason

The wage of 1/- a month (one shilling) is a token wage which legally ascertains that the person named was actually on the ship whilst it was at sea. Such a small wage is often paid to people who work their passage from one port to another. These people may, or may not be qualified as seamen. In the case of the qualified, they are usually obliged to turn to on deck with the sailors. Unqualified men who are often referred to as supernumeraries are sometimes passengers and used as galley hands or any other occupation which may be given to them.

the sailors foc'sle was full, was because only four apprentices were in the half-deck to make the crew of 22. The ship sailed 3 days later on 1 August for Sydney, a port she arrived at on 28 October 1893 after 88 days from Antwerp. Once there John Johnsen a 50 year old Swedish AB was paid off and Francis Ernest Dunnett an apprentice deserted. They were replaced by two ordinary seamen W Woodford and JA Smallbrook. After having discharged and on being too late to get a wool charter for the London sales, her agents managed to get one for Hull. On that occasion, a record number of 5,010 bales worth £100,000 were screwed into *Cutty Sark's* hold. Freight charges for the homeward run was a massive £4,000. But the reign of *Cutty Sark* was almost at a close, and when she left Sydney on 24 December 1893 it would be for the last time. But due to inconsistent weather and a foul bottom, the run home was as bad as the one out as far as the winds were concerned, with *Cutty Sark* taking 87 days to make her destination at Hull on 27 March 1894. After discharging at the Alexandra Dock which took 20 days, *Cutty Sark* sailed for London on 16 April where she began loading for Brisbane.

Cutty Sark's last voyage under the Red Ensign began with the signing on of her crew at London on 22 June 1894. According to the records on hand, the ship's complement of 19 for this trip was the smallest yet. From the captain down there were two mates, four apprentices, nine AB's a cook and the steward. If that was the case it is more than likely one of the AB's was appointed as carpenter whilst one of the apprentices went as third mate. Sailing on 25 June with a general cargo for Brisbane, she first stopped off at Gravesend to take on the usual consignment of gunpowder. No problems of note were recorded for the first few weeks, but when the ship hit the roaring forties it most certainly did. Once in that region of the world the usual hard gales and heavy seas were encountered, but through lack of a good overhaul in recent times, *Cutty Sark's* spars and other gear began carrying away. Due to Willis's reluctance to spend money on the ship it meant that *Cutty Sark* could not attain her best speeds, and her captain ruefully wrote that between 20 and 30 miles a day were being lost as he could not carry the required sail in the Southern Ocean gales. With Captain Woodget carrying as much sail as would allow, the martingale was lost, the fore t'gallant mast went over the side, and the main upper topsail yard broke in half. That latter damage resulted in the yard being sent

Captain Richard Woodget

Captain Woodget commanded *Cutty Sark* from 1885 until 1895, and in his ten year tenure of the ship proved to be the best captain the ship ever had. He was also its longest serving crew member, and only left the ship when he did, because she'd been sold to Portuguese owners. He then left the sea to become a dairy farmer at the place of his birth in Norfolk.

Cutty Sark Trust

down before being fished, reset, and sent back up again within eight hours, and all in the raging seas and gales of the forties. In addition to those mentioned, there was quite a lot more damage done to the deck houses as the seas swept the decks, as well as the poorly maintained chain plates of which three carried away. However, poor gear or not, from the Lizard to Brisbane *Cutty Sark* had made the passage in 79 days arriving there on 15 September 1894.

Blackadder was also there at Brisbane to load wool. She sailed for London on 20 October on a passage which was to take her 123 days. But as *Cutty Sark* began her loading one of the AB's named as John Smith deserted on the same day that *Blackadder* departed. With no AB replacements available, two boys named H Dickson and W Hill, both of whom came from Brisbane, were signed on in Smith's place. On 9 December 1894, *Cutty Sark* with a cargo of wool let go her berth to begin what was to be her last working passage under the Red Ensign. Anchoring for the night at the Pile Light due to adverse winds, she weighed anchor on the following day never to see Australia again. Cape Horn was passed after 27 days on 26 January 1895 before an average to slow run was made up the Atlantic. *Cutty Sark* arrived at London and paid off for the last time on 26 March 1895. John Willis the owner of *Cutty Sark* then put her up for sale.

Captain Woodget was astounded when he learned that his ship for the past ten years was to be sold. Willis who had already disposed of most of his fleet, told him that his none of ships were earning a living anymore. The dye was cast and set. Apparently, negotiations had already been started with J&A Ferreira of Lisbon. Those negotiations were successful and *Cutty Sark* was sold to go under the Portuguese flag on 3 July 1895 and renamed Ferreira. After that date a crew was sent over from Lisbon to sail her back to her new homeport on the Tagus. To give the Portuguese some credit the ship was given a thorough overhaul. As for Captain Woodget, he was given command of *Coldinghame*, a ship of sail indeed, but not in any way the same class as *Cutty Sark*. Shortly afterwards Richard Woodget retired to his roots and began farming at Norfolk.

Crew Deserters

In those years of sail and early steam, crew desertions at Australia were the order of the day - on just about every ship that went there. During *Cutty Sark's* many visits to that country a total of 87 men backed out of the ship. There were 62 desertions at Sydney, 24 at Newcastle NSW and 1 at Brisbane. Many of those deserters stayed on in the country, whilst others made themselves available to other ships in order to gain a better rate of pay. Replacements were extremely hard to get for sailing ships after their sailors had deserted, or skinned out or backed out as the saying went. Nevertheless, when sailors did become available to shorthanded sailing ships, able seamen demanded to be paid the Australian wage which was between £4 to £5 a month, instead of the miserable Board of Trade pittance of between £2-10-0 to £3-5-0.

To get his ship away, a reluctant captain was forced to pay the inflated Australian wages, but at the same time he probably held a grudge against those overpaid seamen. Needless to say, if and when the chance came along, those Aussie wage seamen would be replaced for lower paid sailors. *Cutty Sark* had desertions almost every time she arrived in Australia, and on one particular trip under Captain Bruce, nothing was out of the ordinary when half a dozen men went over the rail at Sydney.

It must be mentioned that in comparison to other ships, *Cutty Sark* had a relatively small number of desertions in Australia. On an ill found ship the whole crew were known to have packed their bags to work on the farms. Or before the days of *Cutty Sark* they would work in the gold fields. On the Liverpool ship *Lightning* in the 1850's, her captain the notorious Bully Forbes, had most of the crew locked up ashore on the ship's arrival. Then had them released and escorted back to the ship just before she sailed.

Although sailors made up the majority of a sailing ship's crew, it wasn't always they who deserted. At times those from the catering branch as well as some of the apprentices did the disappearing act, and on occasion one or two from the saloon vanished into thin air as well. On the following page is a list of *Cutty Sark's* Australian deserters.

Cutty Sark - Sydney Deserters

Ainsworth - Charles - London
Anderson - Henry - Norway
Andrews - Charles - London
Bagert - William - USA
Bell - William - London
Bengston - Christian - Sweden
Bosher - JM - Kent
Branks - George - Athens
Brooks - James - London
Brown - David - Ayr
Brown - Joseph - Portugal
Brown - Mark - Dover
Burden - Alfred - Unknown
Burns - George - New York
Calcraft - W - Dover
Connor - James - Dublin
Cooper - Charles - Unknown
Dale - Edward - Kent
Dalgreen - Charles - Sweden
Doughty Alfred - Unknown
Dunn - John - Liverpool
Dunnett Francis Edw - Unknown
Eldon - George - Poplar
Ersson - CF - Unknown
Filgin - Sailes - Finland
Gangstad - H - Bergen
Garey - J - Manchester
George - John - Greece
Gibson - William - Unknown
Hackley - JH - London
Hancock - Thomas - Deal
Harvey - John - Hampshire
Heinn - Heinrich - Holstein
Hunter - James - Glasgow
Johnson - Albarsh - Norway
Johnson - Benjamin - Gothenburg
Johnson - E - London
Johnson - John - Gothenburg
Jones - Frederick - Norwich
Le Conteur - John - Jersey
Mc Donald - Alexander - Aberdeen
McLachlan - James - Glasgow
Maitland - HN - London
Meinke - William - Guernsey
Mortlock - Percy F - Liverpool
Nave - William - Cromer
Nelson - Charles - Norway
Olsen - Edward - Norway
Olsen - Hans - Norway
Owens - Owen - Angelsea
Paris - William - Auckland
Paterson - John - Sweden
Pearce - John - London
Peart - Harry - Melbourne
Poale - William - Unknown
Powell - PR - Inverness
Roberts - Frederick - Newhaven
St Clare - Henry - Edinburgh
Scarbro - Edward - Nevis
Serreus - John A - Finland
Taylor - Samuel - London
Ward - William - Jersey
Watts - John - Redhill
Williams - EJ - Victoria NSW

At Newcastle NSW

Blamire - TC - London
Button - William - London
Casey - James - London
Christian - Chris - Norway
Collins - Thanes - Finland
Dunn - Richard - Berwick
Ellis - Thomas - Sheffield
Harnastron - John - Sweden
Johnson - Inc - Canada
Joseph - Conan - France
Kerry - Charles - Tasmania
Lennox - William - Guernsey
Lingoe - William - Finland
McLane - W - Lincolnshire
Martin - William - Nova Scotia
Mitchel - HA - London
Pedersen - Niels - Denmark
Peterson - MM - Denmark
Rasmusen - S - Norway
Rasmusen - Henri - Denmark
Salmensen - James - Denmark
Sutherland - James - Leith

At Brisbane
Smith - John - London

The End for the Clippers

Up until the time of 1885, the steamers had been limited in their runs by having to bunker at frequent intervals. With the opening of the Suez Canal however, those steamships coming from the UK could take on coal at Gibraltar and Port Said. Then after having passed through the Suez Canal and steamed down the Red Sea, they could top up at Aden and Colombo, then a number of other places like Singapore, Penang and Hong Kong in the far east. The tea clippers as well as other ships of sail could never use the Suez Canal; the towing fee through the ninety mile stretch would wipe out their profits for the round trip. Added to which, once in the Red Sea they'd often be in a windless zone. For ship's of sail, the Suez Canal route was just not feasible.

Furthermore, steam ships had cargo winches and derricks, items which greatly reduced a steamer's loading and discharging times. Whereas the coal burning vessels used steam to power their propellers and winches, the clipper ships in their efforts to sail and discharge cargo had to use 'Norwegian Steam ... otherwise known as muscle power or brute strength. There were those lovers of sail - and a great number of them, who scoffed at the steamships with their palls of black smoke belching from their tall stove-pipe funnels; indeed, stories of their breakdowns and unreliability abounded amongst their adversaries. Many a stirring tale has been told or written, and many a picture painted, of a sailing ship coming up majestically on a steamer that plods along at six or seven knots.

Then after having passed the power driven vessel, the speedy sailing vessel with its quartering wind would often trail a rope over her stern inviting her adversary to take a tow ... then leave her hull down in the same watch! However, what those same writers or artists failed to mention or paint! Is that quite often ... and sometimes only a day or so later, the opposite procedure often took place. The once speedy sailing ship after having taken her tow rope in, may well be caught in a windless zone where no headway can be made. The steam ship then comes up from astern still belching smoke, still making the same six or seven knots - and blows her steam whistle to salute the bygone age of sail.

Although *Cutty Sark's* maiden voyage to Shanghai was not a remarkable one in terms of a fast passage, she did on three occasions make day runs of over 300 miles on sights. That proved that when there was wind she was a fast enough ship. Her best day's work was 360 nautical miles between 13 and 14 of April 1870. During the passage she also proved she could sail well in light winds, could go about with ease and was able to sail close to the wind. On 31 May 1870 she arrived at Shanghai, 104 days from London pilot to pilot.

With regard to showing her speed, *Cutty Sark* never had much success as a tea clipper; the records will show that almost every year some clipper ship or other made it out to the loading ports in less than 100 days, but *Cutty Sark* never did achieve that feat. Much of her problem lay in the fact she never had a captain who could drive her hard, or as the saying goes 'let her have it.' Such captains were few and far between.

After turning to the Australian wool trade it was on that run where *Cutty Sark* really made her mark. Her pseudonym had by that time changed from a tea - to a wool clipper. Captain Richard Woodget who joined the ship in 1885 proved by far, that he was the best commander *Cutty Sark* had ever had. Because not only did he keep a good ship, he also made created a number of sailing records, records for a full rigger to and from Australia that stand to this day. Woodget was the man Willis had been searching for, a man who could show what *Cutty Sark* was really capable of. In Britain and Australia *Cutty Sark* became a household name, and opposed to her ordinary runs in the tea trade, she was constantly in the news winning the wool race year after year.

By 1895 the reign of the clipper ship had long since passed. Moreover, John Willis who was getting on in years had disposed of most of his fleet, and by that time he was left with *Cutty Sark, Blackadder* and the old *Coldinghame*. But old as he was the Scot still possessed a keen business sense and wanted to remain as a ship owner, no matter how small or insignificant it may have seemed. He'd long since been aware that the days of sail were over, and also realised he could no longer afford to keep both *Blackadder* and *Cutty Sark*. Ship owners of the day like all other businessmen past and present, were constantly under pressure to turn money over and make ends meet. Therefore, a change had to be made. The shipping industry was being upgraded faster than ever before, and Willis knew as did everybody else, that the beautiful and elegant clipper ships were a thing for the history books. In financial terms they were an obsolete and expensive luxury, and 'Old Willis of the White Hat,' was one person who needed no reminding that business and sentiment do not mix.

Why he kept the iron hulled *Blackadder* in preference to *Cutty Sark,* can only be attributed to the fact that he'd received an offer for the more famous of the two, or possibly because *Blackadder* was at the time engaged on a voyage. As a matter of fact, *Cutty Sark* who was already up for sale had been laying up idle in the London river since March 1895. She'd been unable to get a cargo or a buyer, but a bargain hunter came forth from Lisbon to open negotiations in April.

The general public were up in arms when it was learned that the famous *Cutty Sark* was to be sold abroad, a feeble attempt was therefore made to raise enough money to keep her for the nation. Unfortunately, the project was never started in time, and neither was it well organised. There were a number of people who thought Willis should donate the world famous ship to the nation, whilst others asked why should he? He himself had worked hard all his life as well as providing work for countless thousands of people around the world. Even so, one would have thought that such a vessel as famous as *Cutty Sark* would have been saved by the government of the day, or by some maritime institution with a view to preservation or even sail training. Indeed, had she been one of HM ships, then no doubt her claim to fame would have ensured her use in some role or other. But even though the mercantile marine had always been a breadwinner for the nation, it was not allowed its moment of sentiment. On 3 July 1895, *Cutty Sark* was sold to the brothers J&A Ferreira of Lisbon for the rather giveaway price of £2,100.

The ship was registered in Lisbon under her new name of *Ferreira,* then after a month in the River Thames, Ferreira Brothers & Co had their new acquisition sailed to Oporto. In her new home port she underwent an extensive survey and refit. It was then discovered that although much of her top hamper had to be replaced, the ship's hull was as sound as the day she'd been launched. The sparkling livery of *Cutty Sark* was retained, and after a period in Lisbon when *Ferreira* looked like a new ship, the former tea clipper put to sea to begin trading under the Portuguese flag.

In those days Portugal had a big training programme for its navy, with sail handling being regarded as a major factor in both character and confidence building. Although *Ferreira* was in the merchant fleet, the Portuguese Navy was then in a position to send some of its new recruits to her for sail training …. whilst the government paid their wages. So Messrs Ferreira as well as getting a first class ship for next to nothing had little in the way of crew wages to pay out! One may wonder why the British government had never adopted this policy. Although at the same time, all credit must be given to the Portuguese for maintaining their long standing tradition of the sea, as well as taking full advantage of such a gift of a bargain. Moreover, had not the Portuguese purchased *Cutty Sark* when they did, the clipper would undoubtedly have ended up as a coal hulk, or in some knacker's yard - in perfect condition like so many other noted sailing ships had ended their days. Meanwhile, in a quest to expand their merchant fleet even further, Messrs J&A

Ferreira hadn't stopped at buying just *Cutty Sark.* Also included in their list of purchases were the ships *Argonaut* and *Otago*, vessels which were also bought for a proverbial song. The Portuguese Navy also added the wool clipper *Thomas Stephens* to their fleet. Then from the Canadians they bought *Thermopylae,* a ship which had been *Cutty Sark's* greatest rival in former years

Note-The 1,048 ton ship named *Otago* had been built for the Albion Line by Alexander Stephen. On being purchased by the Portuguese she was re-named *Amelia*. However, that vessel should not be confused with the similarly named *Otago* in which Joseph Conrad was master.

We now come to those years in which little is known of *Ferreira's* adventures. There are some accounts which include an incident, when the ship was caught alongside in a hurricane at Pensacola. The date was between 25 and 26 September 1906. *Ferreira* was alongside loading a timber cargo when the hurricane struck, the ensuing storm raged through the hours of darkness causing severe disruption to shipping as well as the town. The damage to *Ferreira* was superficial although she did break off her whisker booms, dolphin striker and some damage to her yards and rigging. After the storm she finished up with port list, and what cargo she had in her hold shifted and had to be re-stowed. There are other stories of her being caught moored in another hurricane whilst in the West Indies. Unable to defend herself she was driven onto a lee shore and almost wrecked. In that incident there was quite some damage to her spars and rigging, as well as a smashed rudder and steering gear. Unable to make sail or be steered, she was towed to Key West for repairs.

Ferreira didn't really do a lot of trading during her years under the Portuguese flag, and for long periods she was laid up in the Tagus. Although Portugal had some Indian colonies, there are no records on hand stating she ever went any further than the Portuguese East Africa or the East Coast of South America.

The following passage has been condensed from Brown Son & Ferguson's 'The China Clippers' written by Basil Lubbock. During that time Captain Megano was in command of *Ferreira*, whilst Frederik Vincenzo da Sousa was his first mate This point of interest recorded in May 1913, is described by a deck officer from the British Mercantile Marine, a man who whilst on a Sunday walk along the New Orleans quaysides made an interesting observation. Quote.

Strolling along at a leisurely pace on the waterfront of New Orleans, I noticed the tall tapering spars of a sailing ship standing prominently out from behind an old shed. This class of cargo carrier was an exception at the wharves of the Crescent City, and taking as I do a keen interest in the doings of sailing ships, my curiosity tempted me to investigate. Retracing my steps I made my way through a timber yard eventually arriving at an old dilapidated wharf where the ship lay.

The days of the clipper ships had long since past ... even before I'd commenced my apprenticeship in the modern Clyde four posters. Nevertheless, I needed no telling that this was one of the old timers. The sun was high in the heavens and shone down with a dazzling glare on her weather beaten hull, it painfully emphasized the detail of its shabby exterior and the general air of neglect. Though shorn of her former glory there was the unmistakable stamp of the aristocrat about her, and it shone forth despite her tattered gear and pitted bulwarks. Like an old racehorse that one sometimes sees relegated to the shafts, the breed was unmistakable.

Floating lazily aloft with the shield of Braganza's noble house graven upon it, was the ensign of Portugal. Wondering what clipper she might be I sauntered along admiring her graceful lines. She was ship rigged with single topgallants and composite built, her copper sheathing was visible and apparently intact. Looking at her from forward, her entrance was like the thin end of a wedge filling out gradually to her waist, a little fuller perhaps in the run. She had a handsome stern whilst emblazoned on her deep counter in six inch yellow letters was her name and port of registry. Ferreira - Lisboa

For a figure head she had a comely maiden with a swelling bosom, plentifully daubed with multi coloured paint, her out stretched hand pointing ahead. I searched in vain beneath the name *Ferreira* on her bows for some clue as to her former identity. Making up my mind to go aboard, I glanced around to see if there was anybody in authority who's permission should be sought; however, everybody in the vicinity seemed to be enjoying their siesta. Walking over the gangway, I made my way slowly aft and mounted the poop deck. To give the Portuguese credit, they certainly did devote a little attention to that part of the ship, though the occasional splashes of colour that is so dear to them struck a jarring note.

The upper poop consisted of a raised deck some three and a half feet in height, neatly railed and hammock netted. Along the port and starboard sides were a row of garden seats, I call them that, as they are the type which are of a pattern generally found in parks and gardens rather than on board a ship. Two individuals occupied the poop, one of them was working away goring a topsail, whilst the other was slumbering on one of the garden seats. The running gear all came down to the outer or lower poop from which the mizzen rigging was set up. Walking around this outer poop I came to the after end of the upper one abaft of which was the steering gear. I examined the wheel, steering gear and brass bell with interest, and although they were of the old pattern, I failed to find any trace of the ship's original name.

Advancing on the individual who was goring a topsail, he didn't seem in the slightest perturbed by my presence. I addressed him. "You speak English?" He looked up and shook his head. "Are you an officer?" I asked. "No sabe." Came the reply. "Where is captain." I once again asked. The reply somewhat astonished me. "Me capitan." He replied, then went on with his work. I then made various gestures to signify that I would like to see down below, he nodded, so leaving him to his stitching and the 'una pelota' to his slumbers, I descended the after companion. An alleyway led into the saloon, on either side of which, were doors with cut glass handles. The saloon was a fairly spacious compartment running athwartships; it was panelled neatly in teak with birds eye maple and adorned with much fancy carving. Beautiful as it had once obviously been, it was pretty bare now. The marble topped fireplace, as well as the old brass lamp that swung in the skylight, were probably the only items of original furniture left.

Another alleyway led from the saloon forward, and on passing along it I glanced in through an open door into the captain's cabin. Like the saloon it was stripped of all of its old fittings except for a marble washstand and a heavy teak four poster bed which is not often seen in ships nowadays. Various compartments occupied either side of the alleyway, which at the end another companionway gave egress to the lower poop. Not caring to intrude, I investigated no more of the accommodation beyond noticing over each doorway that old familiar legend 'Certified for one seaman.'

Entering a door under the companion stairway I found myself in the after end of the 'tween deck. Overhead the rust clung in huge scales to the diagonal tie plates and beams. Judging by the feel of the frames they were still in a fair state of preservation, though they hadn't known a hammer or a slice of paint for many a day. Along the port and starboard sides ran a row of ports that were now plugged up, indicating that at one time she'd carried human freight - emigrants no doubt. Coming to the main hatchway, I peered closely at its pitted surface and endeavored to decipher some letters and figures cut in the after coaming, but I only managed to make out 63556 and 921.100 tons. Continuing forward through the 'tween deck which contained the usual collection of miscellaneous old junk blocks and rusty wires, I came to the fore hatch.

As I looked down below at her wedge like entrance I thought assuredly that it really needed tea clipper freights to make the ship pay. So fine was she, that one could hardly have found room to stand up on either side of the keelson. The iron collision bulkhead came down triangle shaped with the apex at the keelson. I mentally compared it with those of some of the modern windjammers which almost formed a square. Retracing my steps aft and climbing through the after hatchway, I reached the deck again where I wasn't sorry to feel the bright sunshine, for the old 'tween deck had a chilly eerie atmosphere about it. Gazing around I found many things to interest me; her decks were badly rutted, cracked and sorely needed oil.

Her rigging, fitted with wire lanyards (a doubtful boon) would have been better off with a little tar and service. As the yanks say, they were 'hell on chains,' chain strops being in abundance, and where a backstay had parted or a fore and after had gone in the nip, the deficiency was supplied in this manner. A very handy device caught my eye abaft the main rigging, viz, a single winch barrel with a double purchase and a handle clamped to the pin rail. Apparently this could be used with equal facility for taking in a bit on the main sheet or bowsing down the cro'jack tack in a stiff breeze. It didn't look as though it had been much used of late. The teakwood stanchions at the break of the poop, once no doubt a mass of shining brass and glistening varnish were now - ye gods - covered with silver paint.

It would have made any old deep water mate grind his teeth to see such a desecration of the time-honoured methods of 'preserving the bright work.' Nearby a row of teakwood buckets stood in racks, these were painted brown and adorned with silver painted bands - too much trouble to scrub them I suppose. As I made my way forward I couldn't help glancing at what must have once been the half deck, the door was open and seeing no one at home I stepped inside. A roomy enough place, it was obviously once the accommodation for quite a number of apprentices, it was now the abode of the petty officers and its old deal table, well worn deck and a few battered bunks reminded me well of old times. In the fore part of the after house, a donkey room was situated containing an engine and winch of ancient pattern. Overhead were the boat skids on which two launches and two boats rested in their chocks, whilst on the deck above the old harness casks were still in existence.

The main fife rail inside of which the original bilge pumps stood was in pretty bad shape, though at one time it must have looked fine with all its brass and carving. Way up above I noticed the lower block of the topsail halyards, a chain pennant from it reached to the deck, a rope saving device no doubt. The forward house was a neatly panelled structure that was identical with the half deckhouse but somewhat larger. The ship was well provided with boats, as there were two more on top of this structure; a wise precaution, as some day like the 'one horse shay' she will go to pieces all at once. Making my way up the ladder I reached the foc'sle head, a pretty bare spot enclosed by sundry rust eaten stanchions with a ridge wire rove through them. Two pairs of hardwood bollards were placed on each side, and on one of them was a solitary brass cap that glistened forlornly.

The old whisker booms were still in use, one out, the other in and all askew; the jib boom was rigged in, and as I looked at the old spar a deep-water song came to mind.

There was no talk of shortening sail by him who trod the poop
As her boom with the weight of a mighty jib, bent like a wooden hoop.

Looking over the side I once again admired her clean entrance and knife like bows; the old wooden stocked anchors hung at the cat-heads and the ring stoppers were fitted with a patent 'tumbler' releasing gear, eliminating the use of the time honoured maul. Coming down from the foc'sle head, I'd almost made up my mind to go when something which I'd overlooked caught my eye. Standing in pathetic solitude, suspended by a solitary cast iron dolphin was the forward bell; surely I thought this would give me a clue as to the ship's name.

Ferreira suffered superficial damage during the 1906 hurricane at Pensacola. In the above picture the fore royal mast can be seen hanging askew, as well as some sails that have been blown from out of their gaskets, the port whisker boom and dolphin striker have been dislodged whilst the timber cargo has shifted to port.

Photo - Frank Richardson

I went up and examined the bell closely; its surface at first sight appeared perfectly smooth and thickly coated with silver paint. At first I imagined I could faintly discern a very faint hint of lettering. I took a knife from my pocket and scraping away gently revealed the date of 1869, I hesitated not daring to further mutilate some Portuguese artistic work, then thought I may as well be hung for a sheep as a lamb and once again applied my knife. A few more strokes with the blade, and there, standing boldly out was a name that was once a byword amongst seafarers.

Indeed, it raised a thrill wit in me, a thrill that the *Mauritania* or *Lusitania* could never raise - '*Cutty Sark.*' I tapped the old bell gently with my knife and heard again the mellow sound which through the trades, the tropics and the roaring forties, had for nigh half a century marked alike the dark and the sunny hours. I made my way ashore and stood on the wharf surveying her now with a much keener interest.

During *Ferreira's* stay at New Orleans in 1913 the ship's bell was stolen. It was then replaced with another, apparently from the Liverpool registered ship *Shakespeare*. The replacement bell had also been painted silver so as not to arouse suspicion. Indeed, it was only after many years that the theft became apparent. However, the person who'd removed the bell, eventually returned it to the *Cutty Sark* after she'd came back under the Red Ensign.

It may well appear, that the gentleman who wrote the past chapter, and a man who has declined to give both his name or the ship on which he was serving, was more than likely involved in the bell's disappearance ... and its return. Due to his knowledge of ship construction, it may also appear that he was a shipwright or carpenter. Moreover, to obscure his identity even further, he describes himself as being a ship's officer. To that end a ship's carpenter is a petty officer and may therefore, be also be termed as an officer. Nevertheless, the same mysterious gentleman whatever rank he may have been was an excellent writer. Author.

A normal sight on all ships of sail in heavy weather were her lifelines. When a wall of water suddenly came over the bulwarks, sailors working on deck could grab hold of the life-lines and hang on …. Sometimes!

The greatest tea race of them all! The contest that began on 29 May 1866 ended in London ninety nine days later. Of the many ships that took part, *Ariel*, *Taeping* and *Serica* arrived at Gravesend on the same day and finished within minutes of each other. There was no finishing line, the winner was decided on which ship was the first to toss a tea chest onto the London quayside. Because of pilots, tugs and lock gates, a clear cut winner was not established. Sailor men of the day however, decided that *Ariel* was the winner. The picture above shows *Taeping* nearest with *Ariel* to leeward.

Author's Drawing

After having been rigged and fitted out at Greenock, *Cutty Sark* sailed for London in February 1870. At the capital city she loaded a cargo for Shanghai, then in the years to follow, proved to be one of the most famous ships of all time.

Cutty Sark **had pleasing lines even when in ballast.** Author's Drawing

Cutty Sark at Sydney

National Maritime Museum

Hove To Author's Drawing

On certain occasions when a ship is under way and it has to stop for the purpose of picking up a pilot, a doctor or for a number of other reasons. *Cutty Sark* in this instance has stopped to buy some of the catch from a passing fishing boat. This was a normal occurrence of buying fish at sea, and after having been under sail for a long period of time …. some times many months, fishing boats with their fresh fish were a most welcome sight for any ship's crew. For a captain to stop his ship, the normal practice was for him to 'heave to' by hauling up his mainsail and turning the main yards into the wind. By this, and as the above drawing shows, the main sail has been loosely hauled up in its buntlines to its yard, while the rest of the mainmast yards are turned around and into the wind. Meanwhile the sails on the fore and mizzen masts are still drawing. But that is enough to stop the ship, and allow for the lowering of a boat to row over to the similarly hove to brigantine fishing vessel. Once the transaction has been completed, the ship's boat is hauled back on board again, *Cutty Sark's* main sail will be hauled down, and the main yards will be hauled around to once more catch the wind. The ship will quickly make way again.

Studding Sails Author's Drawing

The picture above shows *Cutty Sark* under studding sails - or stuns'ls as the rig was known. Studding sails were the norm on most sailing vessels at the time of *Cutty Sark's* completion, and on every tea clipper those sails were a recognised part of the ship's sail plan. In those days when ship's complements were large, studding sails were often and easily rigged to catch the lightest of winds or cat's paws in fair weather. Because they were controlled from the deck and literally flown by the sailors, studding sails were given the slang name of 'kites.' Each sailor on deck may have charge of one or even two stuns'l sheets at the same time. Different variations of stuns'ls may be used by the captain, but to set those on the foremast were the most used. On other occasions just the port or starboard side may have been set. However, due to rising costs and fierce competition from the steamers, and especially those that used the Suez Canal, ship's crews gradually became smaller by the year. Ships that used stuns'ls needed a big crew. Therefore, to keep costs at the required minimum, *Cutty Sark* dispensed with her studding sails and main skysail in 1880. That was the time when studding sails disappeared forever, and also when crews on all other ship's of sail were drastically reduced.

The different appearances of Cutty Sark between 1869 and 1922.

Cutty Sark's Three Appearances

Many ships underwent structural changes during the course of their careers, and no less *Cutty Sark* as well as *Ferreira*, which also altered her appearance at differing times. On the preceding page there are three descriptive drawings showing the changes made during the ship's working life. The image on the left portrays the ship as built and rigged in 1869-70, and as she appears in Greenwich today. One exception however, is the upper top-sail lifts which were supposed to have been altered during or after *Cutty Sark's* first voyage.

At the time of *Cutty Sark's* building, it was the custom to have masts as tall as would allow, but by 1880 when crews were becoming smaller, the practice of having tall masts with moon-sails, stun sails and other kites was not practical anymore. As an example, *Cutty Sark's* main truck was originally 145 above the deck. The extra one ton of weight in mast height, ropes and cordage required to set the sky-sail was quite considerable, especially when considering what little extra speed it produced for the ship.

The centre sketch shows therefore, the appearance of *Cutty Sark* in March 1880 after she'd had her masts shortened. The main-mast truck was then 129 feet above the deck. The lower masts had been cut down by some seven feet, whilst the top-masts and t'gallants were trimmed down accordingly. In all the mast was twelve feet shorter. That was the appearance of the *Cutty Sark* when sold to the Portuguese in 1895 and re-named *Ferreira*, and the way she stayed until becoming partly dismasted in 1916.

After her part dismasting episode in May 1916, *Ferreira* lay at anchor in Cape Town's Table Bay. With the expense of re-rigging the vessel to its former state being too costly, it was decided to obtain the required main and mizzen lower masts from a hulked barquentine. Those lower masts arrived complete with standing rigging. When converted to a barquentine the main truck was then 112 feet above the deck, this being a 33 foot reduction from her original appearance. The main and mizzen lower masts were shorn off just above deck level and the replacement masts slid down into the cavity to the required depth. Wooden topmasts were then added to finish the barquentine rig

The jib-boom was shortened down to compensate for the absence of a royal forestay, and the life boats were moved to the forward deck house to allow for the swinging booms. After all the necessary repairs and alteration had been made, *Ferreira* sailed from Cape Town in January 1918. Sold to Da Silva of Lisbon in 1920 the ship was re-named *Maria di Amparo* and given painted gunports. As the drawing on the right shows, that was the appearance of the ship when Captain Dowman purchased the vessel for Britain in 1922.

Circular Quay Sydney. On the top picture, *Cutty Sark* **is positioned between and outside the two sailing vessels. Bottom also at Circular Quay, shows** *Cutty Sark's* **port bow whilst loading wool. Note: Her jib-boom has been hauled inboard.**

National Maritime Museum

Ferreira's Dismasting

The story of *Ferreira's* part dismasting is taken up from the time when she was under the command of Captain Fernando Domingues Megano, an experienced man of sail who had joined the ship in 1912. Under her new Portuguese owners *Ferreira* was partly manned by naval reservists, but she didn't travel far or for long periods. She sailed to the Portuguese colony ports of Africa, Brazil, West Indies, the Gulf ports, West Africa, and also showed up in the UK from time to time. In her visits to the UK shores, she brought cargoes to and from South Wales, London, Hull, Newcastle, and the Mersey. Any kind of a sailing ship in those years was something of a rarity, and because of her past career as *Cutty Sark, Ferreira* was a major attraction at every UK port she visited.

Her penultimate visit to the UK as a full rigged ship was to the Mersey in June 1914. By that time however, she'd been relegated to carrying any kind of cargo available, and in that instance the one time pride of the red ensign found herself carrying a mixed cargo of whalebone and cased whale oil from Mossamedes to Birkenhead. Her appearance brought scorn and derision from those old diehards of sail who remembered her, because although she looked good from a distance, a close up view of her was one of neglect and dereliction. After discharge *Ferreira* loaded a cargo of coal, cement and bricks for a return passage to Mossamedes, an open roadstead port where she arrived in October 1914. But by the time of her arrival the First World War was in progress.

As there were no berths at the Angolan port, *Ferreira* had to load and discharge at her moorings in an open anchorage. Mossamedes is noted for the occasional huge Atlantic ground swells, and is indeed a place where the danger of being driven ashore is highly possible. After discharging the cargo into barges with the use of her dolly winches and yard arms, and then after having almost completed the loading of another cargo of case oil for the Mersey, the barometer glass began falling rapidly.

In view of an impending storm that would blow his ship aground, Captain Megano needed no second telling by quickly breaking his two bower anchors at their joining shackles, and none too soon as the weather reared up! The passage back to the Mersey was normal enough, but when she arrived there in February 1915 without a full cargo or any ground tackle, the Jollife tugs of Liverpool were quick to claim she was not under command and the ship became an acrimonious subject of a salvage claim.

On the following month history was made when *Ferreira* sailed down the River Mersey in March 1915, because this was the last time in the history of sail that a fully rigged clipper

When *Ferreira* passed between Lundy Island and Hartland Point in March 1915, it was the last time a fully rigged clipper ship would ever be seen in British waters Oil Painting by the author

ship would ever be seen in the river. A month later as *Ferreira* passed between Lundy Island and Hartland Point with a cargo of Welsh coal from Newport for Lisbon, it was the last time a full rigged working clipper ship would ever be seen in British waters. On her arrival at Lisbon on 2 April 1915, Captain Megano was relieved by his first mate Frederic Vincenzo da Sousza. The new captain from Lisbon had served in the ship for four years.

Top: Five days after passing Lundy Island, *Ferreira* arrived at Lisbon with her cargo of Welsh coal.

Ferreira then resumed trading to the Portuguese African colonies with her first stop being Mossamedes. However, whilst sailing off the Cape Verde Islands she hit bad weather and lost both her fore t'gallant and rudder in heavy weather. With the use of a sea anchor until the weather quietened down, the rest of the passage had to be steered by sail and drogues. Sailing by drogue requires seamanship of the highest quality, with much of that skill depending on the direction of the wind and sea. On occasion Captain da Sousa used a drogue and otter slung from each side of the fore-yard arm. With a tripping rope suspended from each end of the mizzen yard for lifting one of the drogues at the required time, progress continued towards his destination. The weather was kind for the rest of the passage and *Ferreira* arrived at Mossamedes on 10 June after not having lost too much time. A telegraphic cable was then sent to the Lisbon owners to inform them of the rudder loss.

There were no facilities at Mossamedes for the construction of a new rudder, the only alternative was to have one made and shipped out by steamer. Whilst laying at anchor at the Mossamedes roadstead, a wait of four months was experienced before a replacement rudder could be shipped out from Lisbon. In the meantime most of the cargo was discharged, with just enough left in the forward part to keep the ship down by the head.

When the rudder did arrive, it was discovered that the pintles had been incorrectly positioned to line up with the gudgeons, but when that fault had been rectified the rudder was shipped and the last of the cargo discharged.

After a fifteen day passage *Ferreira* arrived at her coal loading port of Delagoa Bay in October 1915. However, no sooner had the anchor touched the bottom than a delegation of Portuguese government officials boarded the vessel. Captain da Souzsa was then informed by the authorities of Portugal's entry into the war against Germany. He was also reminded about the terms of the naval reservists, and advised they must be made available to the Portuguese Navy with immediate effect. Furthermore, the retainer which Ferreira Brothers & Co received from the government for training their sailors was to end forthwith. Much pleading and wrangling by the captain bore no fruit, he claimed that some of the crew were foreigners ... or like the cook too old. He even suggested that such a war would possibly only last a few weeks. At first, the authorities had wanted to take every single man including Captain da Sousa off the ship, they declared that the role *Ferreira* would play in the war was negligible, and her cargo carrying capabilities not worth the number of men who had to man her

It was a tough ordeal for the captain, but after a couple of bottles of the finest wine from the captain's locker had been opened and drunk, the authorities relaxed their stance a little, and then on the continuance of wine to soften their inflexible attitudes, the shore side men had an amazing change of heart. The result was that Captain da Sousa was allowed to stay aboard his ship with a small number of his crew. Eventually, a number of men believed to be eight of his sailors and one of his mates, were transferred to a Portuguese warship on station at nearby Lourenco Marques. The Man O' War had only been carrying a peacetime crew at the time, but as a state of war currently existed, every effort was made to replenish the warship to a full complement.

Captain da Sousza was allowed to keep his ship, plus two foreign sailors, the cook and six company apprentices who were indentured. Unfortunately, the removal of nine men had left Captain da Sousza too shorthanded to sail his ship. Ten men to sail a fully rigged ship was too inadequate by far. Crew replacements were virtually impossible to obtain as all able personnel had been called to arms. *Ferreira* lay at anchor until quite some months later, her captain managed to round up half a dozen local tribesmen and a couple of native fishermen; all of whom showed an inclination to becoming deep water sailormen. They each signed on with a thumbprint. The crew then numbered eighteen, not nearly enough of what in reality was required for comfort.

At her moorings in Delagoa Bay which is just to the south of Lourenco Marques and now named Maputo, *Ferreira* began loading a cargo of coal for the return passage to Mossamedes. It is not known whether it was the local stevedores or *Ferreira's* own sailors - or both - who loaded the cargo which mounted to 1,140 tons, but it was later discovered that the cargo had been badly loaded. When a ship such as the *Ferreira* is loading coal at her moorings from barges, the normal method is to cock bill the lower yards and use them as derricks.   A coaling gin is then made fast to the outer end of each lower yard, and by using the hand powered dolly winch, the coal is hoisted aboard from a barge alongside.   The coal comes aboard in baskets that hold two or three hundred weight at a time, and after they have been lowered to the top of the bulwark, the baskets are emptied into the lower hold via a wooden shute.   With three cargo hatches to her single hold *Ferreira* loaded all hatches at the same time. The general procedure being, that as the coal is being tipped into the lower hold, a number of men known as trimmers or coal heavers, would be responsible for spreading the coal evenly around the hold to keep the ship in trim. Unfortunately, problems arose when those trimmers who were probably the new crew members - tended to leave mounds and hollows, as well as voids in the cargo on the ships side.

The task of trimming coal even in normal temperatures can only be described as being most unpleasant. But when the hold is full of blinding choking coal dust with the trimmers having to work by lantern and candlelight or even in the dark, those poor conditions would be an awful lot worse. This work was also carried out in tropical heat, it is therefore no small wonder, that coal trimmers just throw in the coal to keep the ship on an even keel and vacate the hold as soon as possible. Unfortunately, and perhaps what was not known to those trimmers, was the fact that when the ship puts to sea and begins rolling, the poorly trimmed coal moves around due to the hollows, mounds and voids, then in order to find its own level and sometimes with dire consequences, the ship develops a list! -

(It may well be possible that the coal was just thrown in and not trimmed at all.)

In his book   'Last Of The Windjammers'   (Brown Son & Ferguson) Basil Lubbock describes how some sailing ships were loaded with coal on the Australian coast. When the sometimes badly loaded vessels left port and encountered heavy weather the coal inevitably shifted. The ship with its list would then be forced to make for the nearest port or bay, or any other refuge to have her cargo re-stowed. But if the ship was too far away from land, the crew would have to trim the ship at sea. This of course was a most difficult or impossible task in heavy weather, and needless to say, a great number of those badly laden ships were never heard of again. Basil Lubbock also states that many a furious ship's captain had managed to return to the same port at which he'd been loaded, then pointing to his ship's heavy list had blamed the loading stevedore.

In those circumstances however, it must be explained there are two sides to the story. In the case of the stevedore whose job it is to load the ship, he'll tend to fill the hold as quickly as possible and get the ship away, get the next one in, and so enhance his wage packet. On the other hand and more importantly, it is the ship master's responsibility to ensure his vessel is loaded correctly. Whether he details one of his mates to supervise the loading and trimming or leaves it to the stevedore, or even supervises the operation himself; it makes no difference whatsoever, the final responsibility - right up until the present day - has always been the master's.

When *Ferreira* picked up her anchor to leave Delagoa Bay on the 23 April 1916, she was the last of the clipper breed sailing the seven seas. Most unfortunately and quite unknown to *Ferreira's* crew at the time, the only other vessel synonymous with *Cutty Sark* was the Portuguese *Pero D Alemquer* - formerly the *Thomas Stephens*. But she'd been lost with all hands a few months earlier in the North Atlantic. Therefore, *Ferreira* or *Cutty* Sark, call her what you will, had outlived every single clipper ship ever built. Furthermore, and even at forty seven years of age she could still make a good speed, and given the wind, still had the ability to outrun any tramp steamer and many a passenger liner.

Despite her makeshift crew all went well for the first few days. The newcomers were given a crash course in sail handling, steering the ship, and all the other sailorising jobs so necessary to keep a ship at sea. The new crew showed remarkable skill and agility in going aloft, and soon learned to handle sail in good weather. However, a couple of the new crew members appeared to know more about the jungle than the ship, and soon after leaving port began to feel the effects of the ship's motion. The senior apprentice had been given the vacant first mate's position, and Captain da Souzsa worked watch and watch with him. The captain was looking forward to a fair weather passage in order for his new sailors to become acclimatised. Unfortunately it was not to be, because after about a week at sea when with *Ferreira* somewhere off the South African coast of East London, the weather took a turn for the worse and the ship began rolling heavily on a beam sea.

The vessel was heading southwest in the same direction from which the wind coming; progress became slow by sailing tack on tack under topsails. On the next day when *Ferreira* was between Port Elizabeth and East London, the weather worsened drastically and the seas swept her decks from stem to stern. The ship was pitching and rolling heavily and the temperature dropped noticeably. The chicken coops on either side of the mizzen mast had been hit by the onrushing seas in the hours of darkness. The port side coop was just driftwood with chicken feathers floating around the decks; there was also some of the running gear which having been washed from their belaying pins was swirling around in the water. The strong gale increased to force ten, and with the ship pitching and rolling the way she was, no work was forthcoming from the new hands. Furthermore, and except for two of them who had been fishermen, they were huddled together in a state of terror in their foc'sle refusing to come out. The ship continued to plunge into the cold black seas, and in so doing the air was filled with a spray and spume that greatly reduced visibility. With the dark nimbus clouds tearing past it appeared as though they were brushing against the mastheads. No midday fix on the sextant was possible.

With the captain lashed down and two apprentices occasionally on the wheel, the work of the ship which was mainly sail handling was left to the other young apprentices, two sailors and the mate. The Captain of a heavily rolling ship with a bulk cargo will be constantly monitoring the situation in an attempt to determine whether or not his cargo has shifted. Captain da Sousa was also concerned with the fact that with the lower hold being full, and nothing in the 'tween decks, his ship was too stiff. Such a situation increases a pendulum effect and induces continuous heavy rolling.

If a ship is rolling twenty or twenty five degrees each way, it may be regarded as normal in heavy weather, but when the same ship rolls thirty degrees one way and just twenty the other ... under the same circumstances - then it's obvious that a list has developed. When a ship is rolling and pitching in the conditions described, it so happens that every now and again she'll give one huge roll to one side or the other, and that is exactly what happened to *Ferreira*. It resulted in her rolling right over to port with her lower yard arms dragging in the water. She encountered that gigantic roll whilst on a starboard tack, thereby causing the ship to develop a port list. When Captain da Sousza realised his cargo had shifted, he tried to get onto the other tack to take the weight off the port side, but due to the list the helm refused to answer. In the heavy weather he was compelled to take a chance and wear ship to get the weather onto the port side. The captain knew full well his ship was in the middle of a busy shipping lane, and also knew he was heading directly towards the nearby South African coast, added to which, he'd have to heave his ship to then get the coal re-trimmed before he could resume his course.

At the forward end of the cabin accommodation there is a small hatch door leading into the 'tween deck, and it was from there that entry could be gained into the 'tween deck. A quick survey by lantern revealed most of the shifting had occurred in the forward section of the hold, but even though the ship was hove to, the fore hatch could not be stripped due to the large amounts of water coming over the foc'sle head. Added to the fact that each hatch coaming was only twelve inches high. Eventually just one corner hatch board was taken off which allowed sufficient light into the hold for the task of re-trimming. After a short while a deluge of water entered the hold from where the hatch-board had been removed, it was quickly replaced and the hatch battened down again.

The task of re-trimming then had to be carried out using both a hurricane lantern and tallow candles. Most unfortunately and due to the ship surviving on an extremely tight budget, the ship only possessed one hurricane lantern. Probably, fifteen or twenty tons of coal had shifted over to the port side causing the list. Although it may not seem a lot in a ship carrying 1,140 tons of it, the difference between the port and starboard side then amounted to thirty to forty tons, and on a small ship like *Ferreira,* that is quite significant. Furthermore, such a list would only worsen with the ship's rolling momentum if action was not taken immediately. Whilst the ship was still rolling wildly, there was always the risk of her taking another of those massive rolls, a roll where another fifteen tons or even more may go over to the port side, then there would be little or no hope of stabilising the ship.

Hove to with the captain at the wheel, it took most of the day to get the ship back on an even keel, and indeed, it was the apprentice boys to whom the credit of the re-trimming the ship belonged. While those lads were working frantically to save the ship, the other unfortunate souls who were making their first trip to sea were still huddled up in their foc'sle, suffering the dreadful effects of both seasickness and terror. *Ferreira* resumed her course on 3 May, but after further heavy rolling during the hours of darkness, she once again developed a port list. Captain da Sousza considered taking his ship into Port Elizabeth to have his cargo re-stowed, but such things cost money. The ship had previously been idle for six months at Delagoa, then four months at Mossamedes where she'd awaited the arrival of her new rudder. There was no money available!

Because of the dangerous Thunderbolt Rocks which lay outside Port Elizabeth, Captain da Sousa decided it was too risky to attempt entering. His apprentices had done sterling work so he decided to carry on hoping the winds and seas would abate. At first light on 4 May, those gallant apprentice boys who must by then have been feeling the strain, were once more down in the hold hurling and shovelling coal from one side of the ship to the other. With the captain constantly at the wheel, the mate also added his presence down below. Indeed, he was fully aware like everybody else in the hold, that if the ship did suddenly heel over and capsize they'd all be entombed. But nobody needed to tell those men that even if she did go over, it would hardly make any difference if they were down in the hold or up on deck. There would be no chance of getting a boat away due to the fierceness of the wind and the high seas and their end would no doubt be the same. The sea-water which had entered through the open hatchway only added to the burden of those trimming, that water would eventually seep into the bilge and contribute to the ship being down by the head - unless it could be pumped overboard. But the pumps could not be manned due to the big green seas which swept across the ship, those huge deluges of water would surely smash any body up against the bulwarks or wash them overboard. The hard gales, squalls, and mountainous seas continued, and this just added to the misery of a thoroughly cold hungry and exhausted crew who were by then soaked through. The heavy weather continued as did the shifting of the cargo. Time and again those boys were sent down to level the coal, young boys who by then were grasping at every opportunity to snatch a few precious moments of sleep ... wherever they might be at the end of each session. When the opportunity did arise, none of them even bothered to take off his oilskins or their sodden clothes beneath.

Then to make matters even worse, the only working lantern was lost and buried beneath the coal, then the candles which were few in number gave out. The weather was extremely cold as the month of May is almost mid winter in South Africa. Captain da Sousa knew he was 'out of season' with the weather, and also knew he'd have a south westerly wind in his face all the way to Cape Town and beyond. On May 6 Captain da Sousza who hadn't seen the sun for a few days, assumed by dead reckoning his ship was some 100 miles south of Mossel Bay. By that time she'd been pitching and rolling heavily for over a week making little if any progress. The captain had great fears for the masts which were stayed by rigging much in need of repair. The ship had been hove to on many occasions, although in an attempt to make a bit of headway the foresail was set whenever possible. During the day she took one more of those huge sickening monster rolls, a roll that sent her almost on her beam-ends.

Once again the coal had shifted to port. This time the degree of list was far too great to even contemplate trying to level the cargo. The sea was sweeping over the port rail resulting in the port side deck being full to the gunwhale tops. The only way any light could be admitted into the hold was through one of the hatches, the problem was, that any attempt to open any of them would result in the hold flooding in next to no time. Captain da Sousza realised there was only one hope left to save his ship, the removal of some or even all of the top hamper. Therefore he reluctantly ordered the braces, sheets and backstays to be let go, and fore topgallant mast cut away.

The necessary gear was let go to allow for free running, and the fore t'gallant back stay lanyards were cut away. It was hoped that as the spar came down, it would be blown far away from the ship. But due to the way the ship was pitching and rolling, not all the running gear could be released. The fore t'gallant mast broke off at its cap, and as it fell forward it hit the fore lower topsail yard breaking it off at the slings. It then continued in its fall over the port bow, breaking off the whisker boom before going over the side. Fouling itself up with loose running rigging, it dragged alongside the ship until breaking free. The fore lower topsail yard which carried away at the slings, came down with a crash and lay straddled across the foc'sle head and the fore hatch.

After the melee had been somewhat sorted out, the main t'gallant mast was cut away in the same fashion, this time it broke off clean at the cap and was blown well clear of the ship. Despite the obvious weariness of the crew, work went on at a frantic rate to clear the decks as there was still plenty to do. Then to put as much weight as possible on the starboard side to help counter the list, the fore topsail yard which had landed across the fore hatch and the foc'sle head, was lashed down beneath the starboard bulwarks. It was soon discovered however, that the reduction in top weight was nowhere near enough to make any noticeable difference to the trim of the ship.

At first light on 7 May, Captain da Sousza ordered the main lower mast and its top mast to be cut away in one piece. Once again those weary apprentice boys sprang to life whilst the ship reared and plunged like a wild mustang. They released every thing possible that connected the mainmast to the ship - before hacking through the lanyards of the starboard side main shrouds. They had to hang on in the blinding spray and abide by the unwritten law of the sea - one hand for the ship, the other for yourself. Working furiously to cut through the lanyards, it was then realised they'd been rove off with wire rope instead of the traditional tarred sisal or manila rope, their task was then made much more difficult. The starboard lower shrouds were eventually severed with the fire axe, but most surprisingly the mast refused to go. Meanwhile an attempt was being made to cut through the iron lower mast at its base with the axe, and sparks flew as those apprentices hacked away at the base of the mast at a point above the deck partners. With no shrouds to support it, a mast would normally go over the side on the first or second roll, but it was some time before that main mast began to move, and when it did, it moved in a most surprising way. Because instead of breaking off at the deck partners, the wrought iron lower mast actually bent halfway up and leaned over the port side.

The list was then worse than ever, and even without rolling, the ship had a list of twenty degrees. The general belief amongst sailors is, that once a ship rolls more than thirty-three degrees either way with an unstable cargo, it won't return to stability and the vessel will capsize. *Ferreira's* list went well over the point of no return each time she rolled to port, and although she was virtually on her beam-ends with the port bulwark underwater, she still managed to remain afloat. Those facts in themselves were true testimony as to the way the ship had been designed and built. The bent mainmast contributed enormously to the ship's list until finally, and after much hacking away with the axe, it eventually began to break at the deck and go over the side - in a most miraculous manner!

Due to the rolling and pitching of the vessel, there could be no reliable way of predicting in which way the mast would fall. All those men on the ship could do was to hope and pray for the best, and most fortunately for them that's just what happened. The mast toppled over the port side with a crashing roar, missing the pumps, boats and their skids by inches. It didn't go alone however, because since it was still connected to the mizzen mast by its topmast and t'gallant stays, the whole lot went over in one huge tangled mess. The mizzen topmast broke off at its cap, which in turn took the mizzen t'gallant as well as its gaff and boom. The crojack yard was ripped off breaking at the slings and ended up cock-billed in the starboard mizzen shrouds. Meanwhile, to stop any water getting into the hold, an old sail was quickly jammed down the partners where the mast had broken off close to the deck The port waist was filled with sea water to the top of the bulwarks when she rolled over to port, yet when she went on a starboard roll, the ship only came to an even keel, hardly allowing time for the water to run out through the freeing ports. To exacerbate matters even further, the decks were extremely slippery causing the crew to slip and slide. Ships with wooden decking should be wet down every day, and although *Ferreira's* decks were getting plenty of wetting, they'd become slimy with not being scrubbed or holystoned. *Ferreira's* decks were made of teak a type of wood which is unfavourably noted for the problem. The iron mainmast, which had been the ship's main driving force for the past forty seven years was now her worst enemy, evidence of this was when it began to rear up then drag and slam against the ship's port side.

The wooden upper part of the main mast ... its topmast - had submerged, whilst the iron lower mast was still connected to it. This was straddled across the badly smashed up port bulwarks whilst some of the port lower shrouds were still secured to it. The heavy iron mast which as well as trying to drag the ship under, was ranging up down the ship's side in a violent movement, grinding the top-rail away whilst threatening to gouge holes in the ship's side. Furthermore, the water which was waist deep made any attempt to dispose of the mast extremely hazardous.

Once again the ship's only axe was wielded, cutting through wires, lanyards and ropes as they lay taut across the top rail that was now a chopping block. There was no let up and nor could there be one, because with a rolling list of 45 degrees the ship was about to capsize at any time. As the ship continued her wild pitching and rolling, work went on cutting, hacking, and chopping the bonds which still held the mast to the ship until they were finally severed and the mast sank. In all her years, as either the *Cutty Sark* or *Ferreira,* the ship had been involved in a number of narrow escapes, that one however, was the closest the ship had ever been to disaster.

Although plunging wildly and still in mortal danger, *Ferreira* righted herself to some extent when the mast had sunk. It was then felt the worst was over. But there was still the problem of the list to be sorted out. Once again every available man was sent down below into the hold for what was to be the last time in levelling the coal out. The rest of the daylight hours were spent in saving as much as possible of the cordage and associated gear which lay strewn around the decks. The next day saw the weather improve, but by then it was too late for the rig or what was left of it. Indeed, *Ferreira* would never again sail as a fully rigged ship. The seas were still too high to make work comfortable, therefore, it took the rest of the daylight hours to clear up the decks.

Whilst every effort was made to sail the ship, it was a most difficult task because only the foremast and its topmast were capable of carrying any canvas. The wind had subsided to a light gale from the west, and the beleaguered ship had to tack with just her fore course. Work carried on in the uncomfortable weather right through the hours of darkness. By the morning of 9 May the fore upper topsail had been bent on with its sheets rove through the lower yard where the sheets of the lower topsail sheets should have been. The fore topmast staysail and the inner and outer jibs were set, the flying jib-sail could not be set because there was no royal mast to support it.

Captain da Sousza surveyed his ship and the damage caused by nine days of heavy weather, nevertheless he was quite confident of sailing his battered ship into Simons Bay with a wind from the right direction, or maybe even make Cape Town if he could possibly get a tow in. Ships were sighted but were too far away to recognise the distress signals of the crippled *Ferreira*, which although floundering and wallowing, was still was making slow progress towards False Bay.

Very early on the cold and windy morning of 10 May 1916, contact was made with the SS *Kia Ora*. A Shaw Savill and Albion cargo passenger ship, which having recently taken on coal bunkers at Cape Town, had sailed only a few hours earlier on passage towards Sydney. The very port where *Ferreira* in her prime as the *Cutty Sark,* had been the envy of every sailor who cast their eyes upon her. In the big swell *Kia Ora* came as close as safety would allow, signalling that Captain da Sousa should come aboard the steamer. With his ship hove to under the fore topsail, a boat was lowered and Captain Da Sousza was rowed across by four of his trusted apprentices, one of whom could speak English. Although the wind had gone down a lot, the sea was still running high which made the rowing none too easy.

Meanwhile, word had gone through the mail steamer that the rescue of a battered old sailing ship was about to take place, and all on board came out on deck see the ship in distress. What a sorry sight she must have made to those steamship seamen, who were not to know at the time, that the bedraggled looking hulk they were looking at, was once the pride of the British sailing fleet. The bearded captain of *Ferreira* with his English speaking apprentice were welcomed aboard the *Kia Ora*, and after having been escorted to the bridge were met by the mail boat's captain. Captain da Sousa then made a request to have his stricken ship towed into Simon's Bay or Table Bay. The steamer's captain however, who after having had a good look at the *Ferreira* and noting her condition, reluctantly refused the plea on the grounds that the old sailing ship wasn't worth the time or trouble.

He reminded Captain da Sousza of the war in progress, and as he was responsible for a large number of passengers and crew, his ship would be a sitting duck for any one of the submarines or surface raiders suspected of being in the area. He then added that only if he'd been heading towards Cape Town, would he, or could he have obliged. He then suggested that Captain da Sousza should open his hatches and let the ship go under, he would then give him and his crew a passage to Australia. It took no time at all for *Ferreira's* captain to refuse this generous offer. He was quite determined to get his battered but not beaten ship into Simonstown which was much nearer than Table Bay The distance was only about 60 miles to False Bay as it had been for the last three days. But after what the *Ferreira* had been through if given wind from the right direction, Captain da Sousa was quite sure his ship could make it.

Not having been able to fix his position whilst sailing on dead reckoning for the past few days, Captain da Sousza was given his position by the *Kia Ora's* master. Taking his leave from the steamship by way of her pilot ladder, Captain da Sousza was pleasantly surprised to find his boat had been loaded with a sack full of fresh bread and other dry stores. As Captain da Sousza was being rowed away from the mail steamer and back towards his own ship, he was given three hearty cheers by all on board the *Kia Ora*, who had by that time heard the full story of the events leading to *Ferreira's* shabby appearance. The *Kia Ora* then gave three blasts on her steam whistle as she began making way, but by the time Captain da Sousa's boat had reached his own ship, the SS *Kia Ora* was out of sight.

Once back on board *Ferreira,* her captain set his two square and three head sails in another attempt to make False Bay. The wind came up again - but from the wrong direction, and *Ferreira* could only wallow in the big swell. As the galley had been almost inoperable for some days, the only food eaten had been hard tack, But then the first meal to be eaten for over a week was enjoyed by the cold, we and famished crew. It was only then that the newly signed on 'sailors' who had eaten nothing during the catastrophe, made their emergence from their foc'sle.

In the next forty eight hours little or no progress was made and the wind which then came from the west reached gale force. On 13 May with a strong wind and high seas, The foremast lookout reported land on the starboard side. This aroused fears that the ship was liable to run onto a lee shore. Sailing was not easy, because with only the fore mast carrying any canvas steering was most difficult. The coal no longer posed a threat of shifting due to the ship's pitching into the head seas. However, she took quite a lot of water over the foc'sle which made life difficult for those working the head sails. *Ferreira* was slowly drifting in towards Cape Aghulas, a lee shore, rocks and certain shipwreck. She was less than ten miles away in the forenoon watch when the foremast lookout reported a steamer coming up from astern. This time and none too soon, the disabled veteran who had her ensign upside down, two black balls and a distress pennant, was recognised as being a ship in distress and requiring assistance.

The steamer was the *Indraghiri* of the Liverpool Indra Line. She was under the command of Captain Thomas Pilcher on passage Durban towards Cape Town. Captain Pilcher's offer to tow the stricken ship into Table Bay was gratefully accepted, but to throw a heaving line across was too difficult as the sea was still running too high for the big *Indraghiri* to get close enough. Estimating *Ferreira's* drift, the steamer then positioned herself ahead of *Ferreira* and floated a cane fender down wind attached to a messenger rope. It took some time to grapnel the line and get it inboard, but a towing line was eventually set up with the steamer's towing wire.

The SS *Indraghiri* which was on charter to the Blue Funnel Line was equipped with radio. A message was therefore sent to the harbour authorities at Cape Town to advise of the rescue and a request for a tug as soon as possible. The tow which began in the afternoon went smoothly enough and ended at the entrance of Table Bay at noon on 15 May 1916. The grateful crew of the *Ferreira* slipped the towing wire of the *Indraghiri,* which then went to the coal berth to load bunkers for her run to Liverpool. The tug *Ludwig Weiner* which was waiting made herself fast to *Ferreira's* port shoulder and guided the crippled veteran to her moorings in Table Bay.

Reflecting on the past month's events, Captain da Sousza said if his sailors had not been taken from him in Lourenco Marques, he would by that time have been discharging his ship in Mossamedes. In the first instance the coal would have been properly loaded, and even if it had shifted at sea, his old hands would have soon re-trimmed it properly. The heavy weather experienced wouldn't have been a problem; *Ferreira* would normally have taken such conditions in her stride. The ship in the course of her career both as the *Cutty Sark* and *Ferreira* had seen far worse and come through it all. Indeed, she had been designed and built to withstand the worst the elements could offer. That episode however, was the closest she'd ever been in coming to her end. But there was no doubt in Captain da Sousa's mind, that the heroes of the ship's survival were his teenaged apprentices.

The fact of the matter was, there hadn't been enough competent hands to sail the ship, and under those same circumstances, Captain da Sousza decided he would never again take such a risk. The catastrophe itself could only be put down to his own error, and no blame could be attached to the ship. Indeed, under the same harrowing circumstances many a ship would have foundered. Many accidents and dismastings can be put down to the human error, and it wasn't the first time the ship had been dismasted.

Heavy weather had been the cause of *Ferreira's* cargo shifting, and although this could have been prevented with the use of shifting boards, *Ferreira* like many other small ships never used them. They took up too much space in the 'tween decks, and in being heavy would reduce the amount of cargo which could be carried. For long periods they would not be in use, they were costly, and the *Ferreira* was living on a shoe-string budget. Therefore, *Ferreira* like any other ship of her kind never carried or used shifting boards.

After *Ferreira* had been safely anchored in Table bay, a survey was later carried out by

Captain John McKeown, an experienced sailing master from the Liverpool firm of Peter Iredale and Porter, and late of the full rigged ship *Ainsdale*. Captain McKeown was acting on behalf of the underwriters for the insurance company with which *Ferreira* was insured. His findings didn't make happy reading, because in his report he commented on the lack of maintenance over a long period of time.

Although the whole insurance claim for £1,800 was paid out … the actual figure the ship was insured for, it was nowhere near enough to have *Ferreira* repaired to her original status of a fully rigged ship. Estimates to the whole repair programme were given at well over £3,000. However, even if such money was available, repairs were out of the question due to the First World War being in progress, as well as the war at sea that was raging in the Atlantic. It would appear that when the ship had been purchased twenty-one years earlier, not only had she been under insured in the first place, but since 1895 the insurance premiums had never been increased to allow for inflation.

Considering the amount paid out by the insurance company, as well as the unavailability of materials to repair the ship, there was the feeling that *Ferreira* would have to either lay up until the war was over, use her as a coal hulk, or break the vessel up. But nobody knew when the war was going to end, moreover, the new masts required could not be supplied due to the shortage of material. The war was in progress, and *Ferreira* with its cargo carrying capabilities was deemed as not being worth the effort. However, later enquiries by Captain da Sousa revealed there was a barquentine which had recently been hulked in the Table Bay area. Negotiations were started to acquire its lower main and mizzen masts, the result of which, was *Ferreira's* eventual conversion to a barquentine.

Ferreira's foremast was re-headed without its royal mast. This would exclude both the fore royal sail, as well as the flying jib-sail; due to this the jib-boom was shortened accordingly. The replacement steel main lower mast was ninety-six feet in length from heel to cap with its wooden topmast being fifty-five feet from table to truck. Allowing for the depth of hold and the doublings, the final height of the mainmast truck above the deck was 112 feet, 39 feet shorter than when built as *Cutty Sark*. The new main and mizzen lower masts from the hulked barquentine was specially selected by Captain da Sousa. They was smaller in diameter than *Ferreira's* originals, and for that reason could be slid down into the existing cavity of Ferreira's lower mast. New deck partners would have to be fashioned by the shipwright who had been taken on for the re-rigging, and that was the cheapest way to repair the ship. The iron wire lower shrouds which had arrived with the main-mast were the wrong length for *Ferreira* and these had to be adjusted accordingly with chain strops. Despite the fact that a newly made lower main-mast was out of the question, due to both cost and priority of the First World War being in progress, it remains to be seen why Captain da Sousa chose that particular replacement main lower mast.

As there are no records available, it can only be assumed that quite possibly it was the only suitable mast available; then again, it may have been for the purpose of cost cutting on fitting. Then again it could well have been the case that Captain da Sousa had purposefully chose that mast because of its smaller diameter. Because the remainder of the old mast could be sheered off at the deck, and the new mast slid down into the cavity of the original mast and packed with sand and cement. On the other hand, had it been the case where the replacement mast was fitted in the normal manner, then the cargo of coal which was still in the hold would have to be discharged, then loaded again on completion of the re-fitting task. That would have meant a lot more expenditure which the captain was desperately trying to avoid.

The boat skids were moved from the after to forward deckhouse. This was to allow for the swinging of the main mast lower boom. The patched up repair job to *Ferreira* took over eighteen months in all, most of which time was spent anchored in Table Bay. However, during the month of January 1918 *Ferreira* sailing as a barquentine finally resumed her passage to Mossamedes ... With a crew of twelve! Whilst in Cape Town the natives who had signed on at Delagoa Bay were paid off, and although there is no record, it appears most unlikely that they carried on with their new maritime careers. By all accounts, there was only the captain, a shipwright, and two of apprentices left on board during *Ferreira's* long stay in Cape Town.

Although the vessel had been out of service for longer than at any part in her career, the very fact that her cargo had shifted which resulted in her part dismasting, may well have been a blessing in disguise. This is because in the Atlantic where *Ferreira* was doing most of her trading, sailing ships were easy prey for submarines when caught in a windless zone. Subsequently, *Ferreira* had spent the year of 1917 which turned out to be the worst part of the war in Table Bay.

After the SS *Indraghiri* had dropped *Ferreira* at the entrance of Table Bay, the Cape Town tug *Ludwig Weiner* strapped herself on to *Ferreira's* port shoulder then guided her to an anchorage. As can be seen in the above photograph from the Cape Town Argus, the ship was by that time on an even keel. Also visible is the cro'jack yard still lying askew of the mizzen mast.

The main damage to *Ferreira* had been the loss of the mainmast, fore t'gallant mast, and mizzen topmast with its t'gallant. Superficial damage was the loss of nearly all her yards and sails, damage to the rigging and badly stove in port side bulwarks. There was also much minor damage which included a broken port whisker boom.

After an insurance claim had been filed, Captain John McKeown from the Liverpool sailing ship *Ainsdale* acted on behalf of the insurance company. His report stated that *Ferreira* had been neglected over a long period of time. The ship was grossly under insured but the £1,800 claim was paid out. The cost of refurbishment to the state of a full rigged ship would have been well in excess of £3,500.

Ferreira

In the top photo taken at Table Bay when *Ferreira* was owned by Ferreira Brothers, the differences in diameters between the lower main and lower foremast is clearly visible. The lower main and lower mizzen masts were acquired from a hulked barquentine at Cape Town in 1917.

This replacement masts were smaller in diameter than the originals, and the shrouds which came with the masts were of different lengths and necessitated adjustment.

The main and mizzen masts were fitted with wooden top masts, whilst the fore mast had a stump t'gallant added.

The flying jib-sail was dispensed with and the jib-boom was shortened accordingly. The lifeboats and their skids were moved forward to allow for the swinging main boom.

The photo on the left which shows *Maria di Amparo* with her mizzen shrouds frapped in, was taken at Falmouth in 1923.

Maria di Amparo

May 1916

Arrivals in Table Bay — Departures

Date	Name of Vessel	Tonnage	Name of Captain	Where from	Cargo	Agents
9	Alnwick	12234	J.E. Crosbie	London	gen	Anderson
	Grysevale	4213?	J.W. Steel	Natal	"	Rennie & Co
10	Agnar	427	Brytan	Knysna	"	Thesen
	Rimutaka		F.A. Hemming	Australia	"	Westray Bell
	Maloppo		A. Bergner	New York	"	Bucknall
	Tydeus	7441	W.H. Wallace	Dakar	"	M. Cotts
11	Kwarra	4441	D.S. Davies	St Johns	"	Attwell & Co
12	Suquehanna	3711	D. Samuel	New York	"	Union Cast
	Britania	1525	V.F. Sparks	Cable Service	"	Cable Co
	Port Kembla	4700	Hoad	London	"	Bucknall
	Corfe C.	4592	G. Vivens	Coast	"	Union Cas
13	Outeniqua	1019	A. Pedersen	"	"	Thesen
	Ingerid	204	A.H. Wallin	"	"	P. Leon
	Hawyl	3592	J.V. Ward	Durban	"	M. Cotts
	Orestes	4653	J.W. Clark	Natal	"	Union Cas
	Durham C.	8228		"	"	Thomson W.
	Kathiawar	4456	R. Ro...	Mossel B.	"	Thesen &
	Nautilus	360	H. Ischel	Port N.	"	Parry Leon
	Ardoyne	4315	P.H. Bar...	Natal	"	Johnson
14	Clan Ferguson	4808	R.C. Jones	New York	"	Thesen
	Karratara	540	J. Marteson	Saldanha B.	"	M. Cotts
15	Machaon	6738	W.P. Bevan	Natal	"	M. Cotts
	Indraghiri	5723	Pilcher		"	
	Oranje	4437	W.A. Beijer	Natal	"	M. Cotts
	Tamba		J. Holland	Singapore	"	"
	Ardangorm	3570	F.J. Ogilvie	Natal	"	Thomson W.
	Clara	763	J. Blonde	Knysna		Thesen & Co
	Kazembe	4658	J.W. Anderson	New York	"	Bucknall
	Sabine	3805	A.A. King	Coast	"	Union C.
16	Mashima Maru	8512	S. Wada	London	"	M. Cotts
	Tattarax	6217	W. Reid	To Saldanha B.	"	"

The above document has been obtained from the Cape Town Harbour Master's records. It records the arrival in the port of the Liverpool steamer *Indraghiri*, a ship which towed the disabled Portuguese *Ferreira* to safety. The reason *Ferreira* is not listed in the arrivals column, is because she was not destined for the port as well as the fact that she lay outside in the anchorage.

Masting

Before the days of iron and steel coming into the ship yards, ship's hulls and masts were made of wood. The method of manufacture for wooden masts depended on the size of the ship, and whereas smaller vessels were able to make a lower mast from the single stem of a tree, mast construction for big ships was a time consuming and expensive undertaking. Big ships like the *Schomberg* had to have 'made masts' for their lower masts sections. This was because of the huge diameter and length of those mast portions. A 'made mast' is one which is made up from a number of squared off baulks of timber. These large timbers are scarfed together … then after being covered with rounded off segments, they are banded together with rope at intervals of about three feet.

When iron came into the ship yards, ship's hulls, masts and yards could be made of iron. Another innovation was a ship's standing rigging made from iron wire; both the iron wire and its long splice were the invention of the German mining engineer Wilhelm Alberts in the 1820's. *Cutty Sark's* standing rigging for her lower masts which is otherwise referred to as the shrouds, are of five in circumference. Like so many other ships of the day *Cutty Sark* was built with iron lower masts, whilst she also adopted the new style of iron wire for her standing rigging. The objective of the standing rigging is to support the mast to which it is assigned. It does not move like running rigging and is set up permanently with lanyards and dead eyes. The three lower masts of the *Cutty Sark* are tubular or hollow inside, and each has a thickness of about one inch for the whole of their lengths from heel to cap. When they are being fitted the lower masts were secured into a tabernacle at the keel of the ship. The built up junction where the mast passes through the deck is known as the 'partners.' Each mast of *Cutty Sark* was built in three sections, the lower mast, topmast, and top gallant—royal mast. Those above the iron lower mast were made of wood which is lighter, cheaper and more expendable than iron.

More modern ships like passenger liners have a ladder on the inside of the steel tubular mast leading to the crows nest.

Ships like *Schomberg* pictured above were fitted with made masts. The diameter of the main lower mast on that ship was 42 inches or about 132 inches in circumference. The white painted bandings are visible on each of the lower masts.

On the left is the base of *Cutty Sark's* main mast. The projection at the base of the mast where it meets the deck is known as 'the partners.' Partners are designed to stop leakage into the hold.

When *Ferreira* was being re-masted in 1917, the remaining portion of the mast was sheered off at the top of the partners. The replacement mast which being smaller in diameter, was then slid down into the cavity of the original tubular mast.

After being lowered into the cavity, the replacement mast was laid on top of a concrete filling. By that method the exact height required for the lower mast hounds could have been obtained. An unusual but cost effective method!

Author's Drawing

Severely shorthanded on leaving Delagoa Bay, *Ferreira's* captain shipped half a dozen hands with no sea experience. The first few days went quite well in the good weather, and the new hands appeared to be quite content in the new maritime home. The apprentices carried out most of the work on deck whilst the new hands learned their trade.

Author's Drawing

But when somewhere off the coast of East London, *Ferreira* ran into heavy weather and difficulties. The badly stowed cargo shifted in the heavy rolling and the ship developed a list to port. The new sailors were terrified and took refuge in the foc'sle. It took the apprentices to bring the vessel back to stability, but that was only a temporary solution.

Author's Drawing

A week of heavy weather resulted in the cargo having to be trimmed on a number of occasions. The fore t'gallant mast was cut away to reduce top weight, but in its fall it broke off the lower topsail yard. In going over the foc'sle head the foreyard broke the port side whisker boom. The foreyard lay straddled across the foc'sle head and number one hatch but was later secured beneath the starboard bulwarks in an attempt to put more weight onto the starboard side.

Author's Drawing

After the fore t'gallant had been cut away there was no apparent difference in the trim of the ship. The main t'gallant was then disposed of in similar fashion. This time the spar went clean over the side and was blown well clear of the ship. But it made no difference at all to the ship's problems.

Author's Drawing

It was then decided to cut the lower main mast away. But the dead eye lanyards were made of wire rope and that caused a considerable problem. Eventually, they were severed with the ship's only axe.
But even without any support, the wrought iron mast refused to go over and bent half way up its length. When the mast did topple, it miraculously landed over the port bulwarks between the boat, and the pumps.

Author's Drawing

When the bent main mast did eventually go over the side, it took much of the mizzen mast rigging with it. Most miraculously the falling mast missed the pumps and port boat skids as it went over, but of the bulwarks were heavily damaged.
Still attached to much of both the main and mizzen rigging, the iron lower mainmast began ranging the port side hull.

Author's Drawing

After the weather had somewhat abated, the clearing up of wires, ropes and broken spars began. With the ship then running into head seas, the cargo was trimmed for what was to be the last time. Lookouts kept a constant watch for assistance as the ship wallowed helplessly in the huge ocean swell. But ships that were visible were too far away to recognise Ferreira's distress signals

Author's Drawing

It was the SS *Kia Ora* of Shaw Savill Line which eventually came to *Ferreira's* assistance. In the deep ocean swell, *Ferreira's* starboard boat was lowered, and Captain da Sousa was rowed across to the SS *Kia Ora* by four of his apprentices. The steamer's captain offered to take the whole crew off the beleaguered ship and let her go under, but Captain da Sousa refused and went back to his ship.

Author's Drawing

With the rocks of Cape Aghulas visible things were looking bleak for Ferreira. But The Blue Funnel steamer Indraghiri en route Durban towards Cape Town was then sighted. Captain Pilcher offered to tow the stricken ship into Table Bay, but in the heavy swell it proved most difficult to get a line across. To get a towing wire aboard the stricken *Ferreira*, Captain Pilcher of *Indraghiri* had to float a cane fender down wind with a messenger rope attached to it.

Author's Drawing

On the following morning, the SS *Indraghiri* delivered the damaged *Ferreira* to the entrance of Table Bay. The Cape Town based tug *Ludwig Weiner* then towed her to an anchorage.

Author's Drawing

On leaving Cape Town in January 1918, *Ferreira*, rigged as a barquentine had a total crew of twelve

Author's Drawing

Nevertheless, and despite her cut down rig, *Ferreira* could still make twelve knots with ease.

The SS *Indraghiri* had been built in 1912 at Govan for Thomas Royden's Indra line of Liverpool. Off. Number 131424. Letters - HVJW. Nett 3,600 - Gross 5,723 Dim. 430.5 x 53.9 x 30.3 -- At the time of rescuing *Ferreira* she was on charter to the Blue Funnel Line. After the charter she was purchased outright by Alfred Holt with a name change to *Eurylochus*. She lasted until 1941, when off the Cape Verde Islands she was intercepted and sunk by the German surface raider *Kormoran*.
Photo - Frank Richardson

The SS Kia Ora was built by Workman Clark of Belfast and completed in November 1907. She served the Shaw Savill & Albion Line until 1935 when she was sold to an Italian company, renamed Verbania and registered at Genoa. On 10 June 1940 whilst at Port Said, she was taken prize and renamed Empire Tamar. On 9 June 1944, she was scuttled as part of Gooseberry 5 at Ouistreham, Normandy.
Photo - Frank Richardson

Left:
Arriving at Mossamedes in 1915. Minus her rudder! From the Cape Verde islands *Ferreira* had used drogues and sail to steer the ship.

Bottom:
After breaking both her anchor cables and escaping the heavy weather at Mossamedes, *Ferreira* sailed without her bower anchors. Arriving at Birkenhead with less than a full cargo, she then went to Newport after discharge to load coal for Lisbon.

Photo - Frank Richardson

Maria di Amparo at London in 1922 It can be seen in the top photo that the mizzen mast is not visible due to the mainsail being hauled up

Shabby and threadbare, *Maria di Amparo* **is dry-docked for repairs in 1922 at Surrey Commercial Docks. In this series of photographs, the differing diameters of the lower masts can once again be seen.**

Maria di Amparo   Cutty Sark Trust

After her dry-docking at the Surrey Commercial Docks, *Maria di Amparo* was sailing back to her home port of Lisbon. But in some ferocious English Channel weather. she was forced to take refuge in Falmouth Harbour.

It was while she was laying at Falmouth that Captain Dowman opened negotiations for her purchase.

Captain Wilfred Dowman

After *Ferreira* had been re-rigged as a barquentine, she left Cape Town docks on 10 January 1918 with a total complement of twelve. Her charter was then completed when she arrived at Mossamedes to deliver the coal which had been in her hold for nearly two years. After her arrival at the Angolan port on 21 January, the coal was discharged in the old fashioned manner of gin blocks, baskets and hand winch. *Ferreira* then made a return passage to Mozambique for another cargo of coal.

From then on there is little in the way of records as to where *Ferreira* traded, the next news of the ship being in 1920 when she arrived at London from Pensacola, Florida. Then to Swansea for a badly needed bottom scrape and other maintenance. From the Welsh port she loaded a cargo of coal for Lisbon, then more coal from Newcastle to Lisbon. But Ferreira & Co were not making money on their ship any more, the government subsidy and the training programme they once had was not to be renewed, and neither was it likely to. Then there was more news of *Ferreira* in 1922 when after being dry docked at the Surrey Commercial Dock she took an English Channel hammering and struggled into Falmouth Harbour.

As she lay swinging on her anchor in the Carrick Roads awaiting the inclement weather to subside, she was espied by Captain Wilfred Dowman who lived at Trevissome near Falmouth. He had a strong affection for the shabby looking ship anchored in the bay. Indeed, the retired master mariner was fully aware that the ragged looking ship had once been the illustrious *Cutty Sark*. He remembered that ship only too well from the days of his apprenticeship which was 38 years previously. That was in 1894 when he was serving in *Hawkesdale*, a time when *Cutty Sark* under Captain Richard Woodget had overtaken and left his own ship out of sight in the same watch. No sailor of any ship ever enjoyed being passed by another ship of sail, indeed, it left a tinge of envy or embarrassment in them.

But to be passed by *Cutty Sark* was no shame at all, and in many ways it was an honour to be in the same company as the world's fastest ever tea clipper. Nevertheless, that long gone day of 1894 when *Cutty Sark* swept past *Hawkesdale,* had left an indelible mark in the memory of Wilfred Dowman. At the time he was involved in training ships and assisting boys who wanted to make a career at sea.

In 1920 J&A Ferreira & Co sold *Ferreira* to a fellow Portuguese ship owner named da Silva, the owner of Companhia Nacional ce Navagacao of Lisbon. But instead of da Silva giving his new acquisition some kind of an overhaul, the new owner did nothing more than to change *Ferreira's* name to *Maria di Amparo,* and have a row of gunports painted on her sides After having taken her refuge at Falmouth, *Maria di Amparo* continued to Lisbon before taking another load of scrap iron to Hamburg. Shortly afterwards whilst the sad looking ship was discharging at the scrap iron berth in Hamburg, Captain Dowman opened negotiations to purchase the shabby looking barquentine.

It has been said during the sale negotiations, that the ship was in a squalid condition regarding her hygienic conditions as well as the absence of any planned maintenance. Pigs were living under the foc'sle head, whilst poultry roamed in and out of the sailors' foc'sle and around the decks. Dried out cracked and rutted decks which had not seen oil for a long period of time, were there for all to see, and the once glistening bright work of the ship had long since been painted over in gaudy silver paint.

But da Silva who had no sentiment for the ship itself, must have known that just by owning the sailing pride of the Red Ensign, he possessed a commodity of both great sentimental value and of historical importance. It may well appear that in being a business man, da Silva had bought the ship with the sole intention of re-selling it to a sentimental buyer, and if they were his intentions then that gamble was to pay off handsomely. There is no record of what da Silva actually paid J&A Ferreira for *Ferreira,* but by the time *Maria di Amparo* had left the scrap iron yard at Hamburg and arrived back at Lisbon, the price wanted for *Maria di Amparo* by da Silva, must have been an awful lot more than what he had paid for her.

In comparison to the £2,100 that J&A Ferreira had paid John Willis for *Cutty Sark* in 1895 - when she was a fully rigged ship in a reasonably good condition, and the agreement price reached between da Silva and Dowman, the £3,750 must have been quite a staggering amount. Inflation had not risen to any great extent during the intervening years, as well as the fact that *Maria di Amparo* was in an appalling condition. There was also the ship's towing charges by the tug *Triton* from Lisbon to Falmouth, as well as the passage back to Lisbon for those who had manned her whilst under tow.

Then before the ship had left Lisbon for Falmouth, the enterprising da Silva went as far as removing the ship's bell then demanded an extra £500 for that. But it later transpired that the bell which da Silva wanted to sell was not the genuine article. The original ship's bell which had been on *Cutty Sark's* foc'sle since 1869, had been so heavily daubed with silver paint whilst under the Portuguese flag, that the ship's name on it was completely indiscernible. Apparently, when *Ferreira* was at Pensacola in 1913 under J&A Ferreira's ownership, a visiting British seafarer who recognised *Ferreira* as being the former *Cutty Sark,* decided to remove the foc'sle head bell for his own personal gain. No doubt the robber waited until the most appropriate time, then after having brought along a similarly gaudy painted silver bell he swapped them over.

The replacement of the bell went completely unnoticed, and all because the polishing of bright work had never been on the ship's agenda. Indeed, the theft was not discovered until ten years later, a time when the greedy da Silva the current owner, wanted to sell what he thought was the real ship's bell to Denny Bros & Co; the firm who had finished the building of the ship in 1869. Apparently, da Silva's demands for £500 were rejected as being out of hand - and just as well, because quite soon afterwards the genuine bell was returned to the ship after Captain Dowman had assumed ownership. More than likely, the person who stole the bell from *Ferreira* had done so in all honesty, because indeed, under both the Red and White Ensigns, the ship's bell is the pride of the ship and deserves a much better existence than to be daubed over by sloppy sailors. Hence its removal, and hence its return.

On assuming ownership of *Maria di Amparo*, it was Captain Dowman's intention to first have her renamed back to *Cutty Sark,* then restore the ship to her 1869 appearance. It was indeed a costly exercise, all of which came from the pocket of the retired ship master himself. During her refurbishment at Falmouth, little in the way of repairs or replacement records are available. It can be assumed however, that after the ship had been gutted and refurbished she was crewed by trainees. By that time the new lower masts would have been manufactured, and more than likely would have been fitted by the trainees under the guidance of a shipwright and a couple of riggers. To this end there is photographic evidence of *Cutty Sark* with her new masts which were fitted whilst she lay in Falmouth. Whilst on the River Fowey *Cutty Sark* was thereafter used as a training ship for boys, but in 1938 Captain Dowman died at the age of 62. His widow donated *Cutty Sark* to the Incorporated Thames Nautical Training College. For the upkeep and general maintenance of the ship, she also donated £5,000.

Captain Wilfred Dowman

Above - The re-rigged and refurbished *Cutty Sark* taking steam from Falmouth to Fowey. On that occasion Captain Woodget took command of the ship for the 20 mile passage.

Below - Whilst on that 1924 passage of the ship he knew and loved so much, 79 year old Captain Richard Woodget touches the binnacle bell with fond memories.

The Master of the Cutty Sark.

Although he is nearer eighty years of age than seventy, and has been farming in Norfolk for over twenty years, Captain Woodget, of the Cutty Sark, is to have the command of his wonderful old ship for one more trip. It is a very short passage, it is true, to be towed from Falmouth, where she is now refitting, to Fowey, where she is to act as flagship for the yacht-racing, but it is giving the veteran captain charge of the ship, to whose fame he contributed more than anybody else, and he is happy.

When he took command of her in 1885 she was very much cut down in rig, and she had been under the command of masters who had not got the best out of her. He had his own ideas on rigging, gained by hard experience in the North Sea coal trade, and when he had her refitted to his satisfaction he drove her for all he was worth. He revelled in a blow that laid the old ship over and raced her through the water, hanging on to the weather rigging with one end of his moustache in his mouth and driving his men in a manner that would never have been stood from anybody who was not such a superb seaman as he was. He spoke to them as they understood him, but he never got excited, and would often leave the deck in command of a much less happy mate and spend part of his watch below quietly reading his Bible.

In spite of his reputation as a real "hard case," while he was at sea he never smoked and he never drank, and was seldom if ever seen to read anything but his Bible. It is told of him in sailor quarters that he once kept a supply of tracts on the poop and scattered them into the sea astern whenever he passed another ship, as he knew perfectly well that every man in her crew was blaspheming.

A newspaper cutting from 1924

"CUTTY SARK" MOVES TO REST

Shortly after 11 o'clock on December 10, the *Cutty Sark* left the East India Dock in tow of the tugs *Gondia* and *Java*, for her permanent berth in the new Greenwich drydock. The passage from Blackwall to Greenwich was made as planned, and at noon the *Cutty Sark* was in position at the entrance to the dock. Tugs were slipped and the ship was hauled into position in the dock. By 2.30 p.m. the ship was on her keel blocks and timber shores were rigged to support the hull. The dock was then drained and a temporary gate placed in position.

The move was to have been made considerably earlier but exceptionally high winds compelled postponement of the event on more than one occasion.

On passage to Greenwich the *Cutty Sark* flew the houseflag of her original owner, Capt. John Willis, and her "number" in the international code, JKWS. In order to lighten her, upper masts, yards, deckhouses and ballast were removed. The work of refitting and rigging her will begin shortly.

It is planned to use the *Cutty Sark* for educational purposes, in co-operation with the L.C.C. and local education authorities. *Cutty Sark* bursaries are being created at certain leading nautical training schools. A first bursary has been awarded in co-operation with the Corporation of Lloyd's to Cadet A. J. R. Watson of Folkestone, now in his first term at the Nautical College, Pangbourne.

A newspaper cutting from 1953

National Maritime Museum

Seen here at London after reverting to her original name of *Cutty Sark*, the t'gallant masts were sent down for the duration of WW2.

With blackened masts, *Cutty Sark* had some close calls from bombs during WW2.

Below - *Cutty Sark* moored alongside the training ship *Worcester* at Greenhithe.

The top photo shows a type of shed built onto the after end of *Cutty Sark's* No 2 hatch. It was more than likely used as a store while the ship was under re-construction.

The bottom photo shows the open No 3 hatch, before the visitor's companionway was constructed on top of it. On each side of the mizzen mast base, can be seen a chicken coop.

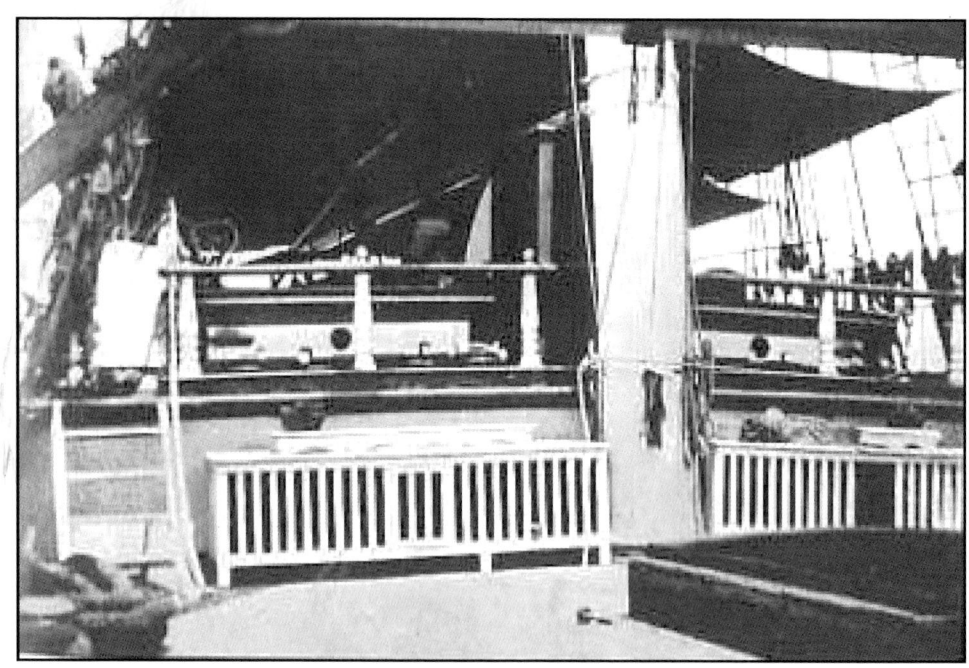

The picture of *Titania* on the left shows her with the jib-boom run in whilst in dry-dock. It also shows a set of sheer legs in the background. Sheer legs are used for heavy lifts and the fitting of masts; such items were used by many of the big ship-building and repair firms of the day; they are usually set in a fixed position. Their main advantage and quite unlike a mast house, is they can be erected to a required size, then dismantled and moved to another site in a relatively short space of time.

The picture below shows the crew of the training ship *Herzogin Cecile* anchored off Montevideo carrying out their own repairs. The four masted barque was partly dismasted whilst on her maiden voyage in 1903 Although the steel lower masts were undamaged, the rest of the rig required replacing. As can be seen in the photograph the trainees sit astride the 110 foot lower yards, whilst the fore top mast is slung in the port shrouds ready to be hoisted aloft. A temporary top-mast is in place for the operation. Depending on the circumstances, there were a number of methods used in the re-masting of a ship of sail.
In 1936 *Herzogin Cecile* ran aground at Salcombe in Devon and became a constructive total loss.

Photo - Frank Richardson

Heavy Lifts

Because records of *Ferreira's* long stay at Cape Town do not exist, it is not known exactly how the fitting of her replacement masts were implemented. However, and because she was virtually crew-less, it is most likely she went alongside to a either a mast-house or else used sheer legs to fit her new masts into position. A mast house is a tall purpose built structure with a gantry on its top floor. The picture above shows a similar device known as an 'A Frame.' These were also used for heavy lifts, and in this instance, a large box or block of stone is being discharged from the alongside ship. The A Frame only has two legs, but it can be positioned to swing over the ship's hold to pick up its heavy lift, then swung back again to load it onto a cart. In this instance two Shire Horses provide the lifting power .

Dismasted ships often had to do their own re-masting and jury rigging without any shore side assistance. A Frames and sheer legs were sometimes erected on the deck using the ship's spare yards. In the year 1870, *Blackadder* which was also owned by John Willis was dismasted on her maiden voyage. In Simon's Bay which is quite close to Cape Town, the ship's company did all their own remasting and rigging whilst at anchor in the bay.

Badly Loaded Cargoes

FIG 1 This diagram gives a transverse view of a ship's midship section similar to that of *Ferreira*. The permanent ballast is necessary to keep the ship stable whilst the holds are empty, without cargo, or 'light ship' as the term goes. The permanent ballast is placed into the ship and under the wooden ceiling of the hold when the ship is being built. This may consist of pig iron, boulders, shale, or anything else that's cheap and heavy enough to stabilise the vessel. Without it, a ship like *Ferreira* would be liable to capsize even in port. Indeed, there were many ships even with permanent ballast that fell over on the quayside. When a ship is sailing from one port to another without any cargo, extra ballast is normally carried in the hold. This in the days of sail normally consisted of rocks, sand, and boulders, but such ballast did not come cheaply and the cost of loading was also added. Then on arrival at the ship's destination port there was further expenditure in discharging and disposing of the now useless ballast. Therefore, to get his ship to the next port, a ship's master would load only as much ballast as he thought was necessary. But history tells us some of these captains cut it too fine and ran into unexpected difficulties. There are also many we don't know of or will never hear about.

Fig 2 Here is a simply explained example of a badly loaded cargo where the coal has been literally thrown into the hold without proper care or supervision. To a deck officer looking down from the deck to a completed loading, it might appear that the lower hold is full and any movement or shifting of the cargo not possible. The diagram however, shows there is every chance of the cargo moving to one side or the other if the ship rolls to any great degree, and especially if it is a great distance to its destination port. In some instances where a cargo had been loaded as shown in the diagram, there is always the chance of the ship rolling gently and evenly from side to side, the cargo may then find its own level by trimming itself. Unfortunately this possibility is better suited to steamships and not so much to sailing vessels, because the motion in a seaway is very much different to that of a steamer. If for instance a steamer is under way, and rolling five degrees each side with her badly loaded cargo and a twenty-five knot wind coming from the starboard beam in a moderate sea, then things might not get any worse. However, if a sailing vessel such as *Ferreira* is in similar circumstances, the yards would be braced to catch as much wind as possible and the ship would heel over to port at an angle of ten to fifteen degrees, to which would be added a roll of a few more degrees. This is the way a captain liked to sail his ship if he knows his cargo is secure!

Fig 3 Gives an indication as to how the badly loaded cargo will appear after a period of heavy rolling, or after heeling over under a press of canvas for some time. A problem arises when the sailing vessel is heeled over in the conditions described in fig 2, and although he has his wheel up, the helmsman should be able to 'feel' the list, it may only come to light however, when the ship goes about on the opposite tack or when the yards are squared. The helm will not respond well, and even if the yards could be braced up, the ship would be liable to be taken aback.

Diagram 2 shows just one way in which a cargo may be incorrectly loaded, and this is only a transverse view of one section. In some parts of the hold the stowage might be correct, however, diagram 3 shows the vessel has developed a list of a huge proportions, possibly fifteen degrees. This means that when the ship rolls to port, the angle will be thirty degrees, but when rolling to starboard it only comes back to an even keel. Such a situation could easily be enough to capsize a vessel, and drastic action to reduce top weight is taken, such as cutting away the masts.

Fig 4

Some ships used shifting boards to restrict the movement of bulk cargoes, These boards are normally shipped along the centre line of the hold and may be built up as a solid wall or bulkhead of timbers as diagram 4 shows. Although there are a number of ways to construct this restrictive wall the effects are apparent, for instead of the coal shifting over to one side as in diagram 3, the coal has heaped against the shifting boards in the centre, and even though the vessel has developed a list, it has been reduced to about five degrees instead of fifteen degrees, (as indicated in diagram 3 shifting boards have not been employed.) But in fig 4, the list is manageable, and wouldn't worsen under adverse circumstances, thus enabling the vessel to make port.

However, shifting boards are heavy and take up valuable space in the 'tween decks when not in use, therefore it is most unlikely that ships like *Ferreira* ever carried them. It must be stressed that the diagrams in this chapter are only approximate and are merely to give an example.

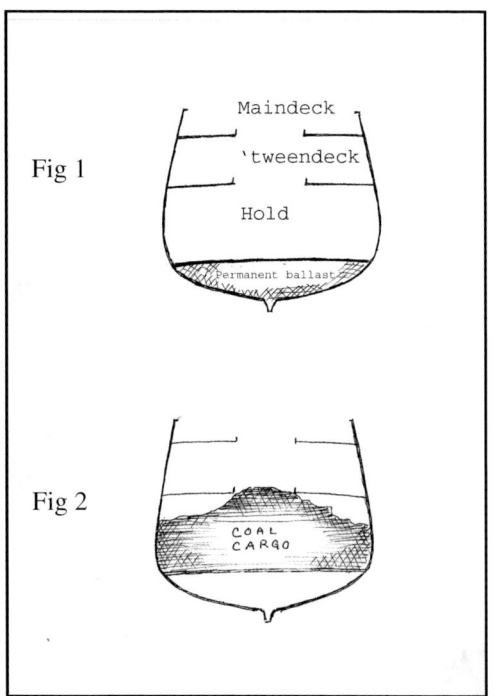

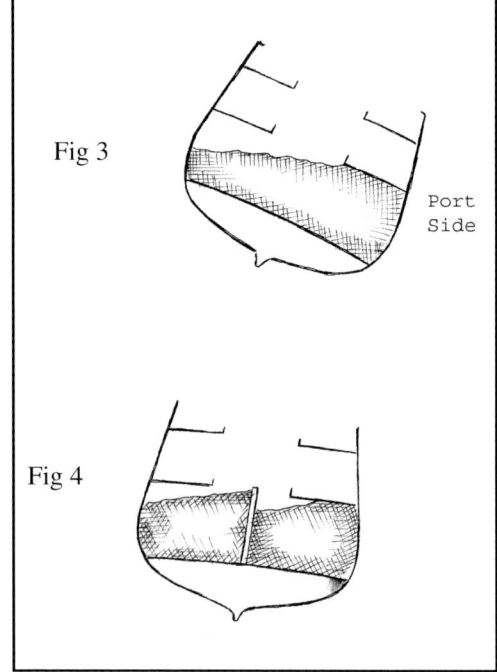

John Robert Charles Spurling

Marine Artist

Of all the marine artists who have graced this world with their talents, John Robert Charles Spurling must rank amongst the greatest. Indeed he was a true artist and not a craftsman, and neither was he one of those Pier Head artist who had never worked the decks of a ship. John Spurling was an artist who created from his own mind and imagination, whilst craftsmen tend to copy the works of others. Modern day marine painter have all the latest copying implements at their disposal, items such as photographic enlargers, epidiascopes and computer aided designers. JRC Spurling had nothing! Just the priceless talents he was born with, talents which were combined with his experiences as a sailor in both sail and steam.

John Spurling was born in London on 12 December 1870 and came from a well found family. His father Charles traded as an import merchant, whilst his mother Mary cared for their two sons and four daughters. John began art lessons in drawing and painting ships as a young boy, then when at the required age went to sea in sail. On his first ship he fell from aloft whilst in the China Seas, then for some months lay hospitalised at Singapore. Returning to London on a steamer, he later became a mid-shipman for Devitt & Moore in their sailing passenger ships. He eventually obtained his second mate's certificate and subsequent promotion to the rank.

However, after seven years he left the mercantile marine. The general talk being, that as well as suffering from the ill health of his childhood, he never really recovered from his first trip accident either. He then began on a new career of painting ship portraits for various shipping companies, but it was only when he met Mr FA Hook, the Public Relations Officer for the P&O Line that he really came to the fore. The mighty P&O line had their own in house magazine called 'Blue Peter, and John Spurling's paintings immediately became a regular feature on its front covers.

As an artist he became a celebrity and was commissioned to paint a series of tea clippers for Blue Peter. So precise were his works in both oil and watercolour, that Mr Hook offered to pay anybody a £1,000 reward, if they could find a single mistake in the sail plans, or in the running and standing rigging in any of John Spurling's works. Nobody to this day ever claimed the reward, indeed, a testament to his previous experience as a sailor. But ill health continued to dog the famous marine artist. He painted the last of his pictures in the early 1930's and died at the age of 62 on 31 May 1933. On the following pages are a number of his many works of art.

Cutty Sark

From a painting by John Spurling

Plate 1

Cutty Sark

From a painting by John Spurling

Plate 2

Plate 3 *Ariel* From a painting by John Spurling

Blackadder

From a painting by John Spurling

Plate 4

Dreadnought

From a painting by John Spurling

Plate 5

Plate 6 *James Baines* From a painting by John Spurling

Sir Lancelot

From a painting by John Spurling

Plate 7

Plate 8 Thermopylae in her race with Cutty Sark From a painting by John Spurling

Salamis

From a painting by John Spurling

Plate 9

Cutty Sark in Eastern Waters

Plate 10

From a painting by the author

When *Ferreira* passed between Lundy Isle and Hartland Point in March 1915, It was the last time a clipper ship would ever be seen in British waters.

From a painting by the author

Cutty Sark

From a painting by the author

Plate 12

Plate 13 *Ferreira passing Table Mountain* From a painting by the author

Stornoway

From a painting by the author

Plate 14

Thermopylae

From a painting by the author

Plate 15

Norman Court

Plate 16

From a painting by the author

Westward Ho

From a painting by the author

Plate 17

Torrens

From a painting by the author

Plate 18

Agamemnon

From a painting by the author

Plate 19

A Sailor From Another Age?

The following passage is taken from 'A Deck Boy's Diary' an April 2000 publication by the author, and a book which relates to *Cutty Sark*. **In this chapter, a small number of grammatical changes have been made from the original publication, but only for the configuration of the text in the passage.**

,,

During my first trip to sea as a sixteen year old deck boy, my ship *Willesden* of London arrived at Tilbury Dock in November 1953. The ship had signed on at Hull in July of the same year, and after a four month trip to India the voyage was almost at an end. However, there was to be the added 'around the land' discharging before the ship paid off. This meant a visit to Antwerp, Hamburg and Hull before paying off at Middlesbrough. Whilst in London some of the crew who were going back on the ship's next voyage went on leave. Two of these 'company's men' were the bosun and my cabin mate the lamp-trimmer. In due course, an AB who was the lamp-trimmer's relief, and one who was to be my new cabin mate arrived on board.

,,,

Tilbury Dock London, 23 November 1953.
A Passage from 'A Deck Boy's Diary.'

Later in the morning, our newly appointed bosun Bill Houston introduced me to my new cabin mate. I'd had so many shocks and surprises during the day with people coming and going, but this one was the best of the lot. My new cabin mate was an old Scotsman named either Bob or Stan Walker. He greeted me with such cordiality it was like someone who hadn't seen his best friend for years. In my opinion, Old Stan must have been at least seventy years old, maybe even eighty, but except for a bit of a hobble he was quite lively as he made his way around. It was really nice to meet Old Stan, and Bill Houston our new bosun immediately posted me in the 8-12 watch whilst Old Stan took my job as the 'peggy.' All the London dockers on the ship knew Old Stan, as well as his previous adventures and escapades, and indeed, it wasn't long before the old sailor himself was telling me bits and pieces of his past life ... in sail! But most unfortunately and amidst his broad Scot's growling accent, I was unable to understand much of his nautical terminology. He told me how after coming from Kircaldy in Scotland, he'd started his sea career at the age of twelve on fishing boats of sail, then at a later date on the big square riggers. He also told me that except for the Sailor's Home in London, he had no home at all but just lived on board ships. He either didn't know or wouldn't tell me how old he was, but did say that the authorities had him down as being sixty seven; a figure he was more than happy to accept. However, even at that age of sixty seven I was more than a little dubious.

Also signed on that day was another AB, this sailor was named Stan Williams. He was the relief of Bill Houston who had taken the bosun's post. These two new AB's were later to be known as 'Old Stan' and 'Young Stan.' They were only on board for the run around the land and would be paying off at Middlesbrough with the rest of us, but what a lively pair they turned out to be.

Old Stan must have received an advance note when signing on, because after making his acquaintances and throwing his gear onto his bunk, he must have awarded himself the afternoon off. At 1 pm when it was time to turn to the bosun asked me if I'd seen the old man, but I could only reply by saying that I hadn't. Later on in the mess-room where the dockers had made themselves at home, and all of whom seemed to know Old Stan, I asked them if they knew of his whereabouts. Those dockers were all highly amused and replied saying that as soon as Old Stan had any money in his pocket he'd make for the nearest pub. They told me that Old Stan, or Uncle Bob as he was generally referred to, had served in sail for many years, and had even sailed on the *Cutty Sark* under the red ensign. They also told me that Uncle Bob hadn't sailed deep sea for many a year, he was far past his best, and was only given around the land, jobs, standbys or night watchman's work by the MN Pool.

Thinking no more on the matter, I went to the cinema that evening with the cabin boy, and it was there that we witnessed John Wayne destroy the Japanese fleet and win the Pacific War. We then went back to the ship thinking the day was over, but it wasn't! Not by a long way! I turned in realising that my new cabin mate was still adrift, but thought nothing of it and soon fell asleep. My cabin was the first in the alleyway at the bottom of the companionway, and sometime after midnight I was awakened by the shore night-watchman. He wanted to know if I knew any body on board named Walker, because if I did, he was flaked out over the accommodation coaming. I arose to offer any assistance I could, but Old Stan weighed about twelve stone, and it took the night-watchman, one of the greasers and myself to manhandle him down below where we laid him on his bunk.

Once all that was over, Old Stan who was rip roaring drunk due to his over indulgence in whisky, came to and started singing sea shanties. He woke the whole crowd up with his Scots gravel voice before finally flaking out again. Whilst he was out for the count, we made his bunk up and proceeded to undress him and put him under the blankets. But when I took his boots and trousers off, I felt really sorry for him. The poor old man had steel callipers on each of his lower legs. My mind wandered back to the previous morning when I watched him hobbling around without complaint.

Next morning I overslept a bit due to loss of sleep, but at 6.30 am after I'd made the tea in the mess-room, and whilst the sailors were holding their hangover heads drinking it, I went aft to wake Old Stan. He was quite cold and still! I shuddered in realisation before covering his chalk white face with the bed sheet. I immediately raised the alarm to those in the mess amidships who arrived at speed to see the corpse. But on clambering down the companionway ladder, a gravel sounding voice with a strong Scottish accent could be heard as the supposed corpse resumed his sea shanties. In the cabin he sat on the edge of his bunk … bleary eyed but full of life again. I myself was given the height of abuse by the sailors for proclaiming that Old Stan had pegged out, whilst the gentleman in question seemed highly amused about it all. He remarked that when he did go it wouldn't be that easy, and in his strong growling voice told me he was ready to face the world for another day.

I later told the bosun what had happened in the small hours of the morning, and also about the callipers on Old Stan's legs. Bill was supposed to report him to the mate for being adrift on the previous afternoon, but in being the man he was he didn't do so. He knew like everybody else that Old Stan was on his last leg of life, that he'd probably served at sea in both World Wars, and if reported he'd be sacked there and then and would never get another job. Therefore I did the peggy's job before turning to on deck. We had a good crowd of sailors, and there were no complaints as we all covered up for the Old Shell Back. By the next day when we were on our way to Antwerp, and after Old Stan had fully recovered from his advance note party, never could a more willing hand be seen. I thought at the time, as I looked at him with his weather beaten leathery face and hands like shovels, that I'd love to read his life story. In Antwerp he went adrift again, then in Hamburg after some fool gave him a sub he once again did the vanishing trick. Nevertheless, he wasn't a slacker and did as much as his old body would allow.

Then on the night before we paid off in Middlesborough in December, where we had finally tied up after what was then a five month voyage, the beer flowed like water and both young and old Stan were the life and soul of the mess-room party. The beer was 18/- for a case of 24 bottles, but as I didn't like beer I was kept busy running to and fro to the second steward for case after case. At that particular time I'd paid scant regard to what the

London dockers had told me about Old Stan serving on the *Cutty Sark*, in fact, in being a sixteen year old, I had never even heard of the ship until that year of 1953. But when I later became more interested in ship's of sail, and thanks to my meeting up with Old Stan, I discovered that the tea clipper *Cutty Sark* was most prominent in the lore of sailing vessels.

Thirty seven years later in 1990 I said goodbye to my last ship, but after having taken a keen interest in painting ship's of sail ... and writing about them, I also decided to take out my diaries and write about my first trip to sea. By that time I'd completely forgotten about the Old Stan incident on *Willesden* in 1953, but whilst I was making preparations for the manuscript of 'A Deck Boy's Diary' the name of Old Stan came up. I suddenly remembered what the London dockers had told me about him serving on *Cutty Sark*, and more in wonder than anything else I made enquiries.

I then acquired a book written by SF Bailey who is a member of the Cutty Sark Society. This publication gives the names of all crew members of the *Cutty Sark* from 1870 until 1995. On page 88 there is an entry stating that a certain R Walker joined the ship as an AB at £3 per month on 2 May 1889. He was born at Kircaldy in 1866 and was 23 years old at the time. On 1 November 1889 he was promoted to second mate at £4-10-0 per month, but paid off at London on 17 January 1890.

Was this the same Walker? Or Uncle Bob as the London dockers called him?

At the time of Old Stan joining *Willesden* in 1953, this would have made him 87 years of age - that's if it was him! And if it was - it most certainly would be no surprise to the author who shared the same cabin with him for a couple of weeks, but most incredible nevertheless.

In those post-war days there were occasionally more ships than sailors to man them ... usually due to a glut of ships arriving in the UK at the same time, but the authorities at the Merchant Navy Pool still had to supply crews for ships. Furthermore, those authorities were noted for taking back handers in their selection of certain men for the more favourable ships. Therefore, as well as turning a blind eye to what was really going on ... when a seaman gave his age that is - it was not uncommon for a sailor who was past the age limit to assume somebody else's identity ... for a fee! Old Stan's discharge book number coincided with a 1947 or thereabouts issue, a number which would have put him in his mid twenties, and yet, he is listed as being 67 years of age on the ship's articles. Even at that age he was well past the age limit. Whichever way one looks at it something was amiss.

....

The document on the following page, supplied by the Archives of the Newfoundland British Shipping Records, is a copy from part of articles of agreement of MV *Willesden's*

1953 voyage. The crew of the 7,043 ton ship was 39 when the articles were signed in July, but replacements were made at Tilbury in November 1953. Number 45 is that of S Walker, an AB who has the Discharge book number of R426819 and given as being aged 67. Also signed on the same day was S Williams who is listed as number 41 on the articles. His discharge book number is R415822 with his age given at 29. In accordance with the issuing of discharge books, This would imply that 29 year old S Williams is older than 67 year old S Walker … !!! ???

MV *Willesden* on which the author made his first trip to sea and where he met Old Stan. *Willesden* was built in 1944 as *Empire Canning* before being ceded to H Hogarth of Ardrossan in 1946 as remuneration for war losses. She later passed to Watts Watts of London and was given the name *Willesden*. Sold out of the company in 1958; after going through five more owners, she was given the names, *Golden Lambda, Marine Explorer, East Vin, Wasa Bay,* and *Golden Wind,* the 7,043 ton ship was scrapped at Japan in 1967.

Page 12 of the articles of the MV Willesden's 1953 voyage. Number 45 which is smudged is probably due to an inebriated hand of the AB Old Stan Walker.

Ref. No.	Income Tax Code	Signatures of Crew and Numbers of Discharge Books	Age	Nationality	Addresses of Master and Crew. Name and Relationship of Next of Kin or Name of Friend and Home Address	Name of last Ship, with Official No. or Port of Registry and year of discharge if more than a year previous	Date	Place
41	517 32 S	S. Williams R415524	29	London	(1) Guardian Mrs D. Scott (2) 215 Hornsey Rd, Southend	Dryden	23/11/53	Tilbury
42	U S	Curren E1682	23	Dublin	(1) W. Margaret (2) 58 Tenison Rd, Whitehall	Twickenham	do	do
43	7063 S	A Gibbs R502228	21	Grays	(1) F. Charles (2) 21 Victory Rd. Grays	Busen Rolla	do	do
44	65 S	T. Grinnell K83413	63	Ballyporeen	(1) Wife Elizabeth (2) 50 St. Chads Rd. Tilbury	Minella	24/11/53	Tilbury
45	S	Walker 72-819	?	?Aberdeen	(2) Dilbrough ?nch ?st Aberdeen		do	do
46	65 S	H. Hayes R39985	??	Rochester	(1) Mother Mrs A. Taylor (2) 20 Longley Rd, Rochester	Regent Knot	do	do
47	52 M	Jim Slater R190139 NP	31	Dumbarton	(1) M. Ellen (2) 24 Countess Rd Dumbarton	Greenwich	7/12/53	Hull
48	S	J R Kane R398496	28	West Hartlepool	(1) M. Jessie (2) 78 Bishopton Rd. M'bro	Brockley Moor	8/12/53	Hull
49	Y S	E. ? R583551	22	Kyle Cockenham	(1) F. Donald (2) 89 Westhowe Ave, Walker	LA ?Grieves	do	do
50	37?? S	P W Wesson R36463	22	London	(1) M. Mary (2) 68 Kenbrook House, London NW5	Zeelan	8/12/53	Hull
51					(1) (2)			
52					(1) (2)			
53					(1) (2)			
54					(1) (2)			
55					(1) (2)			
56					(1) (2)			
57					(1) (2)			
58					(1) (2)			
59					(1) (2)			
60					(1) (2)			

† The capacities of Engineers not employed on the Propelling Engines and Boilers should be described here and in the Certificate of Discharge as Engine Drivers, Donkeymen, should be described as

‡ If any member of the Crew enters Her Majesty's Service, the Name of the Queen's Ship into which he enters is to be stated under the head of "Cause of Leaving"

‡ If the advance of wages is not conditional on going to sea

** NATIONAL INSURANCE.—The Master and all members of the crew are insurable under the National Insurance Schemes. Masters should ensure that issued by the Ministry of National Insurance.

Picture Glossary

Due to the passage of time, and because the age of sail has long since passed us by, maritime expressions are seldom used any more. Indeed, those without seagoing experience, will probably have some difficulty in understanding the dialogue and nautical terms within this and many other marine books.

Therefore, this chapter has been specially designed to help with some of the naming and operating procedures carried out on ships of sail. So as well as a normal glossary where text alone is used to describe an item, the author has been aboard *Cutty Sark* at Greenwich to catalogue a number of items on and around the decks. Consequently, glossary explanations on some of the ship's fixtures are to some degree explained with the aid of a photograph.

As *Cutty Sark,* the ship had her masts shortened in 1880. But when sailing under the Portuguese flag as *Ferreira* between the years of 1895 and 1916, there was little if any difference in the outward appearance of when she was *Cutty Sark*, even the ship's livery was the same. Therefore, and except for the removal of the main sky sail, the picture glossary on the following pages can be used in explaining the ship between the years of 1870 when on her maiden voyage, and 1916 when she ceased to be a fully rigged ship.

Most of the photographs in this chapter were taken by the author on board *Cutty Sark,* albeit on different visits between 2000 and 2004. Others are from the ship's archives

From *Cutty Sark's* foc'sle head the River Thames and Canary wharf can be seen. The two fore stays that are visible ... each of which have four white seizings, are the fore topmast stays.

Figureheads

One thing we never see on ships anymore are figure heads, but this fine collection on display in *Cutty Sark's* 'tween deck must have many a stirring tale to tell. A ship's figure head was supposed to bring good luck to the ship, and as can be seen, those on view are all of ladies. Ship's figure heads were one of the many prides a sailor had in his ship, and indeed it was a great honour to the one who was given the job of painting it when required. Often daubed in bright colours as can be seen above, it has been said that many a lonely sailor had fallen in love with the ship's figurehead.

Nevertheless those figureheads took a fearful pounding off head seas as well as bad weather, and on occasion when a ship had reached port after having been through a fierce storm, it was often discovered that the figure head had been lost. Not all ships had a female for its figurehead, although some people believe that a ship is always referred to as 'she' simply because of the figure head. Also to be seen in the picture above are the ship's side white painted frames as well as the overhead deck beams, all of which were made of wrought iron. Over these frames and beams are laid planks or scantlings to make up the ship's hull. Such a method of wood over iron construction is referred to as composite building.

Cutty Sark's port bow gives a view of her extremely sharp underwater lines. The word 'lines' refers to the underwater shaping of a ship's under-body. This part of the hull where it broadens out as it moves aft is known as the 'entrance.'

The figure arrow near the top points to the port cat-head, this fitting is used as a hauling point when taking in the port anchor.

The anchor cable which comes down through the hawse pipe is usually six or seven shackles in length. Each shackle being fifteen fathoms or ninety feet. The last link in the anchor cable when shackled to the deck of the cable locker is known as 'The Bitter End.'

When the anchor is being hauled in via the capstan, and when it first breaks the surface of the water, the large ring on the top of the anchor is connected to a three-fold purchase block and used in conjunction with the three fold sheaves of the cat-head.

In previous times *Cutty Sark* like most ships of her day had wooden stocked anchors.

The ship's counter stern. This part of the ship also has underwater lines, and in opposition to the previous photograph where the underwater lines are known as the 'entrance' they are in this instance referred to as the 'departure.' Note how the ship's hull further forward bulges downwards and outwards from the level of the deck, this shaping of the hull is known as the 'tumblehome.'

The arrow points to the 'bumkin.' This pole like projection protrudes outboard with a block attached to it . That block is used as a lead for the of the port main brace. As well as the two main top-sail braces. The latter two are presently absent due to current maintenance procedures.

The rudder is that of the 'Oertz' type, although it appears solid and secure, the ship as *Cutty Sark, Ferreira* and *Maria de Amparo* were known to have lost at least three rudders during the course of the ship's trading career.

The gold painted scroll work otherwise known as ginger-bread work, was originally that of a number of naked figurines which caused great excitement … before they were removed!

It can be seen that below the waterline the ship's hull is sheathed with copper plates, these plates which are heavily coated with tallow beneath, are to prevent the teredo worm boring into and destroying the wooden timbers of the ship's hull. Normally only the finest of ships with wealthy owners had their ships copper bottomed. Such a method of waterproofing a ship's side has since resulted in the adage of 'Copper Bottomed Agreements' a term which is often used today. Also on the ship's stern are the self gratifying words of its first owner ;-

'Where There's A Willis A Way.'

Top: 1: The knight-heads, between which the bow-sprit passes. 2: Fairleads through which the berthing ropes pass. 3: The whisker-boom to which the stays from the jib-boom pass. 4: The decorative scroll-work. 5: The anchor cable that emerges from the hawse pipe which is situated between the scroll work.

The picture above gives a view of the starboard side of the fore deck which lies adjacent to the foremast. It shows a number of deck items in which the tarred black standing rigging supporting the foremast is most prominent. The standing rigging is most inflexible, it is made of iron wire, and is therefore not required to bend like steel or flexible steel wire rope which is normally referred to by landsmen as cable. The five furthest away of these tarred black wire ropes are known as lower mast shrouds; their main purpose being to support the lower mast. They are five inches in diameter. The furthest away of the five is known as the number one shroud and is situated directly in line with the centre of the lower foremast at deck level, and directly opposite number one shroud on the port side. The other six of the tarred black shrouds which are nearest, are smaller in diameter, they support the fore topmast and fore t'gallant mast.

Buntlines are ropes which are attached to the foot of a sail for hauling it up to its yard for stowing. They can be seen as being lighter in colour coming down past the black shrouds and through the cup like leads to their belaying pins on the bulwark top.

1: Leads for the buntlines which travel up from the foot of their respective sails, through a block aloft, then down through the leads to their belaying pins on the bulwark top.
2: The five inch diameter shrouds, number one which is the furthest away is normally served with tarred spun yarn.
3: Buntlines coiled up over their belaying pins.
4: The short wooden upper addition to the bulwarks, otherwise known as the top rail.

A view of the same fore-mast shrouds from a forward position. In this picture the deadeyes which are attached to the ends of the iron wire shrouds, can be seen secured to their chain plate poles which are at the bottom of the bulwark. Chain Plates are the final securing point for the shrouds; in this instance they are fastened via an iron rod onto the bottom of the bulwark.

Through the upper and lower deadeyes, tarred black rope is used to occasionally haul the shrouds taut. In an emergency when the mast must be cut away, the lanyards can easily be severed with a knife.

Also on view are the lower mast shroud seizings. These can be seen in both this and the preceding picture as being painted white, three to each shroud. The iron wires of the lower shrouds are not spliced at their ends, they are instead turned back around the upper deadeye, and seized. The seizings are the three white objects above the upper deadeyes.

Above each upper deadeye can be seen a long pole like object which runs horizontally between number one and number five shroud. This is the sheer pole; its purpose being to both keep the shrouds in line and to reduce vibration.

1: Belaying Pins which have many uses, (as well as the proverbial weapon.) In this case the mainmast buntlines can be seen secured to them.

2: The Upper and Lower Deadeyes through which tarred hemp rope passes.

3: Black painted iron bitts. Mainly used for berthing ropes but they can have other uses.

Another view of the deadeyes and sheer-pole. However, this time it is of the mainmast shrouds. There appears to be no difference in appearance, except that in this photo the hempen ropes of the deadeyes have not been tarred, also there are two additional backstays but in this picture the iron chain plate pole is better visible.

1: Upper Deadeye

2: Lanyards

3: Sheer-pole

4: Chain plate pole. Each shroud has its own chain plate pole, which on this ship is fastened to the base of the bulwark. Chain plate poles are extensions which originate from the shrouds, via the deadeyes and the chain-plate pole to the ships side. The combination of supports holds the mast in position.

5: Spider Band clamps. These are made of wrought iron in two pieces on a hinge and are bolted around the lower mast. They normally have cleats and belaying pin sockets on them, and as well as those on the fife rails are used to secure the many ropes which come down from aloft.

This picture of the mainmast shrouds was taken from beneath the starboard boat skids.

In this view it can be seen that there are more shrouds than those of the fore-mast pictures. This is because the mainmast carried a skysail which in turn made the main t,gallant mast taller.

1: The hand winch. This little aid was a great boon for the sailors, its purpose being to take in any slack on the sheets. Although no handle is visible, the same could be placed in the centre of the barrel and turned by one sailor whilst another could haul in the slack around the barrel.

2: The swinging wash ports that open and close with the rolling of the ship, this allows any excess water on the deck to run back into the sea.

3: The forward boat skid. No boat was in position when this picture was taken.

4 : The base of the boat davit.

A view of the starboard mizzen mast shrouds. In this picture the buntlines can be seen to be running through their leads, then secured to the appropriate belaying pins and coiled up. The ratlines which the sailors used as a ladder to climb aloft can also be seen crossing between the shrouds. The deadeyes are also visible, as is the brass hand rail that accompanies the poop deck ladder. Note in which the way the shrouds have been turned around the deadeyes and seized.

The Cargo Hatches

During her working life, *Cutty Sark* had three hatches through which cargo was loaded into the hold below. Like most ships of her day she only had one hold, and therefore had no transverse bulkheads. The number two hatch to the hold which is pictured above was the largest of the three hatches. The other two are presently being used as companionways for visitors.

When a ship puts to sea all its hatches must be securely battened down to prevent any water from entering the hold. Firstly, the three tarpaulin covers of each hatch must be neatly tabled then tucked into their cleats; five cleats can be seen on the near side of the hatch combing. The batten bars which run both the length and breadth of the hatch, are then slid into the cleats and over the tucked in tarpaulin, before their wooden wedges are firmly hammered home.

On long sea passages, the hatches would normally be further protected by having ropes frapped across the canvas, and a solid timber wall built around each hatch by the carpenter.

At just twelve inches in height, *Cutty Sark* like so many ships of the day had extremely low hatch combings. The normal height is over three feet.

When this particular photograph was taken by the author, the ship was undergoing her annual refit. The hatch itself was opened each day to carry out various tasks, and due to this the hatch had been battened down in a rather makeshift manner

The Starboard Lifeboat

The starboard lifeboat lays between, and on top of, the two angled heavy wooden beams which are known as boat-skids. The boat itself is secured on four points by chain and lanyard, as well as the large wooden chocks that keeps the boat in place when the ship is rolling.
The inside of the boat is somewhat protected from the weather by a strong-back supported canvas boat cover, which as can be seen, is secured by a lanyard all around.
After the boat cover has been taken off and when the boat is to be launched, the lanyards holding the chain supports are removed or cut through. The black pin which is visible on the nearside out-board chock is knocked out, likewise the pin on the after outboard chock. Both out-board chocks are then knocked forward on their hinges which allows the boat to swing free. The boat is then lifted at both ends by just a few inches on the boat falls.
The forward radial davit is then allowed to run free, whilst the after davit which is pointing inboard is hauled aft. At the same time, the forward end of the boat is pushed outboard and aft. When the forward end of the boat is over the ship's side and clear, the after davit is then swung forward until both davits are pointing outboard.
According to the deck arrangement the whole procedure can be reversed. After the davits are secured by their guys, and the fore and aft painters are positioned, passengers embark and the boat is ready for lowering on the boat falls.

Above; Looking aft from the starboard cat-head. Protruding from the cat head is the whisker-boom, through which two stays from the jib-boom pass before being secured to the side of the foc'sle head.
Below: On each side of the capstan there are two massive timber cat head supports.

Left - The foc'sle head capstan. Although it has other uses, The main purpose of this capstan is for hauling the anchor in. To raise the anchor a number of sailors would insert capstan bars into the slots on the capstan head. The sailors then walk around to turn the capstan turning a shaft which goes to the windlass below. *Cutty Sark's* capstan has seven capstan apertures for bars; these can be double banked by up to fourteen men if and when required.

Left: A view of the rocker arms or 'Jiggy Jig.' This is used to gather up the slack from the anchor cable after it has been hauled in by the capstan. It is operated by two sailors whilst the anchor chain is being hauled in via the capstan.

With a sailor on each side, each man positions his shoulders into the U shape on the large bracket bars to move the bracket arm up and down.

Their movements result in the black and white painted iron rods taking the slack chain from the windlass into the cable locker.

Modifications

This picture on the left which was probably taken in the 1920's, gives a view of what the ship looked like after her 1923 refit.

The windlass beneath the break of the foc'sle can be seen with three turns of the anchor cable around its barrel.

Also to be seen is the large ventilator on the foc'sle head, an item which was once used to ventilate the accommodation in the 'tween deck.

The rocker arms and the ship's bell can also be seen.

In conjunction with the photograph above, a scuttle hatch has since been constructed abaft the windlass.

The foc'sle head framework which once surrounded the windlass on both its sides has been removed.

On the right foreground the edge of the scuttle hatch which was built on top of number one cargo hatch can be seen.

The arrow points to the rocker arms.

Fairleads

The foc'sle head fairleads in this picture show the three barrels, they are used when or heaving or warping the ship alongside. After the berthing rope which is on the left has been taken to its point, which is usually a bollard on the quay or a tug that is towing the ship in or out of port, the rope is taken through the fairleads to the capstan for hauling in.
On top of each of the barrels a greasing point can be seen. Regular lubrication meant easier turning of the fairleads
The guardrails with its wire mesh is a child safety precaution. During her working life, *Cutty Sark* like al other ships of her day used stanchions and chains as guardrails.

Taken on an unidentified ship, this photo shows a group of sailors working the capstan to haul the anchor in. The first mate who is otherwise referred to as the chief officer, leans over the guard rail to watch the anchor's progress. Other points of interest are the two white painted cat-heads, the open hatch and the pin-rail situated forward of it, The pin rail is used for securing the sheets of the head sails.
Sheets is the name given to the ropes which are attached to the corners of the sails

Beneath the ship's foc'sle head, which is otherwise referred to as the anchor deck or monkey foc'sle, the space shown in this photo is about four feet in height. In that small space is the windlass, bow sprit sheath and anchor cable. The anchor cable in view would normally be stowed in the cable locker. Note the spurling gate through which the anchor cable passes after the anchor has been dropped. When the required amount of cable has been allowed to run out, the press on top of the gate can be clamped down to restrict any further cable running out.

The large white painted sheath covers the bow sprit which protrudes forward of the ship's stem by twenty feet. From beneath that sheath it goes under deck where it is secured to a large baulk. The bow sprit holds the wooden jib boom which in turn holds the fore and aft head sails. In the background can be seen riveted iron plates. That line of plates is an extension to the starboard bulwark.

Anchor Cables

The picture below shows the forward scuttle hatch which leads to the 'tween deck. This wooden structure has been added since the ship's 1953 restoration, its purpose being to facilitate the passage of visitors down to the 'tween deck. As can be seen, this scuttle hatch has been built on top of the iron hatch combing, which was in fact the number one cargo hatch when the ship was trading.

To the left of the scuttle hatch is a section of anchor cable on a wooden grating, this cable comes from the windlass beneath the foc'sle head, otherwise known as the anchor deck. Forward of this cable is a four rung ladder leading to the foc'sle head. Nearest to the camera on the right is the double barrelled hand cargo winch. This was used for loading and discharging cargo from number one hatch, as well as transferring the anchor cable from the windlass to the cable locker. After hauling in the anchor with the capstan, the cable would come up through the hawse pipe, then with the use of the rocker arms, it is transferred to the windlass. The cable would then be hauled along the deck to the drum end cable holder of the winch, and as the photo on the next page shows, is fed through the navel pipe and into the cable locker.

This photo as a sequel to the picture on the previous page, shows the anchor cable bent around the drum end cable holder. It also shows the cable being fed down through the navel pipe and into the cable locker below.

At the bottom of the fife rail there are three sheaves which are used in conjunction with a three fold purchase block under the mast table or fore-top to haul heavy lifts aloft. These heavy items are usually the foreyard or topmast.

Above is an interesting and detailed view of some of the deck arrangements which are synonymous to those of *Cutty Sark*. The picture taken during the 1930's is of the Swedish *Frideborg*, a vessel which began her career in 1866 as the barque rigged tea clipper *Cleta*. The photo shows the ship when she was employed in the Baltic as a timber carrier.

On the right bottom corner can be seen the number one cargo hatch with its tarpaulin loosely covering it. Directly forward of the hatch is the hand operated cargo winch which is not dissimilar to *Cutty Sark's*. The two wire ropes seen to be coming down at a 45 degree angle are the lower foremast stays. The wooden barrelled windlass which is situated at the break of the foc'sle has three turns of anchor cable on it and has the foc'sle bell before it on a dolphin. In front of the bell are the curved rocker arms with pawl post which rotate the windlass barrel. Further forward is the capstan.

The anchor cable in the foreground appears to be ready for stowing in the cable locker.

Wooden Decks

Ship's wooden decks are made up from planks which are normally five to six inches wide and four inches thick. *Cutty Sark's* original decking was three and a half inches thick and made of teak wood. When laid over iron frames, the deck would be waterproofed between the ⅜ inch spaces in the decking with a combination of oakum and pitch. The oakum is tightly packed down between the planks with hammer and chisel into half of the space. The ship's carpenter who would be in charge of any such decking operation, would have a brazier fire lit on the deck for the purpose of boiling the pitch. The boiled pitch is poured down the space on top of the oakum, into the remainder of the space between the planks to form a seam. When set and as the above photograph shows, the excess pitch is scraped off by the sailors.

Until recent years, the wooden decks of all ships were regularly oiled with an equal mixture of raw linseed oil and turpentine. This operation was to stop shrinkage and rot. That practice now seems to have ceased, because the time honoured practice of boiled pitch and oakum has been replaced with plastic strips being inserted between the planking. Neither can decks be oiled anymore, as the raw linseed oil rots the plastic strips away. After a ship has been in heavy weather for some time, and when it has not been possible to scrub the decks, they tend to become slimy. Ship's wooden decks were once scrubbed and holystoned at regular intervals, both to give both a clean appearance and to avoid the men from slipping.

Although *Cutty Sark* has recently adopted the new method of seaming with plastic strips, the photograph on the following page shows the age old method of pitch seaming to the deck.

This photo taken on *Cutty Sark's* saloon roof also shows pitched deck seaming. The residue of pitch is normally scraped off before the wooden deck is holy-stoned to present a clean white appearance. In good weather, *Cutty Sark's* decks would be scrubbed daily with sand and seawater. Note the difference in the widths of the deck planking.

Three different views of the galley which give an indication of what life was like for the ship's cook, a man who had to work within those confines as he slaved over a hot stove in all kinds of weather. The cast iron galley stove which burned wood (or coal if that was the cargo) may well be the same one since *Cutty Sark* was a new ship. Galleys on all ships of sail were most uncomfortable, sweatboxes in the tropics and dangerous in heavy weather. Indeed, when those ships rolled heavily, or were heeled over under a press of sail, the galley would be fraught with danger. This being if a pan of scalding water or other slid off the stove when the ship rolled. For the cook to stop his pans from sliding off, range bars which can be can be seen on top of the stove were fitted. The cook was at times the steward as well, and on most ships the most respected man on board. Normally he would not allow anybody into his galley. He himself would light the fire in the morning watch to prepare for breakfast, whilst the watch on deck would supply him with wood or coal from the bunker for his stove. When their clothing was soaked which was quite often, the sailors with the cook's permission, would hang their wet gear in the galley to dry. After meals had been cooked, the steward would tend to the captain and mates in the saloon, whilst the watch on deck would do the same for the sailors.

Top: The donkey room. Inside was a steam engine which provided power for heavy lifts, such as stowing the anchor and its cable. The large wooden frame in front of the door is known as the fife rail to which ropes from aloft were belayed.
Bottom: The sailor's foc'sle. Situated at the fore part of the forward mast house, it was where the sailors ate and slept. There are two compartments, one for the port watch and the other for the starboard. They have six bunks in each.

This picture which was taken from the quayside shows part of the foremast and some of its associated rigging. Between the second and third shrouds the red port navigation light holder can be seen. When the oil lamp light of this fixture was in place and when the ship was at sea, it gave an arc of visibility through its red glass, from right ahead to two points (22½ degrees) abaft the beam on the port side. A similar light on the starboard side which was green provided the same for that side. Each morning the ship's lamp trimmer would trim the wicks and provide colza oil to the lamps. Ships of sail do not carry mast-head white lights, which means that power driven vessels must give way.

Also in the picture can be seen the lower yard stun sail boom and the upper topsail stun sail boom at the top right. These spars could be hauled outboard to provide extra sail area in good weather. Ships with stun (studding) sails required large crews of sailors, but *Cutty Sark* dispensed with her stun sails during her rebuilding in 1880 due to ever smaller crew numbers.

When disaster is about to strike, "All Hands to the Pumps" is and was, a cry next only to that of "Abandon Ship." It meant that the hold is being flooded, and the only way to discharge the seawater is to pump it over the side with the bilge pumps. All ships past and present have bilge pumps, a bilge is in fact a well which on most ships is situated at the bottom of, and on each side of the hold,. However, because of their large dead-rises, ships like *Cutty Sark* had centre line bilges.

A most necessary piece of any ship's requirements is its pumps. The picture above shows the huge iron wheels which when turned, draws up any water up from the bilges, allowing it run out through the pipes situated between the wheels and onto the deck. At some time during each watch … in port or at sea - soundings were regularly taken to ascertain if there was any water in the bilge, and if so, the pumps would be manned to discharge it. On heavily leaking ships those pumps would be manned for long periods. But if the strum boxes of the bilges were choked the pumps would be useless and many a ship has foundered through having blocked bilges. Such a task of manning the pumps was never popular with sailors.

Also visible in the picture above which was taken on board the *Cutty Sark*, are the fife rails beneath the main mast. These fife rails are complete with belaying pins but without any of the ropes that would come down from aloft.

Top: The forward deck house which was not on the ship when she was built. The nearest door is the galley, the middle door is the carpenters shop, whilst the furthest door away is where the sailors were accommodated.

Bottom: The after deck house which was added to the ship when two years old. The donkey engine room door can be seen on the foreside. The bosun, carpenter, lamp-trimmer and cook steward dwelt in the centre, whilst the apprentices had their half-deck at the after end.

Left: Base of the Mainmast.

In this photo a pin rail can be seen holding some of the belaying pins.

At the bottom two arrows point to the 'partners.' The junction where the mast passes through the deck. When *Ferreira* was part dismasted in 1916, it was at this point where the mast actually broke off before going over the side. The port side mizzen stay can be seen in the foreground.

Below: The port side chicken coop.

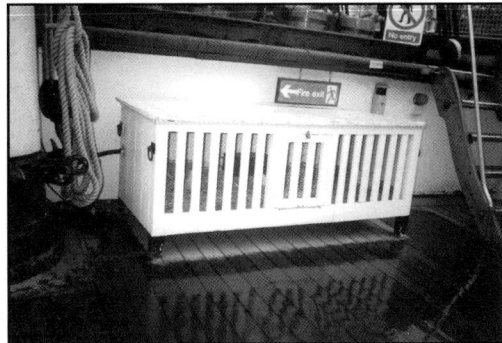

Left: Base of the Mizzen Mast.

The top arrow points to a pin rail, whilst the bottom to a spider band. The latter of these is used for the shackling of heavy items. On each side of the mast, parts of the two chicken coops can be seen.

Top: The sailor's heads. This is their toilet with its hand operated flush pump visible on the after end. The ladder on the right leads to the foc'sle head, otherwise known as the anchor deck.

Left: Directly opposite the sailor's heads on the starboard side is the heads for the petty officers. The arrow points to a rack for seven wooden capstan bars. These are inserted into the windlass on the foc'sle head.

The Ship's Wheel or Helm.

Top: On the after end of the wheel is the steering gear box bearing the ships name on its side. In this box there are a set of gears connected via the wheel to the rudder, thereby making the turning of the wheel much easier.

Left: A different view of the wheel showing the brass compass binnacle in the foreground. The helmsman would normally stand on the foreside of the wheel as he steered by quarter points. This would then enable him to look into the binnacle to check his given course. On some occasions when the mizzen royal had been set, the helmsman would steer off that sail as well as checking his compass.

The Hand Winch

A labour saving hand operated device used for the loading or discharging of cargo, as well as for the hoisting aloft of yards and other spars.

With two drum ends on each side of the winch, those who were working cargo or sending gear aloft had the choice of using the winch gears to reduce their work load.

Handles are inserted into the drum ends on either the top or bottom to gain the required gearing.
Complete cargoes such as 1,100 tons of coal were often loaded using this method.

The three masts of *Cutty Sark*

Top Left:
The fore-mast showing its standing rigging.

Top right:
The mainmast with both its royal and skysail yards sent down.

Right::
The mizzen mast
The arrow in the picture to the right points to the crossjack yard, otherwise referred to as the 'crojack.'

Lahloo

TORRINGTON

In the eyes of many, the schooner rigged *Torrington* was Britain's first ever clipper ship. Others will say that *Scottish Maid* of 1839 held the distinction, then again comes a group who claim *Stornoway* of 1850 held the honour. The truth of the matter is, and as far as British ships are concerned, *Scottish Maid* was the first vessel to be built with an Aberdeen bow which was later to be called a clipper bow; the speedy *Torrington* was also the first to have the underwater lines of a clipper. However, it was the *Stornoway* which became the first fully rigged ship to have the lines, the bow, and to be built specifically for the tea trade.

Torrington was a schooner rigged vessel built by Alexander Hall of Aberdeen to the design of Jardine & Matheson. She was launched in 1845 and listed as yard number 150. At that time there was more than one vessel trading under the name of *Torrington,* and confusion should be avoided. The sleek schooner was 104.6 feet in length, had a beam of 20.2 feet; and was 144 gross tons. She had been specifically designed for speed, her London owners sent her on the far east trade to run as one of the infamous opium carriers.

Captain J. Neill was her first commander, and although his reign on the schooner wasn't a long one, it was most spectacular in some of the smart passages the little ship made between India and Hong Kong. At the time of *Torrington's* trading activities in the far east, there were large numbers of pirates in the China seas. Those parasites preyed on becalmed ships and their crews. For this reason most merchant ships trading in the area carried cannon to ward off any attacks.

The cargoes *Torrington* carried were generally opium, and that led to severe difficulties between the Chinese and British governments, that turn of events eventually led to the ceding of Hong Kong to Britain. As for the schooner herself, *Torrington* was just four years old when she disappeared some time in 1849. It was generally accepted at the time, that it was either the weather or the pirates who were responsible for her loss.

1832   *ANN Mc KIM*   1852

Although not regarded as a true clipper ship, the fully rigged *Ann McKim* was more or less a prototype for the clippers to follow. With regard to both her underwater lines and radical design .... the likes of which had never been seen before, she was a big talking point in American shipbuilding circles. As a fully rigged ship, she was 494 US tons, and built to the order of Isaac McKim, who in being a wealthy ship owner could afford such an enterprise of a new style of ship.

Built and launched by Kennard & Williamson at their Baltimore yard in 1832, she was fitted and furnished with no expense spared. Her rig was standard for the period with single topsails, single t'gallants, royals, and stunsails on the fore and main. She had a length of 143 feet, and a beam of 31 feet, but it was her supposed draught of 11 feet forward and 16 feet aft which raised the eyebrows of other ship builders. The unusual difference in the fore and aft draughts - if it were the case - have in many peoples eyes, excluded her from the clipper ship status.

Isaac McKim named the ship after his wife and had the vessel fitted with 12 brass cannon. This was a necessary feature of the day, and especially in the China seas where piracy was a regular occurrence. In her day she was a remarkable little ship and because of her sharp lines, the passages she made were exceptionally fast by the standards of the day, with the ship owners in America taking a great deal of interest in her.

From 1832 until 1839, *Ann McKim* was engaged in the South American trade. On one particular passage she sailed from Coquimbo around Cape Horn and up to Baltimore in just 59 days. On the death of Isaac McKim in 1837, Howland & Aspinwall the New York tea shippers bought the vessel. The little ship then began in the tea trade to the far east in 1839.

In 1842 - 1843 she really made a name for herself by making the run from New York to Anjer in 79 days, then racing back to New York with a full load of tea in 96 days. In 1847, she was sold to a Valparaiso firm and used extensively in the California gold rush, but the ship had been worked hard and she was well soaked.

In 1852 after just 20 years of existence when after showing her age she was broken up.

Ann McKim

Author's Drawing

1845 *RAINBOW* 1848

When Howland & Aspinwall of New York owned *Ann Mckim*, they realised that as far as speed was concerned, this was to be the future ocean going type of ship. Examples were taken from her lines, and with a few alterations and improvements, the first true clipper ship *Rainbow,* was designed by John Willis Griffiths. The builders of the revolutionary new ship in 1845 were Smith & Dimon also of New York. They increased her size from *Ann Mc Kim's* 494 tons, to 752 tons by lengthening the new vessel 16 feet to 159 feet, on almost the same beam of 31 feet 10 inches.

This extra length gave the ship a length breadth ratio of over five to one, and the critics of the day forecast she would capsize as soon as she hit the water. Howland & Aspinwall began to take notice of those critics, and even sent an emissary over to the UK to an associate to get a second opinion on the new design. Apparently, the delay in the building of the ship was so long, that Smith & Dimon's competitors began building their own clippers. However, when the *Rainbow* was completed, the new ship proved them all wrong by being such a good, fast, and reliable sailer. She had a depth of 18 feet 4 inches which gave her more underwater body than the *Ann McKim,* she also crossed skysails on the fore and main to give her added speed.

Her first captain was the acclaimed 'Old Man Land', and on the ship's maiden voyage he caused a great stir in the shipping world, He went out to the far east and back to New York in 102 days each way, It was a voyage which had all the other shipbuilders changing their plans to the radical new design. The freight earned in just that one trip paid for the building costs of *Rainbow* twice over. During the voyage, *Rainbow* had been dismasted and jury rigged, but still managed to make good speeds, at times the little clipper touched 14 knots, and from the date of her arrival back at New York the clipper ship boom began.

However, and whereas *Rainbow* will go down in maritime history as the first ever clipper ship, her life was indeed a short one. During one of her tea runs to the Far East in 1848, the three year old ship disappeared.

Rainbow

Author's Drawing

1850 *STORNOWAY* 1873

The full rigged ship *Stornoway* is credited to have been the first British ship designed specifically for the tea trade. She was built by Alexander Hall of Aberdeen and launched in 1850, her owners being Jardine & Matheson, a firm which had strong trading links in the Far East. *Stornoway* was 527 tons, had a length of 157 feet, a beam of 25 feet and a hold depth of 17 feet 6 inches. Built of wood with iron fittings, she had hemp standing rigging, outside channels, single topsails and single t'gallants. She also crossed skysails on the fore and main and proved to be an extremely fast little ship. During her trading career she was just one of many which ran from India to Hong Kong with opium, then returned to the UK with a cargo of tea.

The ship's first captain was John Robertson who completed just two voyages before being relieved by Captain Harold Hart. He stayed for a further nine voyages until the ship was sold in 1861 to McKay & Co of London. Later on she changed hands in 1867, this time to Welch & Co of Newcastle where Captain Waugh took command. The ship had by that time come off the tea trade to be engaged in carrying coal from the Tyne to London. In 1871 Chapman's also from Newcastle purchased the vessel with Captain Greener taking charge, she continued as a collier but on 7 June 1873 ran ground on the Kentish Knock and was declared a total loss.

Chrysolite which was built a year later than *Stornoway,* was an identical looking ship and built by the same yard, but for Taylor & Potter of Liverpool. Those two ships were said to be the first British designed tea clippers. Captain Anthony Enright was *Chrysolite's* first commander, but he left to join the *Lightning* of Liverpool's Black Ball Line. Compared with *Torrington* of 1845 which was a schooner rigged opium clipper, *Stornoway* and *Chrysolite* were both ship rigged, a fact which gives added credence to the claim that those two were the first British tea clippers. Whilst transporting cattle *Chrysolite* was wrecked in a typhoon off Mauritius in March 1873 when eleven of her crew were lost.

1858   SCAWFELL   1873

Despite the fact that iron had already been introduced into the shipyards of Britain, many ship owners still chose the time honoured method of having their ships built of wood. One of those vessels was *Scawfell,* a ship built in 1858 by Charles Lamport of Workington, for Rathbone Brothers of Liverpool. Built exclusively for the tea trade, *Scawfell* was extremely well constructed, and as well as having a strong and sturdy frame, she also had oak planking for both her ship's sides and decks. The reason wooden tea clippers were more favoured than those built of iron, was because of a rumour which had been cleverly circulated by the tea clipper owners towards the tea drinkers of the day. The rumour implied … quite incorrectly, that the smoke from the funnels of the iron steam ships, found its way into the tea chests and eventually spoiled the taste of the tea.

Between perpendiculars the little full rigger was 198 feet in length, her beam 32.6, whilst her depth of hold was 21.8. She was 826 gross tons, and because of her incorporation of such items as outside channels, rope standing rigging, single top sails and single t'gallants, as well as triple reef points, she became one of the last … of the first generation of full rigged clipper ships. Nevertheless, she had that stylish and elegant appearance of a tea clipper as well as speed, and this was proved in 1861, when she sailed from Whampoa to Liverpool and picked up her pilot after 85 days.

Captain Robert Thomson had been in command of the ship from new, but he left her after she was sold to Wilson & Blain of South Shields in 1872. *Scawfell* was then employed in the coal trade between the Tyne and London. The new company kept her for eight years before selling her in 1883 to William Hutchinson another Tyneside coal merchant

The ship traded between the Tyne and Thames continued until 9 January 1883, but after having left the Tyne with yet another cargo of coal, the 25 year old ship was hit by a North Sea snorter. Sea water entered the hold, and because of her bilge pumps becoming blocked the ship had to be abandoned. It was not uncommon in those times, for ships which carried bulk cargoes such as coal, grain or guano, to suffer the same fate of blocked strum boxes in the bilges.

1869 *THOMAS STEPHENS* 1916

The *Thomas Stephens* was originally designed for the Black Ball Line of Liverpool, a company which had been so successful with their Yankee Clippers; that the building of this iron clipper was in keeping with the latest designs in passenger sailing ships. She was built on the River Mersey by the noted firm of Potters; but before the time of her launching, in July 1869, the Black Ball Line had found themselves in serious financial difficulties. The London ship owner Thomas Stephens then took the vessel over and the ship was named after himself, the figurehead was also of himself …. complete with top hat and tails. The ship was managed by Bethel & Co, and after her first two voyages from Liverpool, she sailed out of the Thames for the London Line of Packets.

With a gross tonnage of 1,507 tons, she had a length of 263 feet, a beam of 38 feet 2 inches and a depth of 23 feet. Her length breadth ratio was over seven to one, which with her fine lines and large spread of sail contributed to her consistently fast passages.

The *Thomas Stephens* was noted for her lofty rig, she crossed skysails on all three masts, as well as the usual arrangement of stunsails. Her first passage out to Melbourne was made in 82 days. Although this was nowhere near the record, neither were any of her subsequent voyages. She was a steady and reliable ship and never came to any serious grief, and all because she was never driven hard by any of her captains. However, in July 1993, after she had been trading for 24 years, her luck finally ran out. Loaded with Australian grain for the UK, she was caught in a terrific storm in the South Pacific where she suffered considerable damage to her decks and rig. After having taken such a merciless beating, and driven thousands of miles off her course to the north, it was assumed her cargo would be wet - which would in turn result in the ship's sides bursting open. Fortunately, when she made it to Callao, her cargo was found to be as dry as a bone, so after being repaired the vessel resumed its voyage.

On her next trip, she took another battering off Cape Horn where she was partly dismasted, but eventually made it back to the Falklands under jury rig. After having been given an estimate for the repairs at Port Stanley, the ship was sailed to Cape To where the vessel was made good at a fraction of the Falkland estimate. To avoid the possibility of more bad weather off the Horn, and to complete his passage, Captain Belding then sailed east about for his destination of Esquimalt on Vancouver Island. On her arrival back at the UK in 1896, Captain Belding was then informed that the *Thomas Stephens* had been sold to the Portuguese government, for nothing more than the price of scrap. The new owners who were the Portuguese Navy had acquired the ship for £3,500, and she like the *Thermopylae* were to be used for sail training; the sale of the ship took place at Southampton in April 1896. During her delivery passage to Lisbon with a Portuguese crew under Captain Belding, his relief understudy Captain Gomez also sailed with the ship. After leaving the UK and putting the new sailors through their paces fire broke out whilst the ship was in the Bay of Biscay. Captain Belding and his crew extinguished the fire which by all accounts was quite serious. The Portuguese authorities were so impressed with the valour of Captain Belding that on the vessel's arrival at Lisbon on 29 May 1896, not only was he given a high award, but was also asked to assist in the naval training programme. The ship was re-furbished from the fire damage, re-named *Pero d' Alemequer*, and began service as a cargo carrying naval training vessel.

Her first voyage under the Portuguese flag which began on 8 October 1896, was from Lisbon to Lourenco Marques; Captain Gomez was her commander. On the return passage the *Pero d' Alemequer* called in at Luanda with a coal cargo before ending the voyage at Lisbon on 9 July 1897. Her second voyage was to the Portuguese colonies in India, then her third and fourth was back on the East African route with coal for Mossamedes. Used extensively by the Portuguese Navy the vessel didn't travel far, and her long runs out to Australia were never repeated. Like the *Ferreira*, and *Pedro Nunez* her trips were short with long lay ups between them. The *Pero d' Alemequer* was moored for two years in the Tagus from 1909 until 1911, there she was used as an accommodation and training ship.

In 1911 she was taken out of naval service altogether for use as a coal hulk, but in the summer of 1912, the old ship which was then 43 years old, was sold commercially and once again refitted for merchant service. After having left Lisbon in December 1915, she arrived at the USA and loaded a cargo at Boston. On 17 March 1916, the *Pero D' Alemquer,* the ex *Thomas Stephens,* left Boston for Lisbon. The war at sea was in progress as was the North Atlantic weather, and neither the old ship nor any of her sailors were ever heard of again.

Halloween

Thomas Stephens

1869 BLACKADDER 1905

This was another of the John Willis ships, and probably the unluckiest one he ever owned. In the early part of her career, it appears that wherever the ship went or whatever did, she always seemed to find herself in some maritime mishap. It appears that Maudsley Sons & Field her builders, were more renowned for their engineering skills than the construction of ships, and this contributed to her first catastrophe.

Blackadder was built alongside her sister ship *Hallowe'en* at Deptford on the River Thames. Their dimensions were 216,6: x 35.2: x 20.5: both of these ships were 970 gross tons. Like the *Cutty Sark*, the *Blackadder* and *Hallowe'en* had the lines of *The Tweed* built into their construction, and although the three ships may have resembled each other in their outward appearance, there was a marked difference in their fortunes.

Blackadder's bad luck began even before her building was completed. The masts themselves were incorrectly rigged; this being due to the cheeks being improperly secured. Her masts were designed to be stepped in the fashion of a Chinese junk; foremast raked slightly forward; mainmast vertical; and mizzen raked slightly aft. *Hallowe'en* had her masts raked as standard.

Blackadder's troubles first began under the command of Captain Robinson. Basil Lubbock has described this man as being a most incompetent seaman, and one who shirked his responsibilities to the mate whenever good seamanship was required. After leaving the Downs on 24 March 1870, it soon became apparent that the masts were going to give a lot of trouble. However, *Blackadder* made Madeira after ten days, then crossed the line on 19 April in 26 days. But as soon as she hit a full South Atlantic gale on 10 May, any fears that were held about her masts were justified. Then true to all expectations she became partly dismasted. The ship was then jury rigged before struggling to the refuge of False Bay and anchored off Simonstown on 25 May 1870.

After a telegraph had been sent to John Willis, *Blackadder* had to wait three months for replacement masts to be shipped out from the UK. The new masts arrived, but as they were being stepped in Simons Bay, it was discovered they were shorter than the originals.

Therefore, the necessary alterations had to be made to the five inch wire standing rigging shrouds before *Blackadder* could resume her maiden voyage.

Then whilst in the China Sea on her final approach to Shanghai, more bad luck came *Blackadder's* way when she was run down by the SS *Volga* of Marseilles. Both ships suffered damage to their fore parts, and once again the *Blackadder* had to struggle into a sanctuary. This time it was Foochow, where on arrival she was down by the head. After repairs that took three months, the ship finally arrived at Shanghai but missed the 'chop.' *Blackadder* then sailed towards Penang where the unlucky ship was once again involved in a pile up. This time she broke her jib boom, but repairs were at hand and not much time was lost.

Finally arriving in London in November 1871, after a 21 months voyage, Old White Hat Willis informed Captain Robinson his services were no longer required. Captain FW Moore relieved him. During *Blackadder's* maiden voyage, John Willis had filed an insurance claim on the vessel being dismasted. But the claim was rejected in a civil law suit; this being due to the mast cheeks being improperly fitted with the full knowledge of the ship's owner. It was this action that led to Old White Hat Willis from ever having any of his ships insured again, and carried his own insurance.

Under her new captain, the *Blackadder* proved she was indeed a fast ship, and during the course of her second voyage, the only mis-hap was for her to lose the mizzen t'gallant mast. In May 1873 the *Blackadder* arrived at Shanghai under jury rig. Having been dismasted for the second time in three years … she was uninsured. The unfortunate vessel had left Sydney shortly before the *Cutty Sark,* which being on the same charter was also bound for Shanghai. In the China Seas both ships were hit by the same typhoon, but it was the unlucky *Blackadder* who received the worst of it, this resulted in Captain Bisset having to cut his masts away.

After being re-masted she loaded a cargo of sugar for Boston. But whilst off North Borneo her bad luck continued, she hit an uncharted reef and became stuck fast. To lighten the ship, the crew jettisoned as much of the cargo as they could, but it appeared as though she was a total loss. *Blackadder* was abandoned, but whilst the crew were being rescued by another ship, *Blackadder* suddenly came loose, and with some canvas up sailed away with nobody on board. With the help of the would be rescuing ship, it took quite some time to catch the elusive *Blackadder,* but the crew eventually re-joined.

It was later discovered that her grounding had caused no damage, probably the only bit of good luck the ship had encountered during her career. But this was only the start of an horrendous passage, one that continued with the ship being caught in a windless zone of the China Sea. Drifting around windless for weeks on end, the food eventually ran out, and each man was given just enough water to keep him alive. Sugar from the cargo was the only thing to eat, the result being, that *Blackadder* eventually arrived at Boston with most of her crew suffering from scurvy.

On the ship's return to the UK, Captain White took command of the *Blackadder*. He stayed in her for two voyages. The ship showed no sign of bad luck under him, and he even made two profitable voyages, the first money she'd ever made for her owner! Captain Allen took command in 1877, but due to the depression and the increasingly dependable steam ships, the tea trade had by then slumped altogether. *Blackadder* then went on the Australian wool run. This was much easier for sailing ships than steamers, and all due to the lack of coaling stations. On another visit to New York in 1882, *Blackadder* once again found herself alongside the *Cutty Sark*. The latter had arrived from the Philippine port of Cebu with a cargo of jute. But there had been so much trouble on board the *Cutty Sark* during the passage, that Captain William Bruce and the mate were sacked on the spot They were replaced by *Blackadder's* Captain FW Moore and a large number of his crew. In the latter years of her trading under the red ensign for John Willis, the *Blackadder* had run out of her share of bad luck, and although running as normal as any other ship, she carried the name of being a hoodoo ship. John Willis began trimming his fleet towards the end of the century. *Cutty Sark* went to the Portuguese in 1895, whilst the *Blackadder* … the last ever ship of the Willis fleet, went to the Norwegians shortly before the death of Willis in 1900. Whilst off the Brazilian coast in 1905, the *Blackadder* was wrecked off Bahia. The picture below is of *Blackadder*.

1868 *THERMOPYLAE* 1907

It would be hard to write any book about *Cutty Sark,* without the inclusion of her great rival *Thermopylae*. This ship also had her fair share of glory, as well as setting a number of records for a full rigged ship that will never be broken. *Thermopylae* was one of the most distinguished and celebrated of all the British tea clippers, and one which on her maiden voyage, set a record for a full rigged ship that will stand for all time. This was the record run from Gravesend to Melbourne in 63 days. She then created another record with a 28 day passage from Newcastle NSW to Shanghai, before coming home from Foochow to London in 91 days, just two days behind the winner *Sir Lancelot*.

Thermopylae was an extreme clipper designed by Bernard Weymouth, built by Walter Hood, and owned by George Thompson of the Aberdeen White Star Line. *Thermopylae* was laid down at the beginning of September 1867, built composite with her iron frames set at 18 inch intervals and scantlings of yellow pine. She was launched on the 19th of August 1868. Of 947 gross tons, her other dimensions were 212 x 36 x 21 feet. Other measurements include the bow sprit of 21 feet, and a 71 feet jib boom , The overall length from the end of the jib boom to the after end of the spanker boom was just over 300 feet.

Painted in Aberdeen green like all the other ships in the Thompson fleet, she was fitted with single t'gallant sails, and the American innovation of split topsails. In 1871 the t'gallant sails were also split, which to many a sailor spoilt the looks of the ship. Other refinements in her make-up were a Cunningham brace winch, but for the fore yard only, she had an Aberdeen house and her figurehead was of Leonidas the Greek Spartan warrior with his sword held aloft.

After her maiden voyage which began in September 1868, she was seen to have great sailing powers. Her ability to sail close to the wind, to run before it, or to go about, were described by those who sailed on her as exceptional. She had huge staysails which contributed greatly in her sailing close to the wind , combined with her jib boom which was ten feet longer than that of a similar sized ship.

There was great excitement in the shipping world when *Thermopylae* was hailed as the undisputed cock o' the fleet.

There are those who are under the impression that the *Cutty Sark* was built with the sole intention of bettering the feats made by the *Thermopylae*. But as the *Cutty Sark's* plans had been drawn and the keel laid ... before Thermopylae's record run London to Melbourne,

it is not the case. As a tea clipper, *Thermopylae* made ten passages averaging 106 days during her career. Her best performance under Captain Kemball was of 91 days on her maiden voyage, and her longest of 115 days was made three times. In 1878 *Thermopylae* loaded tea for the last time, the trade was completely lost to the steamers so like a few more of her ilk she went on the Australian wool run.

In 1887, and now 19 years old, *Thermopylae* underwent a major overhaul and refit in a London dry dock. During her stay out of the water, much of her planking was removed. This revealed a number of her frames had corroded as well as dry rot that had also taken a hold. When those faults had been remedied, her fore and main lower masts were cut down by some five feet and the rest of her top-hamper reduced accordingly; many of her yards that were also showing the strain of wear and tear were replaced.

After her survey, she was given a new classification and continued to operate for George Thompson junior. But soon afterwards the trade for the sailing ships had deteriorated so much, that in 1890, The Aberdeen White Star Line sold their flagship to the Canadian firm of Redford & Sons. The price was an estimated £5000.

Writing to Sea Breezes in April 1956, H R Bilton gives his account of a four and a half years stay in *Thermopylae.*

I joined *Thermopylae* in Barry Dock on June 6th 1890, my last ship had been the composite barque *Ethel*.

They would not take apprentices because the captain said the ship was to be sold in the near future, so I signed on as Ordinary Seaman. We took coal to Singapore (On the passage H.R Bilton writes about Jenkins as the captain and Wilson as the mate) Captain Jenkins always drove her and the best she made was 14 knots on the log while she was running her easting down. Mr. Wilson the chief officer explained to me that she made more speed according to sightings. The only extra sail we had was the 'Jimmy Green', but one day it carried away the martingale and made a mess of it, so it was the finish. From Singapore under Captain Wilson, we went to 'Frisco with general cargo; then to Hong Kong with flour; then Saigon in ballast where we loaded rice for Victoria B.C. arriving there on 14 April 1892. The Mount Royal Milling Company took the ship over in 'Frisco. It was there that I met Mr Redford the mill owner's son; he was in charge of the mill in Victoria. We loaded flour at the mill and sailed for Hong Kong with Captain Winchester in command. After discharging we proceeded to Bangkok in ballast, then loaded for Victoria with a full cargo of rice where we arrived in July 1893.

It was here that *Thermopylae* was cut down to a barque, and the crew reduced from 30 to 20. Her new owners were Hall Ross & Co of Vancouver, they gave the 24 year old vessel a major overhaul which included, repairing all the rot in her timbers and frames, converting the vessel to a barque, shortening even further the topmasts on the fore and main, and fitting the vessel out as a lumber carrier. It was a common practice to cut bow ports in lumber carriers, and these piercings were made to each of Thermopylae's bows, this enabled the loading of long squared off baulks of timber into the holds which could not be loaded through the deck hatches. From Victoria we towed to the Columbia River, and once again took on flour for Hong Kong; on the return passage we took rice back to Victoria, arriving in February 1894. It was here that I missed the ship on account of sickness, but joined her again in 1895; we towed to Puget Sound and loaded lumber at Port Blakely for Leith where we arrived on 12 December 1895. With Captain Winchester in command, the *Thermopylae* was handed over to the Portuguese.

The *Thermopylae* was a fine sea boat and carried her sail well. She was good and stiff and didn't ship much heavy water; I never saw her pooped in all the time I was in her. We rode out three typhoons in the China Seas, and it was the only time I ever saw her hove to; she made good under goose winged topsails, and was also easy on the steering. After she'd been cut down she didn't steer so well or make as much time, and we had to take in sail sooner because of the reduced crew numbers.

I think Lubbock says in his book that she leaked all the time, the only time I ever saw the pump turn over was for oiling; I never saw them bring up water. I was only shipmates with one officer who'd been in the *Cutty Sark*, he said the *Thermopylae* was a dry ship compared to her. Lubbock was a *Cutty Sark* man.

From Captain H.R Bilton

Now under the Portuguese flag, this once great tea clipper began the final stage of her sailing career. Her 'tween decks were fitted out to accommodate 60 boys, and she was used extensively for training future sailors in the art of sail handling. Those years as a sail training ship saw hundreds of boys learning the rudiments of all types of sailorising, and needless to say, she was kept in pristine appearance. Her trips were short, as far as the Mediterranean Sea but otherwise never venturing far away from the Tagus. .After a survey in 1905, it was discovered that her timbers were beyond economical repair.

The three masted barque was then employed as a coal hulk, supplying the more modern coal burning warships, but her extra lease of life was short lived, and the days of one of the greatest sailing ships were over.

One day in 1907, forty years after the keel of the *Thermopylae* had been laid, the veteran of so much sea lore was towed out into the Atlantic where she was to be used by the navy as target practice. Flags were flying from her masts and crowds of people lined the hillsides, to see the last moments of the holder of so many sailing records. There was many a tear shed by the large number of sailors, as they watched shells and torpedoes rip into their first ship, and send her to a sailor's grave.

Thermopylae

The above picture shows *Thermopylae* at the end of her maiden voyage in 1869. As can be seen she has single t'gallants on all three masts, but this sail plan was quickly changed ... and as the above photograph shows, the t'gallants on the fore and main were split into upper and lower t'gallants.
In 1887 the rig was shortened when the masts were cut down. Then after she came under Canadian ownership in 1895, the rig was cut down even further and *Thermopylae* was converted to a barque. That was the appearance of the ship when she went under the Portuguese flag.
Some writers and historians have compared *Cutty Sark* and *Thermopylae* as the greatest rivals in the tea trade. Whereas this may be true, the fact that Cutty Sark was specifically designed and built to rival *Thermopylae's* maiden voyage records are not true. *Cutty Sark* was still under construction before her rival had broken any of her records.

CLIPPERS' SPEEDS

I agree entirely with Mr. T. A. Porter whose letter appeared in the October issue of "Sea Breezes". Most of the writers who are so eloquent in their praise of the *Cutty Sark* and her consorts never had anything to do with ships and the sea. I have been connected with the sea for over 60 years and can support much of what Mr. Porter states. Most of the sailing vessels I saw were verminous and their crews were over-worked and underpaid.

In the latter days of sail many ships were under-manned and this undoubtedly had some bearing on the number of vessels which went missing. The *Cutty Sark* has been credited with almost phenomenal powers regarding speed—17½ knots. I do not believe she ever did 17 knots in all her life unless she had a three-or-more-knot tide with her. If she was as fast as her admirers claim how is it that she does not hold a single land-to-land record?

She never did anything wonderful in the China tea trade nor did she establish any records to or from Australia. The 362.23 sea miles credited to her is bunkum. The late Capt. Andrew Shewan showed that up by stating that the difference between their observations and dead reckoning was 40 miles. When she lost her rudder, the *Thermopylae* only beat her by six days although the *Cutty Sark* was kept down to about eight knots. Does not this show that the speeds of these ships were nothing like those credited to them? And the *Thermopylae* was reckoned one of the fastest of them. The *Clan Mackenzie* passed her however on one occasion with little trouble. I think the *Preussen's* 368 miles in a day is as good, if not a deal better than most. However, the *Preussen* was a vessel of 5,000 tons, over 400 ft. long and fitted to stand up to anything. It is a good job these sailing work-houses are gone and their generation with them.

Southsea   JAMES GREY

From Sea Breezes 1948

In the days of sail when Britain abounded with seamen, those men in their dockside taverns spoke of nothing else but ships! Indeed, they all had their favourites and especially the ones they'd served on. There were many famous names in the lore of tea clippers, the most notable of which, were *Cutty Sark* and *Thermopylae,* to this end *Cutty Sark* had a large following of admirers and supporters, and so too did her rival *Thermopylae.*

So great was the idolisation of those two clippers, that people who'd never even seen either of them tended to support one or the other. The man who wrote the accompanying article on the left was an undoubted *Thermopylae* supporter. Whilst that great writer Basil Lubbock has always been accused of being a '*Cutty Sark* man.'

Regarding the article on the left, it is not always the case, where the best designed ship is faster on the day than a contemporary. The normally slower ship may at the time be loaded with either a full or crank cargo. Or she may well have a foul bottom covered in seaweed and barnacles, such a situation would result in the fastest or best of ships losing a lot of speed. Then again she may be short-handed or have a poor crew at that particular time. Indeed there were times when even the *Cutty Sark* did not have a good captain. The truth of the matter is ... that *Cutty Sark* not only outlived every single clipper ship ever built ... But she is still in existence!

    Author

The above photo shows *Thermopylae's* appearance shortly after coming under Canadian ownership. The royals on both fore and mizzen are absent and the port bulwark has been stove in. The picture below shows her after having had her masts cut down even further and reduced to a barque. This is what she looked like when the Portuguese bought her.

1875 *TORRENS* 1910

Torrens was the last ever composite clipper ship to be built in Britain. This vessel of 1,335 gross and 1276 nett tons, was built as a cargo passenger ship for the Australian trade. Constructed at the yard of Sir James Laing in Sunderland at a cost of £27,257, she was launched in October 1875 and named after one of the prominent Australian politicians, Sir Robert Richard Torrens.

Her managers were Elders & Co of London, and her first captain was Henry Robert Angel; the ship was known as 'The Ship of the Angel Host.' It was he who supervised her building, owned the greater number of shares and commanded the ship for 15 years. A model of *Torrens* is on display at the South Kensington Museum London.

Captain Angel's children were named after some of the Atlantic Islands, and he had the ships figure head made to the likeness of his eldest daughter Flores. He greatly missed his daughter when on a voyage, and his idea of the figurehead, was he could take her with him on each trip. At sea, he would often be seen on the fo'c'sle looking over the stem at his beloved daughter.

Torrens was a fast ship spending most of her career on the run to the colonies. During these times, her longest passage under Captain Angel was 85 days, and this was on her maiden voyage. Her best ever recorded passage was of 65 days from Start Point to Adelaide, and her best ever days run 336 nautical miles. With an average of 74 days over a period of 15 voyages under Captain Henry Angel, these figures were never bettered by any of his successors.

Torrens was a lucky ship in never encountering any noted hardships of dismastings or groundings. She ran a twelve month round trip and made life comfortable for the passengers and crew alike, she was never raced, and under the command of Captain Angel was never under pressure for time. In 1890 Captain Angel retired from the sea for a more leisurely life ashore, he then handed the command of *Torrens* to Captain William Henry Cope. The change over was dramatic! For on Captain Cope's first voyage the *Torrens* was partly dismasted on the 29th of October 1890. The incident occurred 300 miles Northwest of Recife (then known as Pernambuco) and from there she had to limp into the port to effect repairs. Whilst awaiting her new foremast to be shipped out from the

UK, Captain Copes second piece of bad luck arrived. This was when the ship caught fire in port, necessitating further costly repairs The eventual passage from London to Adelaide took 179 days. After his unlucky start, Captain Cope managed to keep up regular services for the next five voyages without further serious incident. He then stayed with the ship until 1896.

The next commander of the popular *Torrens* was Captain Falkland Angel, the son of her first captain, who on his first trip, made the run out to Adelaide in 75 days.

There seems little doubt, that Captain Henry Angel had also called his son Falkland after one of the Atlantic Islands ... as he had his daughter Flores! But he kept up the good name of the ship in making reliable passages without taking too many chances, but disaster was to strike on Angel junior's third outward trip.

Running her easting down in the Southern Ocean in January 1899, the *Torrens* hit an iceberg when off the Crozets Islands. Her bows were stove in, she lost all her headgear, and caused considerable damage to the foremast and the rigging. Nevertheless, she managed to make Adelaide under jury rig after being 103 days out. Not many ships have been unfortunate enough to hit an iceberg, and then to be fortunate enough to make port. The *Titanic* of 1912 wasn't!

Captain Falkland Angel stayed with the ship until 1903, and where the story goes, after taking on a cargo of unused Boer war explosives at St. Helena, the *Torrens* was under tow in the River Thames. Through no fault of her own, the *Torrens* was involved in a collision with a vessel attempting to cross through the tow line, the offending vessel subsequently sank under the forefoot of the clipper.

It was the last straw for old Henry Angel, the ship which had been his pride and joy for so many years, was, like all other sailing ships, costing more to maintain than what they could earn. In 1903 the *Torrens* was sold to the Italian firm of Vittoria Bozza & Guiseppe Mortola for an estimated £1,500, a figure that was hardly a tenth of her building costs! She was then registered in Genoa and used as a cargo vessel. Some time later she ran aground on the Italian coast, then after being re-floated, was laid up for some time before being repaired at great expense in 1907. Not long after, she once again piled up on the beach close to Genoa, where she was scrapped in 1910.

Captain Robert Angel was born at Bridport, Dorsetshire on 8 Oct. 1829 and died at Las Palmas aged 94. His death was a result of an accident which occurred while he was a passenger on board the SS. *Highland Piper* (Captain Collins) on 7 April 1923.

Author's Drawing

Torrens

Captain T.W.Pickard who served the whole of his apprenticeship on *Torrens* writes.
When I joined the *Torrens* in 1885, the main skysail yard was discarded although the ship still carried her fore topmast stunsails. She was also fitted with what is known as parsery booms, which were carried on each bow forward of the fore rigging; these were used to extend the foot of the foresail when the wind was quarterly or astern.

In 1887 when I had attained the dignity of being a second trip apprentice, we experienced a particularly bad passage down the English Channel in the teeth of a sou'wester. Twice we had to put in for shelter; first at Spithead Roads where we brought up with most of our canvas blown away, and later at Portland harbour. Altogether we were ten days beating down from London to Plymouth. After getting away from the land the luck changed with the wind veering away to the Nor'ard and blew us down to the equator in 18 days.

From there, the favourable winds continued and we dropped anchor off Semaphore, Port Adelaide 65 days out; this was the second best passage of her career. Her best day's run on this passage was 321 miles; this distance was never exceeded during my 4 years on board although Lubbock credits her with 326 as her best ever.

Where the *Torrens* scored best against her competitors and especially the iron ships of her day, was her ability to ghost along at two or three knots when there was only sufficient wind to flap the sails. Yet when running her easting down she was as buoyant as a cork Another of her good points was her dryness, even in heavy weather! Never during my term did she ship any heavy water.

In 1888, we were standing in for the Lizard homeward bound; then after hoisting our number and destination we squared away up channel. Just about the same time, the crack P&O liner SS. *Carthage* also arrived from the south. There was a strong south westerly wind blowing and very soon we were racing neck and neck with the lordly liner up the channel. The *Carthage* stoked up for all she was worth, but could not shake off the *Torrens*. Eventually, on reaching Dover we had to shorten sail to pick up the pilot and only then were we left behind.

As long as the *Torrens* was under the Red Ensign, she always remained in the Adelaide trade returning home via the Cape, St Helena, and Ascension Island, completing the voyage in about nine months of twelve monthly service.

Nothing very noteworthy happened during my four years service on the *Torrens,* and looking back, it would appear those four years were the most uneventful period of my sea career. We used to leave London in October sometimes sighting Tristan da Cunha and the Crozets, then return the following June always calling at Cape Town, St. Helena, and Ascension on the homeward trip which made a nice break. Once we called at Port Elizabeth instead of Cape Town; a number of our passengers and the ship's doctor decided to live ashore during our stay. Later on, each and every one of them had to be landed ashore at St. Helena suffering from typhoid. Before leaving Plymouth each voyage, we usually shipped about 50 sheep, several pigs and a milch cow, likewise a similar number of chickens, geese and ducks, all this was for the passenger's consumption, a similar food source was loaded at Adelaide. There was no cold storage or refrigerating apparatus in those days.

Being a passenger ship there was no scarcity of food, which on many ships was a frequent source of trouble. Instead of the usual Board of Trade scale, we signed for 'full and plenty with no waste' Grog was served at 11 am daily, and on Saturday evening in the second Dog Watch. We also had 'smoko' in port and when the ship was shortened down in heavy weather. The *Torrens* was an extremely popular ship with the sailors.

Captain Angel senior was the perfect type of square rigged sailing master mariner, in narrow waters he could handle his ship like a racing yacht and she would respond with the lightest of touches to the helm. Never once did I know her to miss stays or fall in any kind of evolution he did not want of her. He was representative of the type of seaman who flourished in the days of the tea and wool clippers, and with all due respect to the modern mariner, we shall never see his like again. Incidentally, he was the only shipmaster who I have ever seen, who signed himself as shipmaster and owner. As I remember the old gentleman, he did not in the slightest resemble the normal British sailing master. Being rather short in size he made up for it with his powerful voice which was heard at ship's concerts when he usually sang two songs, 'The Sea is England's Glory ' and 'The Lads of the Old Brigade. 'Although he always insisted on his officers wearing a modified uniform on duty, he never wore anything of the same himself, always appearing in mufti and a bowler hat. This attire he wore in all weathers and in a wind he would have the bowler hat jammed down around his ears.

He was the ship's sole navigator, or in other words, did all his own navigating; after taking an observation from the poop, he would slip down the companionway and note the time by chronometer. Never once did I see an officer or apprentice take a sight, and never once did we fail to make a landfall as expected.

I don't think he held a very high opinion of my capabilities; in a reference I received at the end of my apprenticeship, the best he would concede was, I was ' well up on my duties as a seaman.'

Before he died, I'd had command of twenty ships, and all with reasonable success.

Torrens **after her collision with an iceberg**

1869 *NORMAN COURT* 1893

Condensed from an account given to Sea Breezes by P J Salmon

Another of the sailing aristocrats was the Glasgow built *Norman Court,* a ship that was launched in July 1869. Built from the design of William Rennie to the order of Baring Brothers the London bankers, the ship's name *Norman Court,* came from that of the Baring's home. The ship rigged vessel which could carry just over 1,000 tons, had a gross tonnage of 855 and was composite built by A&J Inglis. This ship was just one of a number of such clippers built during the decade, when some owners spared no expense on their craft; these vessels were often showpieces for their owners as well as being possible money earners. Despite the fact that the *Norman Court* had been built for Baring Brothers, the majority of her shares were in fact owned by Charles L Norman a London merchant and business associate of the Barings.

As well as her official number of 260998, and her signal letters WQMD, the principal measurement of the ship was her length of 197 feet 4 inches: beam 33 feet: and depth 20 feet. The height of her mainmast from deck to truck was 141 feet 6 inches; she followed the usual pattern of the modern day clipper ships, by carrying a skysail on the mainmast as well as the normal arrangement of studding sails. A point of interest on this particular ship was her extra long jib-boom which measured 68 feet 4 inches; this may be compared to the *Cutty Sark* whose jib-boom is 60 feet, and Thermopylae's of 71 feet. Apparently there are two excellent models of the *Norman Court* in Baring's offices London.

The first master of the *Norman Court* was Andrew Shewan; he took the ship out to Shanghai in the nominal time of 104 days, and at the end of the voyage gave the following description of the vessel. 'The ship excelled in going to windward and was very fast in light winds, she was staunch and tight, yet at times the whole fabric of the ship would tremble like a piece of whalebone; when diving into a head sea and after recovering herself from a heavy plunge, the after end would vibrate like a diving board.'

On her third voyage in 1873, the *Norman Court* was sailing down the English Channel bound for Shanghai when her captain developed a severe illness. The ship put into Dartmouth where the master was landed ashore for hospital treatment. The question then arose as to who was to take command of the vessel. However, the voyage had to continue, and on the recommendations of the ailing captain, his 22 year old son Andrew who was at that particular time the *Norman Court's* first mate took command of the vessel. The shipping world was astounded that such a young man should have been given command of a crack clipper ship. It later turned out that he followed where his father had left off, and quickly proved to be extremely popular and successful captain. So successful in fact, that he actually purchased the ship from the Baring's in 1877.

By the year 1878 the tea trade was slowly being swallowed up by the steamers, and to compete, the owners of clipper ships were having their ships cut down and converted to barques. After a further voyage to the far east in 1878, Andrew Shewan jnr had his ship cut down and re-rigged as a barque. This was mainly to reduce the crew numbers required for the racing clipper ship, as unfortunately, the once much lauded tea races were by that time at an end. By having his ship re-rigged, Captain Shewan was then in a position to dispense with half a dozen or so sailors which in turn cut down on the high cost of running his ship. Andrew Shewan jnr stayed as captain until 1879. In 1880 Mr C L Norman who had been the *Norman Court's* first principal shareholder re-purchased the vessel. Two years later in 1882 however, the ownership of the former tea clipper changed hands once again.

By that time and as well as the tea races, the tea trade with sailing ships had all but gone, nevertheless her new owner J Grieve of Greenock had another attempt at the tea trade. Captain McBride was appointed as the *Norman Court's* new master, and once again the ship was sent out to the far east with general cargo, in the hope she could secure a tea cargo on the homeward run. But after discharging, the only cargo available was one of sugar from Surabaya for her home port of Greenock. Departing Surabaya on 16 December 1882, the *Norman Court* left port for the last time. The next news of the vessel was at 11.15 am on 30 March 1893, when after having been at sea for 94 days - and almost at her destination, she struck a rock in Cymyran Bay off the Isle of Angelsea North Wales. The ship had been sailing in a stiff south westerly wind, but was hit by a sudden squall and driven onto the rocks; she was doomed, and after firing distress flares the crew took to the foremast rigging.

By then the sea and wind had intensified, and although the Rhosneigr lifeboat put out, it had to return after having filled twice. During the rescue attempts one of the lifeboat's crew was washed out of the boat but was pulled aboard again. The Rhosneigr lifeboat crew then refused to carry on with the rescue attempt, and with the ship's crew still hanging on to the foremast rigging, the crew of the Holyhead lifeboat was summoned to man the Rhosneigr lifeboat. *Norman Court's* 20 men were saved, but the steward and one sailor was lost. For their gallant rescue, the crew of the Holyhead lifeboat received a silver medal, and its coxswain, £3 in cash.

At the inquiry held to determine the wrecking of the ship, Captain McBride was held to blame. However, his certificate wasn't suspended as it was deemed he'd suffered enough already. The ship had been insured through Lloyds for £9,000 and its 1,000 ton cargo of sugar for £25,000.

In 1965 the wreck of the Norman Court was located by divers led by P J Salmon.

In recent times Barings Bank, the original owners of the *Norman Court* have been at the centre of much publicity with the collapse of their banking business.

THE TWEED

Originally a paddle steamer, this vessel was built at Bombay with a sister ship for the Honourable East India Company and named *Punjaub*. At one point in the 1860's the owner's of those two ships put them both up for sale in believing there was no future for that type of sea going vessel. Apparently paddle steamers of the *Punjaub's* size were not in demand and the steamship owners of the day were turning their attention towards screw driven ships. However, the wily Captain John Willis bought the pair for the giveaway price of £40,000, then after having them both surveyed decided on keeping the *Punjaub*. The other vessel was sold to a third party for £42,000, then after the paddles and engines had been removed from the *Punjaub*, he sold the whole lot for a further £10,000.

With the huge profit he'd made, John Willis who believed more in sail than steam redesigned the *Punjaub*. The result was the hull was lengthened, the vessel converted into a three masted full rigger ship and renamed *The Tweed*.

In the mid 1860s when under the command of Captain White, *The Tweed* began trading for her new owner and soon proved to be a resounding success. This was because as well as making money in the tea trade, she possessed excellent sailing qualities; the heavy squared counter stern which helped in preventing the ship being pooped was a noted feature in a following sea; these facts were duly reported to John Willis. The ship soon became his favourite, and when the time came to build the *Blackadder Hallowe'en* and *Cutty Sark*, the lines of *The Tweeds* stern were successfully incorporated into their building.

Lightning — Author's Drawing

The American built *Lightning* was the first of four extreme clippers to be built for the Black Ball Line of Liverpool. On her maiden passage from Boston to Liverpool on 1 March 1854, she logged 436 nautical miles on sightings; an all time record for a British fully rigged ship which stands to this day. Another of her distinctions being she was the first ever ship to be built in America for service under the red ensign; furthermore, at that particular time she was the largest sailing ship in the British Mercantile Marine. *Lightning* was 2,083 US tons on completion. The ship's length between perpendiculars was 243 feet, added to which was a further 90 feet for the bowsprit, jib boom and stern overhang; her maximum length therefore, was 333 feet. The end of *Lightning* came about on 31 October 1869. This was whilst she was at Geelong loaded and ready to sail for Liverpool. But on that fateful day smoke and fire was seen to be coming from her hold. The ship was built entirely of wood, and even despite the fact every effort was made to put the fire out it soon took hold. Because the water in the dock was too shallow the ship could not be scuttled. *Lightning* was eventually towed out into the river and flooded, but alas, too late to save the famous ship. The fire intensified and her foremast came down in the blazing inferno. Much of the cargo was salved but *Lightning* became a total loss.

Westward Ho!

The clipper ship *Westward Ho* was built by the proclaimed ship builder Donald McKay, and launched from his Boston - East Massachusetts yard on 24 September 1852. *Westward Ho* was built to the order of Sampson and Tappan of Boston, a firm who traded between the east and west coasts of America. The ship was 1,650 tons in the old measurement, had a length between perpendiculars of 210 feet, a beam of 40.6 and a depth of 23.6. She was an all wooden ship with hemp standing rigging, and outside channels Her figurehead was that of a full length Indian brave. In those years the Californian gold rush was high on passenger ship's agendas, but to transport the gold diggers from the east to the west, Cape Horn had to be passed. Fast clipper ships were the order of the day, and so too were quick turnarounds.

The ship's first captain was James Johnson who sailed the *Westward Ho* in the fast time of 103 days from Boston to San Francisco. On one particular day during the passage she logged 376 sea miles, which is about 400 land miles. On the second voyage Captain Hussey took command and did the same run in 105 days. These passages being regarded as being extremely fast. From 'Frisco the ship went to Calcutta to load jute for New York then back to Boston to complete a round the world voyage.

The next voyage was to Hong Kong with general cargo, but on discharging and finding there were no freights, Captain Hussey embarked on the notorious 'coolie trade.' On discovering this, the owners sent a telegraph forbidding the practice, but by the time the message was received it was too late. The *Westward Ho* was pulling away, with 800 coolies on board. The human freight was shipped across to Callao where they were much in demand for digging guano from the Peruvian islands. The ship then loaded a guano cargo and made it back to New York in 100 days.

That was the last trip the *Westward Ho* made under the American flag. She was sold to Don Juan de Ugarte and registered in Callao, but retained her name. Captain Jones then took command. The ship went back on the undesirable coolie trade, running between Hong Kong, Callao and Havana. However, on 12 February 1864 when the ship was in Callao ready to sail for Hong Kong, fire was discovered in the hold in the early hours of the morning. With the fire fighting appliances of a few buckets of sand and a bucket chain gang being extremely primitive, the all wooden ship burned to the waterline at her berth.

Index

Abbreviations ;- All Ship's names are in Italics;- SS Steamship;- MV Motor Vessel RMS;- Royal Mail Ship;- Capt Captain;- SBC Ship Building Company

A

Abbotsford - 66
Aberdeen White Star Line - 77, 213, 214
Abram W - 62, 63
Achilles SS- 23
Agamemnon SS, - 22,23
Ajax SS - 23
Ainsdale - 121, 123
Ainsworth C - 87
Alberts - Wilhelm - 126
Albion Line - 91
Alexander G - 52
Alexander Hall SBC - 10
Alexander Stephen - 91
Alexandra - 66
Allen O - 55, 56
Ambrose W - 28, 32
Amelia - 91
Anderson H - 87
Andrews C - 87
Andrewes R - 67, 68
Andrewes W - 68
Angel-Capt. Falkland - 220
Angel Capt. Henry - 219, 220
Angel Flores - 220
Ann McKim 9, 201, 202, 203
Argonaut - 91
Ariel, - 98
Atkinson Y - 73
Australian Crew Deserters - 87
Avebury - Lord 16

B

Bain J - 28, 31
Baring's Bank - 226
Baring Bros. - 41, 225
Bailey SF - 27
Bagert W - 87
Barker J - 56
Barnes Mrs N - 1
Barrett J - 67
Barvig - 62
Bartolomew Diaz - 11, 12
Beaumont WR - 51
Belding Capt. - 208
Benachie-tug - 48
Bethel & Co - 67
Bibby J & Co - 18
Bickford Commander AK - 59
BillingsG - 56

Bilton Capt. HR - 214, 215
Bisset Capt. -
Blackadder - 19, 44, 47, 61, 62, 63, 76, 85, 89, 156, 210, 211, 212, 227
Black Ball Line - 11, 205, 207
Blood W - 56
Blue Funnel Line - 23, 120
Boake BC - 45
Bosher JM - 56, 87
Bowers OJ - 67
Bozza & Mortola & Co - 220
Branks G - 87
Britannia RMS - 73, 75, 76, 77
British Ensign - 65
Brooks J - 87
Brown D - 87
Brown J - 87
Brown J & Co -
Brown Jas. - 16
Brown M - 87
Brown Son & Ferguson - 91, 111
Brown W - 28, 32
Bruce Capt. Wm - 29, 54, 55, 56, 57, 59, 60, 61, 62, 67, 86, 212
Burns G - 87
Burns -Robert, - 25
Bullard King & Co - 65
Burden A - 67, 87

C

Caffey J - 55
Caird & Co SBC - 76
Cairnbulg - 76
Calcraft W - 87
Camando J - 51
Camel SS 18
Canning N - 80
Canty - 54
Carlson T - 55
Carne H - 55, 57, 60
Carson S - 51
Carthage SS - 222
Cassels Janet - 36
Cave JA - 55
Charles Lamport SBC -
Charles Lambert - 66
Chapman's of Newcastle - 205
Christo W - 31, 32
Cleta - 186
Chrysolite - 10, 205

Cimba - 76
Coldstream - 61, 66
Clark F - 51
Clifton J - 82
Coldinghame - 85, 89
Collins - 54
Collins Capt. - 220
Connor J - 87
Conrad Jos. - 91
Conway P - 67
Cook G - 28
Cooke S - 72
Cooper - 28, 32
Cope Capt. Wm -219, 220
Copenhagen - 66
Costello J - 28, 32
Cunningham - 213
Cutty Sark Preservation Society - 5
Cutty Sark Trust

D

Da Silva - 147, 148
Da Sousa-Capt. Emilio - 12
Da Sousa Capt. FV - 98,110, 114, 115, (117 - 122) 135
Davis H - 28
Delaney A - 55
De Lessops-Ferdinand - 22
Denny Bros SBC - 18, 24, 37
Derwent - 76
Dickson H - 85
Dilharee - 61
Dixon TF - 67
Dimmint J - 67, 69, 72
Dolphin - 66
Donald McKay SBC - 229
Dorsey J - 51
Dowman Capt. W - 145, 146, 147, 149
Downie J - 52
Doyle J - 82
Dreney - 62
Drummond W - 67
Dryburgh A - 28, 32
Duke of Abercorn - 41
Dunnet FE - 83
Dunkelly - 11
Dunton T - 56, 59, 62
Durr J - 31, 32
Durant LK - 62

E

East Vin MV -163
Edwards W - 51, 55
Elder & Co - 219
Emmen W - 31
Empire Canning MV 163
Empire Tamar SS
Ennew W - 28, 31, 32

Enright Capt. A - 205
Ersson CF - 67
Esplin - 77
Ethel - 214
Eurolychus SS - 140
Evans E - 31, 32

F

Fairhurst G - 55
Faith - 65
Ferguson J - 28
Fisher R - 28, 31
Fletcher W - 28, 31,
Foley - 28
Fowler Capt - 54
Francis WH - 51, 52, 53, 54
Frank W - 28
Frazer SA - 76
Freak - 66

G

Gerrard W - 55
Gomez Capt. - 208
Gordon RW - 62
Gourlay Bros SBC - 19
Greener Capt. - 205
Grieve J - 226
Griffiths JW - 203
Guilleros F - 56, 62
Guthrie J - 28

H

Hackley JH - 56
Hall, Ross & Co - 215
Hall W - 56
Haloween - 19, 54, 208, 210, 227
Hanlon - 28, 31
Hansen - 54
Hart Capt. - 205
Hartman - 62
Hausen O - 76
Hawkesdale - 146
Heather Bell - 68
Hector Capt - 75
Hegarty W - 28, 32
Hellyer F - 26
Henderson H - 18, 28, 37, 38, 48
Herzogin Cecile - 155
Highland Piper RMS - 220
Hill F - 44
Hogarth H - 162
Holford E - 51
Holt-Alfred - 22, 23
Hood - Walter SBC - 213
Hornberg J - 77
Horning H - 56
Houston W - 159

Howland & Aspinwall SBC - 201, 203
HRH The Duke of Edinburgh - 4, 5
Hussey Capt - 229
Hutchinson W - 206

I

I G Insurance - 11, 12
Indra Line - 119
Indraghiri SS - 119, 120, 123, 125, 136, 137
Inglis JA - SBC - 225
Iredale & Porter - 121
Irving CE - 67
Isabel - 66
Isaac McKim - 201

J

J & A Ferreira, - 85, 90, 110, 146, 147, 148
Jackson GD - 62
Jackson S - 28, 32
Jacques JW - 62, 64, 67
Jansen A - 51, 55
Jardine & Matheson - 46, 205
Jenkins Capt - 214
Johansen J - 67, 83
Johns - 65
Jones Capt - 229
Jones J - 31, 32
Johnson - 28
Johnson C - 28, 32
Johnson H - 32
Johnson J - 229
Johnston A - 32
Johnstone Bros - 28
Jolliffer Towage Co - 108

K

Kellam - 54
Kemball Capt - 214
Kennard & Williamson - 201
Kia Ora SS - 118, 119, 135, 141
Kinsellar - 31, 32
Kirby FFC - 51
Kormoran SS - 140
Korpi J - 28

L

Lahloo - 199
Lampig - 54
Landin C - 67
Laister E - 81
Lauderdale - 36
Larsen - 54
Leary J - 55
Leckie Wood & Munro SBC - 19
Leda SS - 61
Leerberg - 62
Leonidas - 213

Le Norman - 62
Lewis T - 81, 82
Lidget J & Co - 21
Linton Alexander - 18
Linton Hercules - 18, 19, 20, 25, 80
Linton Marjorie - 80
Linton R - 20
Lightning, - 11, 86, 205, 208
Lisbon Maritime Museum - 21
Littman R - 22
Lloyds of London 17, 18
Lively Maria - 36
Liverpool Yankee Clippers - 10
Loch Vennacher - 73, 76
London Line of Packets - 207
Louis C - 51
Low J - 29, 32
Lubbock-Basil - 91, 210, 215, 214
Lubbock Mrs DM - 16
Lubbock Sir John - 16
Ludwig Weiner-tug - 120, 123, 137
Lynch W - 51
Lyvie JP - 62

M

Maguire J - 244
Maitland HN - 81
Marine Explorer MV - 163
Mattince T - 62
Maudsley, Field & Son - 19, 210
Mauritania RMS 86
Mayall T - 69
Meinke - 56
Merse - 46
Macgregor - tug - 48
McCausland W - 51
Mc Bride Capt - 226
McCarthy - 56
McEvoy W - 67
McGregor W - 55
McKay & Co - 205
McLain - 62
McKeown Capt John - 121, 123
McKim - Isaac - 201
Megano Capt FD 91, 107, 108
Miller Max - 34
Moodie Alex - 32
Moodie Capt Geo - 18, 26, 28, 29, 31, 36, 37, 38, 39, 40, 41, 43, 44
Moodie-Janet - 25
Moore Capt. FW - 29, 44, 45, 46
Moore Capt F29, 61, 62, 63, 64, 67, 81, 212
Morris L - 62
Mortlock PF - 81
Morton, Wilde & Co SBC - 19
Mount Royal Milling Co - 214

Murphy J - 67, 68

N

Naylor W - 76
Nicholasen N - 51
Nicol - 56
Nilson - 62
Nina - 66
Norman - 62, 82
Norman C - 225
Norman Court - 41, 215, 216
Nothroth TCE - 51

O

Old Man Land - 203
Ohlensen H - 67
Olivey R - 75
Ormiston S - 56
Orontes - 76
Otago - 91
Owens O - 62, 67

P

Paris Wm - 76
Parker W - 28, 32
Parton H - 51, 56
P&O Line - 73, 76, 222
Paramore F - 62
Pedro Nunez - 208
Pero d' Alequemer - 112, 208
Peace - 65
Peart H - 55, 58
Pickard Capt P - 222
Princess Dagmar - 66
Priscilla - 66
Perry OA - 67
Punjaub SS - 227

R

Rae J - 28, 32
Rainbow - 203, 204
Rathbone Bros - 206
Redford & Son 214
Reindeer - 10
Rennie-John - 25
Rennie Wm - 225
Reynolds J - 54
Reynolds STP - 52
Rhosneigr Lifeboat - 206
Richards W - 28
Richardson Mrs BA - 244
Richardson Capt C - 244
Richardson D - 244
Richardson F - 244
Richardson J - 8
Robertson Capt - 205

Robinson Capt - 210, 211
Robson T - 67, 71, 77
Rodney - 76
Rogers GH - 51
Ross Shire - 16
Rowlands J - 51
Rutland WH - 55, 60
Ryoff FA - 62

S

Salamis - 67, 77, 81
Salmon PJ - 226
Samson & Tappan SBC - 229
Sankey CA - 51, 59
Scawfell - 206
Schomberg - 126
Schubert J - 56
Scott W - 25
Scott & Linton - 17, 18, 19, 24, 31, 37
Scottish Maid - 200
Selbie A - 55
Selby T - 72
Serica - 76, 98
Shakespeare - 86
Sharff C - 54
Shaw Savill & Co - 118, 141
Shewan Capt - 225
Shinper A - 31
Shore J - 54
Sir James Laing
Sir Lancelot -
Sophocles - 76
South African Navy - 8
South Kensington Museum - 219
Smallbrook JA - 83
Smith C -
Smith J - 85
Smith JG - 62
Smith SW - 51, 52, 53, 54
Smith WE - 67
Smith & Dimon SBC -
Somersetshire SS
Spears J 28, 32
Spurling JRC - 249
Stornoway—200, 205
State Line - 41
Stern J - 51
Stoughton HL - 51, 55
Stuart Capt - 36
Suez Canal - 22
Sullivan B - 56
Swart - Johan - 12
Swinson P - 28, 32
Sykes JH - 62

T

Taeping - 98

Tam O' Shanter - 25, 26
Taylor & Potter SBC - 205
Taylor G - 51
Teviot - 61
Thalia HMS - 59
Thermopylae 37, 39, 40, 41, 44, 45, 66, 68, 208, 212, 214, 215, 216, 218, 225
The Tweed - 24, 36, 64, 67, 80, 210, 217
Thomas Stephens - 91, 112, 207, 209
Tiptaft Capt WE - 29, 46, 47, 48, 49, 50
Titania - 41, 155
Thames Nautical Training College -
Thomson Capt R - 206
Thompson Geo Jnr SBC - 214
Thompson G - 67, 213
Thompson T - 55
Thynne Commander TU - RN - 16
Tite C - 77,
Torrens - 219, 220, 221, 222, 223, 224
Torrens, Sir Robert - 219
Torrington - 200, 205
Turner Wm - 77
Tweedsdale - 66

U

Ugarte di DJ - 229
Ulster - 51
Undine - 41
Upjohn H - 62
Usher J - 68

V

Vaughan E - 28, 32
Victoria RMS - 77
Volga SS -

W

Walker - R, or ,Stan - 76, 159, 160, 162, 164
Wallace Capt JS - 29, 48, 49, 50, 51, 52. 53, 54
Walter Hood SBC - 213
Waratah SS
Wasa Bay - 163
Watson JR - 151
Watts, Watts & Co - 162
Waugh Capt - 205
Welch & Co - 205
Wellesley J - 28
Wellesley Nautical School - 8
Wells TW - 51
Wessex Brigade Royal Field Artillery - 16
West E - 62
Westward Ho - 229
Weymouth-Bernard - 213
Weston J - 67
Whicker E - 67
Whiteadder - 46
White Capt - 212, 227

White Star Line - 11
Williams G - 52
Williams - Stan - 163
Willis Capt. John
Willis Robert - 37, 38, 41
Willesden MV - 163
Wilson - 54
Wilson C - 56
Wilson & Blain & Co - 206
Wilson Capt - 214
Winchester Capt - 215
Wittmann R
Woodford W - 83
Woolahra - 76
Worcester - 153
Woodget AS - 82
Woodget H - 76
Woodget R Jnr - 72, 76, 80, 81, 82
Woodget Capt R 20, 29, 61, 65 (66-85) 146, 150, 151

Glossary

It is assumed that the reader is acquainted with the nautical terms contained within this book, if not, then this glossary may help in some way to describe them. In certain cases, a word in brackets translates a nautical word to that of a landsman.

A

A1 At Lloyds A ship's certificate of construction.
AB   Initials for Able Bodied, a qualified first class sailor capable of performing any sailorising task on deck.
Aback   When the sails of a ship are being blown the opposite way to which they are intended.
Abeam At a 90 degree angle to the fore and aft or centre line.
Aberdeen Bow An elegant and stylish looking bow-stem protruding rakishly forward.
Aft To the rear of - Behind -Astern of - Abaft.
A',Lee On the lee side, - On the sheltered side of the ship away from the wind.
Aloft   Above - Higher up - Up the mast.
AMC   Armed Merchant Cruiser.
Anchors Aweigh   When the procedure of hauling in the anchor takes place, the anchor is said to be 'aweigh' when it is just clear of the seabed.
Athwartships   Has a similar meaning as abeam, at a 90 degree angle to the fore and aft line.

B

Back-stay Lanyards   Short ropes that are rove through deadeyes to keep the shrouds or backstays taut.
Ballast   Extra weight such as rocks, shale or sand carried in the hold to weigh the ship down to level of safety.
Baltimore Bow   Same as Aberdeen Bow.
Barque A vessel with at least three masts that is square rigged on all masts except the aftermost mast which is rigged fore and aft.
Barquentine A vessel with at least three masts, except for the foremast it is fore and aft rigged. See the photo of *Maria di Amparo*
Battened Down   Secured, tightened, fastened down.
Beam The maximum width of a vessel's hull.
Beam Ends A ship is said to be on its beam ends when it has capsized and is laying on its side.
Beam Sea   When the waves and the swell of the sea come side on.
Bent On   Secured to with rope, tied to with rope, connected to with rope.
Bilge That part of the ship's hull where all the unwanted water drains away to.
Blue Lights   Distress rockets.
Bottom Scrape   Cleaning the ship's underwater body of barnacles, seaweed etc.
Bow The forepart of the ship's hull.
Bow Sprit   An extension from the foc'sle head. Often used to support a jib-boom.
Braces Ropes or wires used to haul the yards around.
Brig   A two masted square rigged vessel. - A name which is also given to a ship's prison.

Brigantine A two masted vessel. The foremast is square rigged, whilst the mainmast is fore and aft rigged.
Bucko A bully.
Bulkhead A dividing 'wall' between the holds or compartments of a ship.
Bulwark A wall, at and above the level of the deck.
Bunkers Engine fuel such as coal or oil.

C

Caravelle An ancient sailing vessel. See photograph of Bartolomew Diaz.
Carried Away Broken, Snapped, Parted.
Cat's Paw Small puff of wind.
Caught in Stays An erroneous act of seamanship which - when a ship is attempting to go across the wind when tacking, gets caught with her sails aback.
Chain Plates. Fastenings on the ship's side below the channels that take the strain of the lower shrouds and back stays.
Channels See Outside Channels.
Ceiling A wooden decking in the bottom of the hold.(floor of the hold)
Chain Strop A length of chain often used as a temporary repair to standing rigging.
Clipper A term used to describe a fine lined ship of sail built for the speedy carrying of passengers and cargo.
Close to the Wind As a ship cannot sail directly into the wind, it will go on either a port or starboard tack, and often at 4 points or 45 degrees to the wind, A ship which can sail close to the wind was one which could reduce this average of 4 points, some of the fine lined clipper ships could sail between two and three points off the wind. Schooners and fore and afters are best suited for sailing close to the wind
Cloth One width from a bolt of canvas used in the making up of a sail, On British ships these were normally 24 inches in width for square sails, then when sewn together about 21 inches apart. Any reef point would be on a reef band. Smaller stay sails were usually of 18 inch widths.
Coaling Gin A single sheaved block originally used on collier ships for working cargo.
Cockbilled Canted - at an angle.
Collier A coal carrying ship.
Company's Man A seaman who is on a contract with the ship owner
Composite - A composite built ship is one with a metal (usually iron) skeletal frame and planked with timber.
Belaying Pins Short bars of wood or metal that are inserted into the pin rails - being transferable they are used to secure the running gear.
Berthing Hawser One of a number of ropes used to secure a ship alongside.
Between Perpendiculars Abbreviated as bp. The length of a ship taken from the rabbet inside the stem, to the inside of the stern post.

Coppered—Copper Bottomed The coppering of the underwater hull of a wooden hulled vessel.
Cordage Rope or line.
Counter Stern Special shaping given to a ship's stern designed to 'counter' any following sea which may poop the ship.
Course The direction in which a ship is proceeding.
Course also - The large lower square sail of each mast.
Crank A term given to a badly or unevenly loaded vessel that induces poor sailing.
Crew A complement of seamen of all ranks, who make up a ship's company excepting the master who is not a crew member.
Cro'jack Short for Cross Jack. The lower yard of a mizzen mast.
Crossed Yard A yard is said to be crossed when it's shipped into position

Cut Away the Masts A term used when cutting through shroud and backstay lanyards that support the mast. In turn this allows the mast to fall overboard.

D

Dead Reckoning When there is no sun or stars visible to take an accurate fix by sextant, an approximate position is worked out by means of the mileage on the log line, plus any other means of drift, wind, soundings and any currents. Not regarded as being accurate.
Dead Rise That part of the hull which tapers from the rise of her bottom.
Deadweight Tons The weight amount of cargo, stores, and fuel a ship can carry.
Deck One of a number of levels on a ship(floors).
Decking The planking which makes up the deck (floorboards).
Deckhead The underside of the deck above (ceiling).
Deck Hand A Sailor.
Deck House A raised structure on the upper deck.
Deck Partners The watertight position where a mast passes through the deck.
Displacement Tons Determines the amount of water a ship displaces, and constitutes the actual weight of the vessel. Warships that normally have no cargo space are measured in this manner.
Doldrums A frequent windless part of the ocean found around the equator. In the Atlantic, the doldrums are some times referred to as 'the horse latitudes.'
Dolphin A supporting bracket for a ship's bell.
Dolphin Striker Another name for a martingale boom. It is situated at the junction of the bowsprit and jib-boom. See photo in picture glossary.
Doubling The junction where two separate parts of a mast are joined in an overlap. ie. where the lower mast joins the topmast and the topmast joins the t'gallant.
Draught The amount of the ship's hull that is under water.
Drogue A conical canvas sleeve open at both ends and used as a sea anchor.

E

Even Keel When a ship is level and is neither pitching nor rolling.
Extreme Clipper An extremely fine lined ship built for speed. Such vessels have sharp entrances and departures with large dead-rises.

F

Fairlead A guide that leads a rope to its destination.
Fake A single turn in a coil of rope
Fathom A nautical measurement of length which is equal to six feet, or two yards, or 72 inches.
Fidded As in fidded topmast etc. A toggle used to connect two mast portions.
Fife Rail A large frame at the bottom of a mast used for securing ropes from aloft.
Flake - Flaked Out As in rope, laid out on deck.
Flare The overhang of the hull from the foc'sle head deck to the waterline.
Flying-Jib The most forward of the fore and aft jib sails.
Foc'sle The sailor's accommodation, in whatever part of the ship it may be situated.
Foc'sle Head The anchor deck. Also: Abbreviation for - Forecastle Head - The name originates from the early Men o' War, where the ship's soldiers or marines would position themselves for battle.
Foredeck That part of the main-deck which is forward of amidships.
Fore-Foot The lower part of the ship's stem.
Fore-stay The main fore and aft supporting stay of the foremast. It is usually doubled.
Forrard Shortened word used by seamen for 'forward.'
Foul Bottom A ship with an under water body which is covered in barnacles etc.
Four Poster A ship with four masts.

Freeing Port Swinging doors in the bulwarks which allows the water to run off the decks.
Freeboard That part of a ship's side showing above the water.
Fully Rigged A term given to a ship rigged vessel, A full rigger is a vessel with at least three masts, which has square sails on each and a spanker on the aftermost mast.
Furl As in sail, to gather, roll up, and secure to the yard.
Foundered A ship that has sunk.

G

Gaff A boom normally used to hold the head of a fore and aft sail or flag halyards.
Gangway A platform from ship to quayside which enables people to board or disembark.
Gasket A length of line used to wrap around a sail when it is furled on the yard, when the sail is set, it is neatly coiled and hung over the foreside of the sail.
Gear Any moveable items on board ship. Also used as a name for clothing.
Geordie Brig A small two masted square rigger used in the carrying of coal from the Tyne to the London and the South Coast.
Goring Piercing a piece of canvas prior to stitching.
Gross Tons Merchant ships are measured by their cubic capacity. Each 100 cubic feet of space in the entire ship, equals one gross ton. - See nett tons, displacement tons, and deadweight tons
Gudgeons One of a number of iron brackets on the fore part of a rudder blade, to which a pintle fits into.
Gun Tackle A pair of sheaved single and double blocks which is often a luff tackle (Handy Billy) rove to disadvantage. Originally used on Men 'O War to run out cannons after they have recoiled.

H

Half Deck Accommodation for the apprentices in whatever part of the ship it may be.
Halyard (Haul Yard) Rope or cordage used to hoist, such things as flags and yards.
Handy Billy A small rope tackle of two inches or less, consisting of a double block and a single block.
Hardwood Bollards Wooden posts normally used for berthing ropes. (Bitts)
Hawse Pipe The entrance from the ship's side to the foc'sle head through which the anchor chain or cable passes.
Hatch board A section of boarding that fits in between the beams of a cargo hatch.
Head-Sea When the sea or swell comes from ahead.

Headsails The sails which ride on the head stays, from the foremast to bowsprit and or jib-boom.
Head stays The stays on the fore and aft line which lead forward from the foremast and prevent it from falling aft.
Heel, Heeled When a ship is forced over to one side by the wind on the sails, or when a cargo is in imbalance causing the ship to be listed or heeled over.
Helmsman Lashed Down In heavy weather when there is a danger of the helmsman being washed overboard as he steers the ship, he is lashed down to keep him on board.
Helm The ship's steering wheel.
Hemp Natural fibre used for rope making.
Hogging When a ship is lifted by a big sea amidships, momentarily causing the whole weight of the ship to be taken there and causing straining on the hull. Ships can also hog after having ran aground. See 'Sagging.'
Hold The main cargo space of a ship
Holystoned A name given to the scrubbing of wooden decks where the sailors would use blocks of sandstone, also referred to by seamen as 'bible practice.'

Hove To - Heave To When a ship heads into the wind or heavy weather, 'heaving to' keeps her in a stationary position. Also, when a ship stops, eg. to pick up a pilot, boarding party or other.
Hulk A storage vessel - A ship which is out of service, or unseaworthy.
Hull The main body of a vessel.
Hull Down A ship is said to be hull down when it is some distance away, The hull is not visible and only the masts or upper works can be seen above the horizon
Holystoned A name given to the scrubbing of wooden decks where the sailors would kneel down using blocks of sandstone, also referred to by seamen as 'bible practice.'
Horse Latitudes The area of Atlantic doldrums, where horses travelling as cargo, had to be put down and jettisoned through lack of drinking water.
House Flag A flag flown from the mast head of a ship that identified the ship's owner.
Hounds The junction of the lower and top-mast, and or, topmast and t'gallant

J

Jackstay Used as a connecting line between two ships on which stores or personnel may be transferred.
Jackstay on a Yard A rail on the top of the yard used to secure the head of a sail.
Jib sail The royal headsail, outer jib, inner jib or foremast t'gallant headsail.
Jib Boom An extension of the bowsprit, used to position some of the head stays and jib sails.
Jimmy Green An extra sail that's set under the bowsprit in good weather.
Jury-rig A temporary rig

K

Kedge An anchor used for stern mooring.
Keel The backbone and main support of a ship's hull.
Keelson An extra strengthening timber on the keel.
Kites A name given to stun sails or any other additions to the normal suit of sails.
Knight Heads An extension to the stem of the ship that comes up through the foc'sle head deck, it is used to bear the bowsprit, and often as a rail for the jib sheets.
Knots Bends and hitches used in rope handling, Also -A nautical and aero-nautical measurement of speed, One knot is equal to 6080 feet travelled in one hour.

L

Lanyard A short length of line with many uses. Shroud lanyards for example, are the lines which are rove through deadeyes for setting up shrouds to the ship's side.
Lashed Secured with rope, line or cordage.
Lee, Alee The side away from the weather.
Lee rail The bulwark top on the side of the ship away from the wind
Leeward Away from the weather side of a ship.
Light Vessel A vessel anchored and painted red, acting as a beacon and navigational guide.
Light Ship A term used to describe a ship in ballast and without cargo.
Line Cordage which is one inch or less in circumference, eg cod-line. Also, a term used to describe the equator.
Liner A vessel which is on a regular run between ports.
Lines The shaping form of a ship's hull.
List When a ship has more weight on one side causing an imbalance.
Lizard A short length of rope with a thimble spliced into one end.
Livery The colour or paint scheme of a ship.

M

Made Masts The lower masts of a ship were often so large in length and circumference, they were made up in sections and segments, then banded together with iron hoops
Mail-boat A ship which is normally a passenger liner carrying mails
Main Deck The longest unbroken deck of a ship
Making Way A vessel which is moving through the water.
Man O' War A warship.
Master The captain.
Mate The chief officer, The senior deck officer.
Messenger A length of rope used in conjunction with a heaving line and a heavy berthing rope or similar.
Mid-day Fix When the angle of the sun is fixed using a sextant at noon.
Mizzen The third most forward mast.
Mooring Pipe An opening in a bulwark through which berthing hawsers to pass.
Moorings Anchors, anchor cables, buoys, or anything which holds a ship to the sea bed.
Mooring Rope A rope that is used to secure a ship to a moored buoy etc.
Moulded Depth The maximum height from the underside of the deck of the hold, to the ceiling.
Main Spencer A fore and aft sail fitted to the after end of the main mast. Used to assist the ship's steering during heavy weather.

N

Nautical mile - A nautical mile is 6,080 feet.
Nett tons The gross tonnage, minus the spaces used for living accommodation, engine and store rooms
Norwegian Steam Manhandling ropes etc with brute strength.

O

Oertz A type of rudder design.
Outside Channels Channels is short for 'Chain Whales.' Platforms which are built into and on the ships side adjacent to each mast, Their purpose being to provide the shrouds and backstays with a securing point, thus giving a better radius in providing greater stability for the mast. In the later sailing ships they became obsolete.
Old Man The captain.
Old Salt An old sailor of experience.
OS Ordinary Seaman.

P

Parrel A Fitting which holds a movable yard to the mast; it is greased which enables the yard to be hauled up or down.
Partners The junction where the base of a mast meets the deck
Passage A ship is said to be on passage when it is at sea between two ports..
Pennant A short length of cordage or wire rope with a thimble spliced into each end.
Pennant A signal flag.
Pitch When a ship moves in a see saw motion fore and aft. Also - Pitch used in caulking decks.
Point One part of a circle equally divided into 32 parts or known as a compass point - eleven and one quarter degrees.

Poop Deck A raised structure at the after end of the ship. Originally this was the latrine deck where a large box was hung over the stern to act as the officer's toilet. (Still used on Arab dhows.)
Pooped When a following sea over rides and sweeps over the poop deck.

Port The left hand side, when standing aft and looking forward.
Purchase An advantage gained with leverage or a tackle of blocks.

Quarter Either side of the after end of a ship.

R

Rail - 0r Top Rail The upper part of the bulwark, otherwise known as the gunwhale.
Rake A streamlining effect on some part of the ship and masts, often used to enhance the appearance of a vessel.
Range When a ship moves up and down the quayside with the movement of the tide
Raking Masts Those masts that are set at an angle usually towards aft, but sometimes forward. When raked forward the masts are 'stove.'
Rigging See running and standing rigging.
Roaring Forties A belt of the Southern Ocean noted for its prevailing winds.
Rove - Reeve When a rope is led through one or more blocks or leads.
Rovings Short lengths of line used to secure the head of the sail through eyelets to the jackstay of the yard.
Runner A seaman who signs on solely to deliver a ship from one port to another.
Running Gear The ropes and blocks used to alter the sails and yards.
Running Rigging Ropes which run freely between blocks and used to control the spars and sails.
Rove - Reeve To pass a rope through.

S

Sagging When a ship is lifted by its fore and after ends in big seas, leaving the midship part vulnerable to strain on the hull.
Sail Handling Sailors setting or furling sail.
Sail Plan The suit of sails for a ship.
Saloon The officer's and passenger's dining room.
Schooner Rigged Besides the rig name of a fore and aft sailing vessel, this is also a derogatory name passed onto a seaman who is devoid of suitable clothing or tools.
Screwed As in bales of wool or tea—to pack tightly making use of all available space.
Scurvy An affliction brought on by lack of vitamin C causing swollen gums as well as inoperable joints and muscles.
Scuttle The purposeful sinking of a vessel.
Scuttle A porthole.
Seaway Heavy and inclement seas.
Sea Price An exorbitant price demanded or paid for an article, whilst the ship is at sea.
Serving Tarred hemp that is tightly wound around a rope with a serving mallet.
Shackle A length of fifteen fathoms which is usually associated with anchor cables.
Shackle A metal looped link, closed by a bolt and used for connecting chains etc.
Sheerpole A solid metal bar that traverses the bottom shrouds to hold them in place.
Sheave The grooved wheel on the inside of a block, on which a rope will run to reduce friction.
Sheets The name of the rope or chain, secured to a clew on the lower corners of a sail which controls the tautness of the sail.
Shift Cargo moving around the hold. Also, moving ship in port to another berth
Shifting Boards Heavy planks used as a barrier to stop movement of bulk cargoes.
Ship A square rigged sailing vessel with at least three masts, with a spanker on the aftermost mast.
Shoulder The forward part of the hull where it broadens out from the flare of the bows.
Shrouds The large ropes -or wire ropes, which support the lower mast both port and
Skids The platform on which a life-boat rests.
Sky Sail A small sail carried above the royal sail.

Slings The heavy iron chain the holds the lower yards to its mast.
Spanker A fore and aft sail secured to a boom on the aftermost mast.
Split-sail A topsail or t'gallant that's been divided into two parts for easier handling.
Standing Rigging The rigging which consists mainly of the lower shrouds and back stays. It is rigging which is fixed in a permanent position.
Spar Any booms, yards, stunsail yards, Mast sections, gaffs, etc.
Spider Band A fitting with a number of lugs on it, usually made of iron it fits around a mast or similar, and to which stays, blocks, etc, can be shackled or secured.
Standing Rigging Shrouds and backstays that stay in the same position.
Starboard The right hand side of the ship - when standing aft and looking forward.
Starboard Tack A ship sailing close to the wind, with her yards pointing over the starboard bow is on a starboard tack, the opposite is given for a port tack.
Stays Ropes or wire ropes which support the mast on the fore and aft line
Stem The most forward part of the hull which cuts through the water
Stem to Stern From the forward to the rear end of the ship.
Stern The after end of a vessels hull
Stiffening A term used referring to an addition to the permanent ballast which is built into or loaded into a ship.
Storm Sails A number of sails selected for specific use when the ship is in heavy weather; these and are usually the lower topsails and the fore-course.
Stranded When a ship has grounded or beached.
Stun-sail A studding sail.
Swifter Similar to the sheerpole of the mast shrouds, swifters are set on every fifth course of the ratlines

T

Tackle (pronounced taykle) a number of sheaved blocks rove together.
Tack To zig-zag a ship through a headwind with the use of sails.
Tack on Tack A ship is said to be tacking when it is sailing as close to the wind as possible, in order to make headway it will occasionally go on the opposite tack to balance out the course. This common practice is known as sailing tack on tack.
Taffrail The wooden rail that goes around the poop deck.
Taken Aback or Caught Aback When the wind suddenly changes direction and comes from a dangerous forward position - usually in squally weather. This can put severe strain on the forestays and lead to a ship being dismasted.
Taking Steam A term that describes a sailing vessel being assisted by a steam tug or similar.
Tar and Service General maintenance of rope-work.
Tarred Hemp Cordage made of hemp which has been treated - usually with Stockholm tar.
Tender A ship with a crank or unstable cargo. Also - A passenger or baggage boat.
T'gallant Short for a top gallant mast or sail.
The Line The Equator.
The Horn Cape Horn.
The Cape Cape of Good Hope.
Thwart The bench of a boat on which an oarsman sits.
Top The working platform, or 'table' on the upper end of a lower mast
Top Hamper A term used to describe anything above the deck such as the masts, yards, and rigging.
Toprail The upper extension to the main bulwark.
Tramp - Tramping A vessel which is not on a regular run; one which often sails on speculation or hires itself for any type of cargo available.
Trimmed To keep a bulk cargo level. Also to keep sails adjusted.

Truck Found at the top of each mast head, a round plate shaped object which often has a small sheave or two built into it for hoisting flags.

Truss An extension protruding from a mast which is attached to a yard on a gooseneck; it allows the yard to be canted as well as being braced fore and aft thereby keeping it clear of the lower shrouds.

'Tween Deck Nautical abbreviation for a 'between' deck.

Two Blocks When two purchase blocks are rove hard up to each other - Slang, chocker block.

W

Wall Sided Slang - for any ship with no tumblehome showing a large amount of freeboard.

Waist That part of the ships hull at the beam, where the sheer of the deck is at its lowest.

Watch A period of four hours duty; there are six watches in each day. From midnight to 4 am is the Middle Watch, (referred to as the graveyard watch) From 4 am to 8 am is the Morning Watch, From 8 am to noon is the Forenoon Watch, From noon to 4 pm is the Afternoon Watch, From 4 pm to 8 pm is the Evening Watch, From 8 pm to midnight is the first or night watch. On some ships the afternoon watch is split into two parts
called a first dogwatch 4 - 6 pm and the second dogwatch from 6 - 8 pm. The dog watch practice is carried out on warships and allows for a change of watch each day. The first watch is also called the night watch.

Wear Ship - Going about, jibing, a practice used mostly in bad weather when a ship goes on the opposite tack; instead of bringing the ship across the wind, the helm is put down and the vessel goes the long way around to get on the opposite tack. This often used practice is not favoured by the master as distance is lost.

Well Heeled A ship is said to be well heeled, when sailing listed over to one side under a good press of canvas and making good progress.

Wet Down A term used to describe keeping the wooden decks wet daily to stop shrinkage.

Wet Ship A vessel whose decks are continually awash due to lack of freeing ports or poor deck scuppering.

Whisker Boom An extension on the catheads, through which the stays from the jib boom are led to a securing point.

Wire Standing Rigging Shrouds and stays which are made of wire rope, They are in a fixed position and do not move, their main purpose is to support the masts.

Y

Yard The boom or spar which crosses the mast at a 90 degree angle, it can be braced around to catch any favourable wind, it also holds a sail and the sheets of the sail above it.

Yankee Clipper An American built clipper ship of the 1850's.

Yaw - Yawing When a ship slews from side to side in a seaway - often uncontrollably.

In Appreciation

As well as the many maritime institutions and authors whose works have been incorporated into the manuscript of this book, I would like to express my deep gratitude to those who have assisted me in the groundwork for its publication. First and foremost my wife Barbara for her patience and fortitude, then my brother Frank Richardson, who in his Merchant Navy travels has supplied me with a considerable amount of information and documentation. My eldest son Darren for his help in research and computing, Colin the younger son who as a master mariner in sail, has checked, corrected and verified much of the relevant sailing documentation. My late sister Nancy who has supplied the frontispiece as well as many of the photographs within. My cousin Jim Maguire MN Rtd, who due to living in Newcastle NSW has obtained valuable records of Cutty Sark's Australian movements. Dallas Hogan MN Rtd of the Newcastle NSW Maritime Museum. Robert Linton of Southport Lancashire, who as the great grandson of Hercules Linton has supplied much of the family history. Captain Graeme Cubbin of T&J Harrison Lines for his assistance and guidance in the initial stages, and last but certainly not least, Captain Sandy Kinghorn of The Blue Star Line for his encouragement, as well as his final reading and correcting of the completed manuscript.

John Richardson 2007

Sources of Information, Acknowledgements and Assistance

HRH The Duke of Edinburgh
Brigadier Sir Miles Hunt-Davis
Captain AW Kinghorn - Merchant Navy
Captain Emilio da Sousa of Lisbon
Captain G Cubbin - Merchant Navy
Captain Colin Richardson - Merchant Navy
Frank Richardson - Merchant Navy
Mrs A Barnes - Southport
Cutty Sark Trust Greenwich
National Maritime Museum
Lisbon Maritime Museum
Newcastle NSW Maritime Museum
The China Clippers   Lubbock, Brown Son & Ferguson
The Colonial Clippers Lubbock, Brown Son & Ferguson
Log of the Cutty Sark Lubbock, Brown Son & Ferguson
Dallas Hogan of Newcastle NSW
James Maguire of Newcastle NSW
Robert Linton of Southport
Ship's Monthly Magazine
Sea Breezes Magazine
Cape Town Harbour Master
Cape Town Archives

Due to a lifetime of collecting pictures and text for this publication, a period in which the author has amassed a large amount of articles, postcard and photographic oddments, every effort has been made to acknowledge the originators of those items, as well as those who have assisted in the making of this book. On advertising in 'Ship's Monthly' for additional information and photographs for my manuscript, a tremendous response was received from all parts of the world. I am therefore, most grateful to those whose names are listed in the acknowledgements page. However, if there is any text or photographs which have unknowingly or mistakenly printed without the owners or copyright holders consent, or indeed, if there are any mistakes within the text or photographs, then the author makes a full apology. If any person has a just or valid objection to any text or photographs within this book, it will be removed on any future edition.

John Richardson

In this typical dockside scene in the days of the clipper ships, note how the ship on the left has outside channels for her shrouds and backstays. When rigged outside the bulwarks, a better radius to support the mast was obtained.